CHIEF OF INTELL

by

IAN COLVIN

To

H. C. O'Neill

'Strategicus', who said
"Why not attempt a full
study of Canaris?"

MADE AND PRINTED IN GREAT BRITAIN BY PURNELL AND SONS, LTD. (T.U.)
PAULTON (SOMERSET) AND LONDON

ADMIRAL CANARIS

THE INTELLIGENCE GAME

How good was the British Intelligence Service during the Second World War? Did it compare with the legendary reputation of the Secret Service in the past? Did we out-manœuvre the German Abwehr? Did we know what country Hitler intended to attack, and when? It seemed that at the beginning of the war the British Government was surprised by a series of unexpected aggressions.

I was casting these questions over one of the Under-Secretaries of State at lunch when the German wars were over and he rose to the subject, remarking with a certain emphasis:

"Well, our Intelligence was not badly equipped. As you know, we had Admiral Canaris, and that was a considerable thing."

Hitler's Intelligence Chief a British agent? Although I had occasion over a number of years, as a correspondent of British newspapers in Berlin, to catch glimpses of the workings of the Chief of Intelligence Services of the German Armed Forces, it would have no more occurred to me to describe him as a British agent than I would have described Tallyrand as an agent of Castlereagh. Yet the Under-Secretary said "we had Canaris" emphatically, and his point of view was so fascinating that I have begun this study of Canaris by quoting it.

As I walked away from lunch that day it seemed that this must be the best-kept secret of the war. I wondered to what extent the Services Information and News Departments, usually so helpful in historical research, would respond to enquiries about Admiral Canaris.

"You have chosen a difficult subject for us," said Brigadier Lionel Cross at the War Office. "Why not ask the Admiralty? After all, he was a sailor." At length I found an officer in the Admiralty who had made a study of Canaris. "I am afraid I cannot help you much on the aspect which interests you," he admitted, "and I don't think anyone can." I tried the Foreign Office.

"We have a large amount of material on Admiral Canaris—all of it secret," said the Foreign Office. "We could not contemplate allowing you to examine it yourself, and we cannot spare the time of anyone here to look through these papers for you."

"But," I objected, "historians are given access to a great number of documents of recent date."

"We see your point, but we don't see our way to help you."

Was it so deep a mystery? I asked Lord Vansittart if he could say anything of Canaris as a friend of the British. "I only knew of him as an efficient intelligence officer," he answered.

By chance I met a man at lunch who had worked in the Military Secretary's office of the War Office during the war. We fell to talking about the German enigma and I once again mentioned Canaris. The name registered.

"Ah yes," said the man from the War Office, "he helped us all he could, didn't he?" I said I thought that this was so. "What has become of him?" my companion asked.

So the search for Admiral Canaris went on; Germans in remote villages, Austrians, Irishmen, Spaniards, Poles, Swiss, each with a scrap of information to add to the strange portrait of the man who was Hitler's Intelligence Chief and Britain's secret contact in Germany. I had before the war collected certain information when working as foreign correspondent of the *News Chronicle* in Berlin. As correspondent of Kemsley Newspapers in Germany since the war, I have been able to add to that material. The German biography of Canaris by Dr. Karl Abshagen has also given me the broad trend of his career and I am indebted to its author.

Members of the German Abwehr have helped me with their own aspects of the story: General Erwin Lahousen, long his assistant and head of Branch II, Dr. Paul Leverkuehn, his chief in Turkey, Dr. Josef Mueller, special liaison man with the Vatican. Close personal friends of Canaris have helped, too, like Otto John, who worked for him in Portugal, and Fabian von Schlabrendorff, who was entrusted by him with high political secrets.

I expected to be writing this book without any official assistance from the British and had already finished many chapters when the telephone in my office rang, and I realised with some astonishment that someone on our own side had a word or two to say about Canaris. The British Secret Service looked further into the mind of Admiral Canaris than his close German associates were aware. Some of his old British opponents in the duel of wits have helped to correct imperfections in my portrait with a solicitous and friendly touch.

The main records of the Admiral's secret activities, his diary, may have been destroyed by the Gestapo, but there is no conclusive evidence that it may not come to light when the prisons are emptied of the remnants of the Nazis and the world has quietened down. Therefore I have not attempted a full biography of Canaris or even a verdict on his strange character.

The intricate collecting of technical information and the networks of agents and large departments that flourish in the intelligence game are the backcloth, but not the main interest of this book. How we deceived the enemy and rooted out his agents in Britain is a chapter that may be told in the fullness of time. It is the mentality of the man himself, and the web that he wove round Hitler, that seize the imagination. The readers will have to judge for themselves whether Admiral Wilhelm Canaris was a German patriot or a British spy, a European statesman or a cosmopolitan intriguer, a double agent, an opportunist or a seer. It will not be easy for them to make up their minds.

I started the story with my ideas still disordered; then I undertook a journey to Spain and scoured south Germany for the remnants of his Intelligence Service. This was not sufficient—Berlin and the northern provinces had to be reconnoitred. Still the picture blurred and altered. Every German officer I met put a little more into the portrait, but each was sceptical about the lines that his colleague had drawn. "That can't be true—or the Admiral would certainly have told me about it." How often was I to hear that answer! How often I saw their faces cloud with suspicion that their own idea of him was incomplete!

Eventually when I had visited Madrid, Berlin, Frankfurt, Hamburg, Wiesbaden, Munich, Stuttgart, somebody in England who appeared to know more than a little about my subject suggested that I should visit a remote village in Holstein. "Go and see Richard Protze," he said; "you cannot finish your book without him." Who was he? The Admiral's mate when he was a young submarine officer, later by odd coincidence his Chief of Counter-Espionage. I found him at the back of beyond on the Baltic coast, a heavy, white-haired old man with pale-blue eyes that fixed your attention for as long as he cared to relate and had strength to tell the story. "Gaps—there will always be gaps," he said, and he wound back his mind to the time when this intelligence game began, and held me with the eye of the ancient mariner.

"We in England hardly know his name," I said. "Yet some people tell me that he spoiled Hitler's destiny."

"The Germans did not know his name until the end of the war," he said, "because he was the Chief of Military Intelligence. Anyone who knew his name and mentioned it openly would be sentenced to imprisonment.

"He was an officer of the German Navy who served in the General Staff and later in the High Command—but he was not really an officer by nature—a politician rather."

"A politician without a name," I suggested.

"Yes, if you like," and so the story began.

CONTENTS

CHAPTER I

AT THE HEIGHT OF HIS AMBITION

ADMIRAL WILHELM CANARIS was a shortish man of forty-seven, his hair quite white and his face rubicund, lined and benevolently settled, when he entered the four-storey building plain and brown stuccoed that stood alongside the War Ministry at number 74–76 Tirpitzufer in Berlin. It was January 1935 and the bare chestnut boughs revealed the Landwehr Canal and the ornate façades of the Wilhelminian period residences opposite. The room that was his office was small and bare, with a map of the world on the wall and photographs of his predecessors, the Chiefs of the German Military Intelligence Service. The Tiergarten Park where he used to ride every morning was only two minutes' walk from the office, the embassies and legations lay close at hand. It so happened that when I took a flat in Berlin two years later it was within two hundred yards of the Abwehr building. Looking back now, I can see the significance of an incident or two that I noticed as I walked along the chestnut avenue past these offices.

Wilhelm Canaris had reached the height of his professional ambition when he took over the appointment of Chief of Intelligence. Had he been another kind of officer he might have risen to command the North Sea Fleet, or the new German Navy that he had done so much to build up secretly. Although he had sailed in U-boats with credit in the First World War, and risen to command the battleship *Schlesien*, everyone who knew him with whom I have spoken agrees that it was the intelligence game that interested him most of all. He was the son of a Westphalian industrialist with an Italian name, long settled in Germany, who traced his ancestry to Lombardy. He distinguished himself early in his naval career when the cruiser *Dresden* was dodging British warships in South American waters after the battle of the Falkland Islands. His fellow officers were struck by his skill at procuring her coal and victuals from consular agents and Chilean merchants and spreading false rumours of her position. His work later in the Great War consisted in arranging refuelling and refits for German U-boats in foreign bases. It marked him out for a career in the Intelligence. Yet it seemed in 1934 that his last post would be that of Flag Officer commanding *Swinemünde*, a stone frigate on the Baltic coast due north of Berlin in a little resort where the Prussians spend their summer holidays.

They had nicknamed him "Kieker" when he was still a lieutenant—"peeper", because of his insatiable curiosity. The early pictures of him with the tip-tilted nose and inquiring glance show why the name stuck to him. Kieker had a passion for obscure knowledge, which he absorbed and disclosed just as he drew breath.

"I tell them what they want to hear and what they can pass on to others," he explained in later life—and behind his apparent loquacity there lay an immense silence on the matters that he would reveal to nobody.

They were not altogether friendly to him in his own service. Some of his fellow officers believed he had worked with the Vehm murderers in liquidating German revolutionaries. They disliked his easy readiness for secret missions, his fluent approach to complex foreign problems, his familiarity with strange foreigners, and they believed him to be an enthusiast for National Socialism, too. That was still a handicap in the German services in 1935. Then there was the story of his activities in Spain and France during the First World War, the rumours that he had paid and used Mata Hari to spy on the French. It was also said that to escape from an Italian gaol after being arrested as a German spy he had strangled the prison chaplain and escaped in his clothes. Dr. Abshagen, his German biographer, has heard this story and discounted it, and I have had it solemnly repeated to me by a highly intelligent German professor.

Had he not issued false passports as a junior intelligence officer in 1919 to the murderers of the revolutionaries, Karl Liebknecht and Rosa Luxemburg, whose bodies had been thrown into the Landwehr Canal?

Canaris was in 1924 in a position when he might have had to account for this rumour, when he was giving evidence before the Reichstag Commission of Enquiry into the conduct of the war. One of its members, Deputy Moses, hotly accused him of abetting the murderers of the two Socialist leaders, but Canaris was adroit enough to point out that the incident in question did not come within the scope of the Reichstag enquiry.

Had he not negotiated for U-boats of German design to be built in Spain, Holland and Japan during the years after the Versailles Treaty had deprived Germany of these weapons? Had he not taken part in the Kapp putsch of 1920 and forsaken the Defence Minister Noske, to whom he was A.D.C., when Noske fled from Berlin to south Germany? Canaris smiled and allowed these stories to run their course. Not one did he ever trouble to deny, and laughed heartily when they were seriously mentioned, relates his friend, Dr. von Schlabrendorff.

It was a foible of his that his family had connections with that Admiral Kanaris who was a hero of the Greek wars of liberation in the nineteenth century. Perhaps it was also not entirely disagreeable to him to have a number of these tales circulating. Nobody knew which to believe. They earned him a mysterious reputation. They made it less easy for enemies and rivals to take his true measure.

What circumstances had combined to bring the rear-admiral from Swinemünde to this high and secret post in the capital? Admiral Raeder had been obliged to recall Captain Patzig from the appointment of Chief of Intelligence. Field-Marshal von Blomberg, the War Minister, a faithful prop of the National-Socialist regime, had criticised the uncompromising attitude of Patzig towards the security service of the Secret State Police. Reinhard "Butcher" Heydrich, chief of this organisation (known as the S.D.), had complained to his own chief, Reichsfuehrer of the S.S. Heinrich Himmler, that Patzig was obstructing co-operation between the Intelligence Service and the State Police in vital matters of security. The Commander-in-Chief of the Navy did not want to support Patzig, but he hoped to second another naval officer to this important post. To lose it to the Army or the Luftwaffe would be regrettable. Raeder did not consider that the men in field grey possessed the mental horizon to direct a secret service with commitments all over the world.

"That is correct, but not the whole story."

Richard Protze here took up the narrative.

"Our Fuehrer had concluded his treaty of friendship with Poland in 1934. It detached Poland from the ring of enemies round Germany at the price of relinquishing the chance of an understanding with Russia. It removed the threat of partition from Poland for the time being and it enabled Hitler to continue his pose as the true enemy of Bolshevism. A secret clause in the 1934 treaty forbade either party to pursue espionage in the other's territory and substituted an exchange of information."

Captain Patzig called together his heads of departments and acquainted them with the General Staff agreement, but he concluded with the words:

"It goes without saying that we continue our work."

The Abwehr had a reconnaissance aircraft that had been flying over Poland at heights of eighteen thousand feet and above taking infra-red photographs through cloud. It so happened that General von Blomberg, the War Minister, was on a visit of inspection to Holtenau aerodrome in October 1934, when he saw an aircraft standing outside the hangars.

"What is that plane?"

"Herr General, that is Captain Patzig's. We use it for taking photographs over Poland."

Blomberg was extremely angry. His orders had been flatly disobeyed. Patzig must go. Perhaps he had it at the back of his mind that Patzig was being obstinate with the S.S., too. He asked Admiral Raeder, Commander-in-Chief of the Navy, whether he had another officer available.

"I can only let you have Canaris."

Blomberg accepted him immediately. "But within a short time he seems to have regretted his decision," related Canaris to Protze. "He told Raeder suddenly that he did not want me. I was an untransparent character, he said." "The appointment is already made," objected Raeder, and so the War Minister let it be. Had he looked meanwhile into the service record of Canaris?

The service career of Rear-Admiral Wilhelm Canaris could not have appeared so lurid in the official records of the German Navy as gossip in the mess would have it, but it was impressive enough to make Blomberg hesitate. It was an adventurous career with many unorthodox jobs. Dr. Heinrich

Bruening, the last democratic Chancellor of the Weimar Republic, tells me that Canaris had to retire from the Navy in the 'twenties; but Protze describes him as working in Kiel as intelligence officer, Baltic station, and fighting counter-espionage actions with the French intelligence bureau in the Rhineland. To Heydrich, Himmler and Hitler the choice may have seemed excellent. Canaris was known to be an instinctive enemy of Bolshevism. It was he who had suggested selling all the instruments and tackle taken out of the Grand Fleet before it was sunk off Scapa Flow, selling it abroad and using the funds to subsidise the Free Corps against the Bolshevik armies. This man might be an ally for Hitler in the throng of stiff-backed Prussian militarists with their secret penchant for Russia. Admiral Canaris officially entered 74–76 Tirpitzufer on January 5th, 1935, after some weeks of working himself in.

Known as the Abwehr, or Security Service, because the Treaty of Versailles attempted to restrict the German armed forces to counter-espionage as their only legitimate intelligence activity, the Admiral's new command was then probably the best co-ordinated apparatus of its kind in the world and it had the advantage of being small. It was divided into three departments: Abwehr I, to collect information through German and foreign agents; Abwehr II, to manage sabotage; and Abwehr III, to do counter-espionage work at home. One of the concessions made by Hitler to the Commanders-in-Chief when he came to power was the absolute independence of the Abwehr. It was answerable to the service chiefs alone, a secret state within the state.

There was, besides, a Foreign Section of the Abwehr (Amtsgruppe Ausland) which looked after foreign military attachés in Berlin, received reports of German military attachés abroad, and co-ordinated the military with the political intelligence which the German Foreign Office gathered through its own services. The work of digesting and exploiting military intelligence was done by the Great General Staff itself, and later by the High Command of the Armed Forces when Hitler created that organ of war. The three services were thus under one hand in intelligence matters, and there could be no inter-service rivalries, no hoarding of vital intelligence by the Army which the Navy wanted to see, no exclusive air intelligence. Soldiers, sailors, airmen and civilians had to work together, owing to the design of the machine. Hitler gave Canaris a directive to build it up and make it an instrument that could measure itself with the secret services of the Western Powers.

In the first brief calm after he assumed office, while his Abwehr was still fairly small and inviolate, the Admiral must have gazed at the picture of the famous Colonel Nicolai hanging in his room and pondered on the sinister influence that had been exerted from this building on the structure of the civilised world. Colonel Nicolai had subsidised the Russian Bolsheviks in exile, he had undermined the Tsar's state and the Russian war effort to a degree that compares with the achievements of the Nazi fifth columns in the early 'forties and Communism after 1945, and finally he had launched Lenin into the tottering Russian empire in the sealed railway coach that passed through German territory in October 1918. Then there was the inevitable revenge upon a cynical policy. Germany had been obliged to send volunteers to the Baltic states and Finland to try and put the red genie back in the bottle whence it appeared to be moving all over Europe, and Canaris had played an active part. He was attached to the Guards Cavalry Division in 1919 for special duties when it took over internal security in Germany for a short while after the Kaiser had abdicated.

By the late 'twenties the Reichswehr had forgiven the doctrinal errors of Marxism sufficiently to negotiate a secret military training agreement with the U.S.S.R., so that they could try out new and forbidden weapons in Russia unobserved by the Versailles Treaty powers. Many of the officers of the General Staff believed even in the 'thirties that it was quite possible to achieve a working alliance with Russia, despite the fact that Hitler wound up the German-Russian military agreement soon after he came to power.

Admiral Canaris, turning over the reports at his desk above the Tirpitzufer, looking at the old map of the world and the faded photographs of service chiefs, staring out across the chestnut trees over the Landwehr Canal, was confronted with the problems of a situation that he had dearly wished and worked for since the second Reich had collapsed. A man had emerged who was preparing to make Germany powerful again and great. The German Navy would be expanded, the U-boats that Canaris had hitherto helped to lay down secretly in Spain and Holland would be assembled at Hamburg, Bremen and the Baltic ports after being prefabricated at inland factories. There was order again in Germany and employment, cleanliness and efficiency; there were no strikes, no labour unrest; and foreign powers were watching her in apprehension. Her neighbours were being polite and willing to be friendly, though still on their guard. To the eastward lay nervous Poland and, beyond, Russia, mistrustful and inscrutable. France, preoccupied with petty squabbles at home, still maintained a large conscript army with a mass of reserves, and behind her lay Britain wielding naval supremacy and the threat of the blockade. The British exerted economic and financial influence all over Europe and the world.

Further yet lay America, lazy and delightful, a potential world power but still far keener on producing prosperous families than directing world politics. It was England, no doubt at all, the Admiral thought, that by reason of her traditions, her toughness and her far-sighted statesmanship, would offer Germany the greatest resistance or the most solid friendship.

Study of an operation in the early life of an officer often gives us the clues to his future promise, and his service with the cruiser *Dresden* in the South Atlantic and Pacific in 1914 and 1915 indicates the strong points of Canaris. I enlarge upon this period of his early life as one of the few which is fully documented, seeing so much else is hearsay. He was Flag Lieutenant and Intelligence Officer to Captain Lüdecke at the Battle of Coronel and wrote home to his mother in November 1914 in a cautious vein of optimism:

"A fine success certainly, which gives us breathing space and may have an effect on the general situation. Let's hope we continue in this way."

On December 8th Admiral Sturdee caught the German squadron off the Falkland Islands after false wireless signals had deceived von Spee as to his enemy's position. The *Dresden* was the only warship that escaped from Sturdee. She ran into Punta Arenas and refuelled before slipping through the Straits of Magellan to hide in the steep bays and inlets of the Chilean coast.

According to the official British naval history of the First World War, the British Consul in Punta Arenas, who happened to have had a German partner in business, soon picked up her whereabouts, but he was disbelieved in the Admiralty which had received other reports. The Germans were spreading rumours that she was in deep, uncharted culs-de-sac, which in fact she was, but the reports were so various as to bewilder the search and the true report was soon lost in the false. (One of these leg-pulls said that she was in Last Hope inlet.) I fancy I see here a technique that Canaris developed later to perfection. The cruisers *Glasgow* and *Kent* searched the coast for hundreds of miles until March 1915 without finding the *Dresden*, though they were very near her at times. At length they caught her in Cumberland Bay outlined against the precipitous cliffs within territorial waters but obviously getting up steam and prepared for action. Captain Lüdecke had refused to land parts of his machinery and accept internment, though the Kaiser had signalled to him permission to do so.

Captain John Luce of the *Glasgow* straddled the *Dresden* with his first salvo at 8,400 yards and the *Kent* opened fire with her six-inch guns. The *Dresden's* fire control, intercom. and two of her guns were quickly knocked out. Captain Lüdecke signalled that he was prepared to parley, but in the confusion of battle he had to hoist a white flag before the British cruisers ceased fire. The *Dresden's* steam pinnace then brought a German lieutenant alongside. His name is not mentioned in the British official report. It was Canaris, who spoke excellent English and had already shown his skill in various negotiations. He was to ask for terms, but when taken to Captain Luce he first tried a stroke of guile, declaring that the *Dresden* was already interned by the Chilean authorities and could therefore not be attacked without breach of international law. It was certainly a plausible lie, but Luce appeared to have other information and would not believe it. He could see that the *Dresden* had been getting up steam.

Canaris tried the argument that she was in territorial waters, but Luce was not disturbed by this either. The *Dresden* had been infringing Chilean neutrality for months, he pointed out, and he had his orders to sink her wherever he might find her.

They then came to discuss terms.

"Captain Luce's answer was—as the tradition of the service required," relates the official British naval history of the First

World War, "that he could treat on no basis but that of unconditional surrender."

With this answer Canaris returned to the *Dresden* and Lüdecke thereupon decided to blow up his forward magazine and scuttle the ship. She would not have escaped for as long as she did, his fellow officers agreed, had it not been for the skilful work of Canaris in securing supplies, gathering intelligence, and sending out deception reports.

I imagine from some of his later reactions that his visit on board the *Glasgow* left a lasting impression on him of the power and determination of the British. Her officers showed him frigid courtesy as he stepped aboard her quarter-deck, but they spoke a language which he understood well, and when the action was over Captain Luce sent his surgeon officers ashore to tend the German wounded. He then demanded internment of the crew.

Lieutenant Canaris slipped out of internment, crossed the Atlantic in a British ship and escaped through the blockade with a false Chilean passport as Mr. Reed-Rosas. Still posing as a Chilean, he worked in Madrid against the Allies during 1915 and incited Arab tribes with subsidies against France and Britain in Morocco and West Africa.

France no doubt blamed Spanish connivance for these activities, for France and Spain had always been rivals in Morocco.

"He blew up nine British ships from his base in Spain," said Protze. "Don't forget to mention that."

When Madrid became too hot for him and after he had nearly fallen into the hands of the French on his way back to Germany, Canaris served in U-boats and his patrol reports attracted the attention of the Kaiser. "Is this a descendant of the national hero of the Greek War of Independence?" the Kaiser wrote in the margin. Perhaps it was in a subsequent moment of vanity that Canaris let it be thought that he was descended from Konstantin Kanaris.

Such is the outline of his early career. An original mind, initiative, resourcefulness, and a high degree of cunning—his personal integrity still difficult to assess.

"Promise me that you will look after him!" said Patzig to the old bloodhound, Richard Protze, as he handed over office. He had a premonition of calamitous times ahead when the nervous, agile Canaris would need a steady guide, and Protze promised that he would serve him faithfully.

It seemed to me extraordinary after following some of Canaris's adventures in the Second World War to turn back the pages of history and read how his first personal encounter with the British in 1915 ended with "unconditional surrender". These words re-echo in our story.

CHAPTER II

OPERATION KAMA

NEITHER DID THE Poles take too seriously the agreement
with Germany not to spy on each other. We shall see that the
Polish Intelligence Service continued to search by the most
daring methods for the true intentions of the German General
Staff. It did not relinquish its suspicion that, despite Hitler's
assurances, Germany intended to partition Poland with Russia.
But whereas the German Intelligence Service specialised on
aerial reconnaissance of terrain, in the offensive sense, the Poles
concentrated on discovering what plans were being made in
Berlin against Poland and what arms were being developed.
The activities of Captain Jurek von Sosnowski were directed
to that end. This was the first big espionage case that fell into the
hands of Canaris, half finished by the service under Patzig.

Canaris himself sat high above the police work that un-
ravelled this extraordinary scandal, and his name was never
mentioned in connection with it.

His appointment was a special secret, the post was secret,
and the Third Reich with its treachery laws was a safe reposi-
tory for secrets. The British Admiralty which had come across
the activities of young Canaris in neutral countries during
the First World War and followed his career, lost sight of
him between 1935 and 1939. It did not note a change of
appointment from *Swinemünde*. The Embassies and Legations of Berlin simply knew him as a naval staff officer working
in the German Admiralty, in contact with the attaché section
of the War Ministry, and his personal liking for small intelligence
missions made it difficult for those foreigners who came into
contact with him in the course of their duties to guess that this
was the Chief of the Intelligence Service himself.

Canaris moved his family from Swinemünde to a little house
in the Dollestrasse, in Sudende, and lived there the simple,
somewhat austere life that was traditional to the German

services. These Berlin suburbs with their wooded gardens and pleasant architecture were an example to the world of how to make a suburban life delightful. He soon discovered that the Chief of Prussian Secret Police and later Chief of the Reich Security Service, S.S. Group Leader Reinhard Heydrich, occupied another house in the same street as himself. It was plain that the Chief of the Military Intelligence and the Chief of the Gestapo Security Services must be on calling terms. With Frau Canaris and his two daughters the Admiral used to stroll up the road on a Sunday afternoon for a game of croquet with the Heydrichs. We shall see later that there were lunches with Heydrich to which the senior men of the Gestapo and the Intelligence were invited.

Reinhard Heydrich had been one of his first visitors at the Tirpitzufer, to discuss a serious espionage affair that raised the whole question of responsibility for security in the Reich. He was not a pleasant man to encounter: of hawklike features, slightly unsymmetrical, a straight and thin-lipped mouth and hard, cruel eyes. Heydrich was tall and bony, with angular shoulders; with him silence prevailed mostly and this cold silence made it difficult for his colleague to settle problems on a basis of friendly compromise. The Admiral was small by contrast, voluble, spoke softly and gesticulated a little. They were as little like as mallet and hoop, and, though outwardly polite, each made reservations about the other.

Heydrich had come to him asking for access to the files of Abwehr III, where the agents of foreign powers in Germany were listed and classified. This had been the subject of his contention with Captain Patzig, and he gave the new man no respite. He wanted to know who were the foreign agents in Germany, and a scandalous espionage affair that had been tried in camera during 1934 lent weight to his request. It concerned the Poles.

It was noticeable that Canaris treated Heydrich on the footing of an officer who had been at sea with him. He remembered Heydrich from the year 1922, when he had been First Lieutenant of the training cruiser *Berlin*, and Heydrich a naval cadet, and no doubt he said so, leaving Heydrich to guess what was in his mind. He had obtained Heydrich's service papers from the German Admiralty and refreshed his memory on the court-martial that had found Heydrich guilty of moral delinquency in the late 'twenties, which led to his dismissal from the naval service. The papers showed him another interesting fact: the father of Heydrich, an operatic tenor in Halle-an-der-Saale, was a half-Jew. Canaris gave the service records of Heydrich to a staff officer and instructed him to keep them in his safe. He noted of Heydrich in his diary: "a violent and fanatical man with whom it will be impossible to work at all closely." But he was destined in the next eight years to share many high secrets with this violent man—and the first of these was the extraordinary story of Captain von Sosnowski.

The military men of all nations were not quite rid of the nightmare of trench warfare. They were still impressed by the memory of the huge burrowing armies of the First World War and the hopeless interlocked bloodshed that even tanks and aircraft had not broken up into a war of movement. France drew the conclusion that she must build a defence line in concrete, a national trench, the Maginot Line.

But in 1934 it was rumoured that Germany was following a new theory of rapid armoured warfare and building a hard core of three armoured divisions, a Panzer fist, that would smash through trenches and concrete fortifications. The Italians were highly alarmed, and General Roatta of the S.I.M. or Italian Military Intelligence Service went to Vienna himself to see what he could learn from Erwin Lahousen, his Austrian colleague. Lahousen, Chief of the Austrian Military Intelligence, was bound to work with the Italians, because as long as Mussolini was determined to keep Austria as the buffer state, as long as he was prepared to send his own armour to the Brenner Pass in a crisis as he did when Dollfuss was murdered, as long as the Stresa front was possible, the General Staffs of Rome and Vienna had common interests. On intelligence matters there happened to be a secret agreement between Germany and Austria to exchange information on Central Europe and the Balkans. This made some contact on other matters possible. Lahousen understood the international freemasonry of intelligence services and promised Roatta what help he could.

The Poles had no such opportunities. Their intelligence work was more daring and original. Among others, Jurek von Sosnowski, a man of handsome appearance and dashing temperament, was sent into Germany posing as a cashiered officer who had disgraced himself by an affair with the wife of his regimental commander. He crossed the frontier leading two horses, as a man starting a new life, and he calculated that he would do best to find women who would work for him.

"Let me tell this story," said Richard Protze, ex-Chief of Counter-Espionage. "It was I who laid Sosnowski by the heels."

He put his nose down to the table of the inn in Holstein where I discovered him, like a hound taking up the scent, fixed his formidable blue eyes on the listeners and traced out each footstep that the Pole took.

"There were two Polish intelligence officers in Berlin in those days. Lieutenant Griff-Tschaikovsky had no idea how to begin his work, so he came to us fairly soon and confessed that he could not do the job. He asked us to give him information.

" 'You shall have plenty of material, my lad,' we told him. 'Right about turn. Now you work for us.'

"Probably the most interesting section of the General Staff was I.N.6, at this time under Colonel Heinz Guderian. It was an experimental section developing armoured fighting vehicles. It had also to be acquainted with the areas in which these vehicles would operate and the type of warfare that was envisaged. I.N.6, therefore, was kept informed of operational planning and of Operation Kama, the secret development of forbidden German weapons in Russia. My branch, Counter-Espionage III F, went to Guderian for false information to pass on to Griff-Tschaikovsky. He made photo-copies of it and took them to the garden of the Polish Embassy, where there was a dark room.

"Judge his astonishment and ours when one day he found hanging up in the drying room somebody else's films, of which he copied one off the clips and brought it to us—it contained *genuine* material from Section I.N.6. After that we watched visitors to the Polish Embassy closely, and after hours we also watched the lights of the basement windows. But we still had no idea how the Poles had got photographs of these documents.

"Jurek von Sosnowski was a handsome devil, brave and cool, with a charming smile and cold eyes that made you shiver. He seemed to have plenty of money, played about the world of film and fashion, gave parties in his ornately decorated flat. The women could not resist him. He consorted openly with a society woman of Swiss birth, Frau von Falkenheyn née Zollikofer, divorced Schmidt, who became Baroness von Berg. Sosnowski worked in the grande couture, and these two were often seen at the races, at theatres, in night clubs together.

"One summer day in 1934, Jurek espied a little Hungarian dancer, Rita Pasci, in a Budapest hotel and invited her to dinner. When he left Hungary a few days later Rita went with him in the car, to dance for him in Berlin, but soon Jurek explained to her that her real work would be espionage, and she noticed that he surrounded himself with a host of elegant women.

"Frau von Falkenheyn set about this work without any misgiving.

" 'I have a friend in the War Ministry,' she said. 'I will see where she works.'

"She invited Frau von Natzmer out to bathe in the Wannsee Lake and as they lay on the beach they chattered about her work.

" 'You work with Colonel Guderian in I.N.6?' On a subsequent bathing party Frau von Falkenheyn exclaimed:

" 'Do you know that you are working for the Russians? My Conservative friends are quite scandalised at this business. I belong to a patriotic group of Germans.' Gradually she drew out of the widow Natzmer the business of her branch, a sketch map of the offices she worked in, and then she set about obtaining the papers of Operation Kama.

"Before long she was persuading Frau von Natzmer to bring out documents from I.N.6 for the patriotic German group that was working against the Bolsheviks. She paid her for them, but immediately ran her into such debts by taking her round expensive shops that she became more than ever dependent on her friend. Then came the big shock. Benita von Falkenheyn told her that they were both really working for a Polish intelligence officer. If she wished to be released from this contract, she must enlist other girls in the War Ministry who might be hard up and work them in to replace her. Frau von Natzmer dared not go back on her bargain. She sought out one Fräulein von Jena and three others whom she knew to be in need of money. Jurek was busy, too. He found a Colonel in debt, Colonel Biedenfuhr, started a liaison with his wife, bribed a Lieutenant Rotloff, who also worked in the War Ministry, and within the space of one year he had obtained 150 secret documents, the keys of

Colonel Guderian's safe, and the German outline plan of attack on Poland.

"It was then that jealous Rita Pasci went to a theatrical agent with the complaint that she was being asked to spy on Germany. The agent came to us and asked for the assurance of pardon, if she did what she was told.

" 'You shall have that,' we said to Rita. 'But now you turn about and work for us. Find out the names of those with whom this Sosnowski is working.'

"One day Rita Pasci rang us up and asked: 'Do the names Frau von Natzmer and Fräulein von Jena mean anything to you?' I felt weak at the knees as I heard these names—I knew that these were War Ministry secretaries in charge of confidential work.

"Sosnowski arranged a ball in the Bach Hall for the film and fashion world of Berlin. I sent my wife to it to see who would be there. I arranged with the S.D. to raid Sosnowski's flat that same night as he was holding a supper party after the ball in honour of Rita Pasci."

Sosnowski paid great compliments at the ball to Helena, Richard Protze's wife, a shrewd-looking woman with a steely eye, whom he had never met before. She said quite truthfully that she was working for the War Ministry.

"I hope we meet again," he said.

"Probably this evening," she answered with a smile.

Richard Protze sat shaking in the Abwehr offices. "We'll catch the band tonight or never," he muttered.

Rita Pasci rang up from the flat: "Jurek is uneasy . . . he's packing his bags."

The Gestapo, led by Richard Protze, knocked at the door of Sosnowski's flat, just as the champagne supper was beginning. Jurek in dinner jacket opened the door himself and the Gestapo lined up hysterical women and white-faced men while they searched the flat.

"You are a spy," shouted the Gestapo at Jurek.

"No, no, nothing of the sort," he replied coolly.

"Then you are a confidence agent."

"You are quite mistaken," said the smiling Sosnowski.

"I'll tell you what he is," said the quivering Protze. "You are a Polish intelligence officer."

When this accusation was repeated in court some months later, Sosnowski clicked his heels and sprang to attention. There was dead silence.

"Yes, that's what I am."

The People's Court was crowded with high party men and the young German intelligence officers were detailed to attend proceedings as a lesson in intelligence matters. Frau von Falkenheyn and Frau von Natzmer were condemned to death, Fräulein von Jena to penal servitude for life. Hitler thwarted an attempt to marry Captain von Sosnowski and Benita von Falkenheyn in prison, a stratagem by which she hoped to save her life by obtaining Polish nationality.

As she was led out of court for the last time she cried: "I die gladly for my new Fatherland," and Jurek, deeply moved for the first time in the proceedings, stooped to kiss her hand. Both women died by the axe in February 1935. The furious Colonel Guderian broke off all social relations with the Poles, and there was anger and consternation in Reich government circles that such a fantastic scandal should have marred the new German-Polish treaty of friendship.

It took Richard Protze the best part of a day to relate the Sosnowski story from beginning to end, and his narrative differed notably from the sparse accounts that have hitherto come to light. I have therefore retold this story at some length, because it is all part of the struggle for mastery in the Third Reich, and also because we catch our first glimpse of Canaris in office through a Polish diplomat.

The Polish Ambassador in Berlin, Josef Lipski, remembers clearly how this awkward case brought him into contact with Canaris.

"It was about this time I was visited by an elderly, white-haired German Admiral," Lipski related to me. "Sosnowski was still in prison. I was struck by the soft, benevolent manner of this Canaris. He talked as if he was enlisting my sympathy by an especial degree of confidence. He seemed to be searching for the most sensible course of action for us both. I never dreamed for a moment that this was the Chief of German Intelligence.

"He suggested that Poland should exchange a German woman spy who was held in Warsaw for Captain Jurek von

Sosnowski. The Polish Government agreed with this suggestion and the exchange took place.

"Subsequently I invited Admiral Canaris to the Embassy and he came once or twice to dinner with his wife. I still had no idea of his identity."

What of the 150 documents and the plan of attack on Poland? As in so many cases of first-class espionage, the General Staff receiving the information refused to believe it. Sosnowski on his return to Poland was kept in a fortress while the Polish Intelligence Service tried to determine whether his documents were genuine, whether those of Griff-Tschaikovsky were genuine, or whether both were false.

"We suspected that Sosnowski had been transmitting misleading intelligence prepared by the Germans," Lipski told me.

General Lahousen, head of Abwehr II, was given Sosnowski as one of his principal intelligence targets when the Wehrmacht attacked Poland in September 1939. "But when we reached Warsaw," he said, "we found that he had been moved eastwards and had fallen into the hands of the Russians."

The unimaginative Griff-Tschaikovsky was hanged for treason; no particular benefit to Poland was gained from Sosnowski's daring work. As for Rita Pasci, the Hungarian dancer, when I last heard of her she was back in ruined Germany dancing with a gypsy band.

CHAPTER III

THE SPANISH ADVENTURE

WHEN THE SPANISH CIVIL WAR erupted in July 1936 few people in the outside world knew what was afoot, but it was very soon suspected in London and Paris that Germany had been the instigator of the Generals' revolt. Now that the archives of the German Foreign Ministry have been published (*Germany and the Spanish Civil War*)[1] it is plain that every foreign government was taken by surprise, Germany, too, but that Hitler was quickly advised and made his decisions within a few days. It appears also from other testimony that Canaris urged Hitler and Goering to support General Franco and acted as personal emissary to the Caudillo during the whole of the Civil War.

The spark that set the land aflame on July 16th, 1936, was the murder of the Conservative politician, Calvo Sotelo. He was called for in Madrid by the Spanish republican police and found dead next morning. That was the signal for civil war.

The war in Spain lasted from July 1936 until the spring of 1939, when Madrid fell. During those three years that span the time between Hitler's march into the Rhineland and the beginnings of his final mobilisation for war, a million Spaniards fell in battle against each other, the airmen of four foreign powers—Germany, Italy, France and Russia—were engaged, besides technicians, volunteers and foreign contingents of all sorts. The war correspondents of the world followed the battles and sieges in the peninsula and the diplomatic correspondents of all nations reported the work of the Non-Intervention Committee. During all this time Canaris came and went in Spain, sometimes under the pseudonym Guillermo, without being discovered either by the republicans or the world press.

The part of Canaris in deciding Hitler to act is described by Lieutenant-General Bamler, one of Canaris's departmental

[1] Documents on German Foreign Policy 1918–1945, vol. iii.

chiefs, and Colonel H. Remer, former German military attaché in Tangier, who asserts that Canaris obtained Goering's support for Franco and helped to get Italian aid for Spain. The official documents also show that Hitler and Goering, though taken by surprise, acted quickly and failed to exact hard political conditions from Spain as the price of their aid. At that moment the German General Staff was all for caution after the move into the Rhineland. The German Foreign Ministry was not anxious to have Germans fighting, and its Political Department on July 25th advised against supplying any arms to the emissaries of the rebels. The Reich was utterly unprepared for a general war, her western frontiers were unfortified and remained so until late 1938, her Army was less than half the size of the French Army. Admiral Raeder was against intervention.

I can find no statements that any highly placed German argued for quick and active aid to Spain except Wilhelm Canaris.

Lieutenant-General Bamler, then a major and departmental head of the German military security in Abwehr III, has given in Soviet interrogation an account of what Canaris did in July and August 1936. Bamler left his command and went over to the Russians during the last stages of the Eastern campaign. *Pravda* has printed his story, of which I give the main points.

"Spain interested me," related Bamler, "because I had previously been rapporteur on Spanish affairs in the third section of the General Staff. Canaris told me that he knew Spain particularly well. He said that he had good and wide contacts which he trusted in Spain, Spanish Morocco, and Rio de Oro." He maintained these contacts personally, and indeed his closest collaborators were not informed of all his contacts.

"Canaris was sent by the German Naval Intelligence Service to Spain in 1916 on a particularly important secret assignment. There with the help of Germans residing in Spain, and Spanish friends, he successfully prepared the setting up of a supply base for German submarines; he prepared a ramified system for observing the movements of British and French ships in the Mediterranean, especially off Gibraltar. From Spanish Morocco and Rio de Oro, he directed uprisings of Moroccan and Arab tribes against the French and the British. From then on, as Canaris himself told me, began his secret collaboration with Franco, who at that time was serving in the Spanish Army in Morocco in the rank of Major.

"After the Primo de Rivera Government was overthrown and the Republican parties came to power, Franco (who had since risen to become Chief of the Spanish General Staff) was sent to the remote Canary Islands. Another friend of Canaris, General Martinex Anido, who was Minister of the Interior under Primo de Rivera, quit Spain and lived in Portugal. Canaris had meanwhile restored his own intelligence system in Spain, making frequent trips for the purpose, and he kept up his contact with Franco."

The narrative of Bamler, which appears correct in its main facts, though possibly coloured by internment in Soviet Russia, continues that two agents of the insurgents arrived in Berlin to see Canaris as soon as the Civil War started.[1] Then Franco sent to inform him that he flown from the Canary Islands to Morocco and wanted military assistance and air transport for his troops to subdue the Republicans in Spain.

"I myself was a witness of how Canaris brushed aside all other questions and spared neither time nor effort to have the leading men of Germany and Italy interested in his plans. Canaris explained everywhere that although Franco was unknown as a politician he deserved full trust and support as he was a tested man with whom Canaris had worked for many years."

Canaris impressed Goering with his ideas. There were conferences in Goering's home, Karinhall, on the Spanish war and in the offices of the Prussian Prime Minister, one of Goering's many posts.

Canaris asked for Junkers transport aircraft to fly the Moroccan troops and the Spanish Foreign Legion across the Straits of Gibraltar to Spain. Goering was at first dubious of such a venture. Then, says Bamler, Canaris went straight to Hitler.

It is appropriate here to say something of the relationship between Canaris and Hitler. General Jodl, when he was asked by the Nuremberg tribunal whether he passed on the reports of Canaris to Hitler when they told unpleasant truths, replied

[1] Probably Langenheim and Bernhardt, whose names are revealed in *Germany and the Spanish Civil War*.

that Canaris had direct access to the Fuehrer whenever he
wished. This was so, and if in later years Canaris failed to
report directly to him it was because they had instinctively
fallen out of sympathy. At this moment, in 1936, Hitler was
still honouring his agreements with the General Staff; he was
not interfering in military matters; he had not begun to arm
the S.S., he had not yet accepted perjured evidence against
his Commander-in-Chief, General von Fritsch.

Canaris and his master had in common an intuitive hatred
for Bolshevism and a leaning towards the British in their
political theory. They were both possessed of strong suggestive
powers, but whereas Hitler streamed out his hypnotics to the
masses and to small audiences alike and all the time, without
breath or pause, Canaris worked upon the individual with
softness and flattery in an infinity of degrees. During military
conferences it was noticed that he had a curious soft eloquence
that attracted and quietened Hitler.

"You can talk to the man," he said. "He can see your point
of view, if you are careful not to irritate him. He can be reasonable."

The story of the agents from Spain is borne out in a document
of the Reich Chancellery dated July 5th, 1939, which reveals
how the decision to intervene in Spain was taken. It recom-
mends two Germans living abroad to be decorated for services
in the Spanish Civil War and states in a preamble:

"At that time (late July 1936)[1] Herr Langenheim and Herr
Bernhardt, members of the Foreign branch of the Party,
arrived in Berlin from Spain with a letter from General
Franco to the Fuehrer. . . . The first interview with the Fuehrer,
on which occasion the letter was delivered, took place in
Bayreuth . . . after the Fuehrer's return from the theatre.
Immediately afterwards the Fuehrer summoned Field-Marshal
Goering, the War Minister, General von Blomberg and an
admiral who was present at Bayreuth. That night support for
the Generalissimo was agreed to in principle, while additional
details were worked out during the course of the following
day."

It is probable that the admiral at Bayreuth was Canaris.
Colonel Remer's statement is also emphatic that Canaris was a

---

[1] The German Consul in Tetuan reported on July 24th that they were on their
way by air.

decisive influence with the Reich Government and with Italy in the Spanish affair. If the documents hitherto published in *Germany and the Spanish Civil War* do not bear this out, that is perhaps because the Chancellery and War Ministry correspondences are not included.

According to Bamler, the Fuehrer asked Canaris for a detailed report on Franco. The Admiral obtained permission for military assistance for the insurgents, and for himself special authority to act in these secret operations with Spain. Then he was off to Italy to meet his Italian colleague, General Roatta, and convince him that Mussolini must support Franco as well. Gone were the days when Roatta peered anxiously northwards over the Brenner Pass and asked Lahousen in Austria to find out more about the German armoured divisions. The dispute over Abyssinia had made Germany and Italy allies.

Canaris was received by Mussolini to expound his case on Spain and flew back to Berlin to supervise further operations. He helped to organise Hisma and Rowak, Spanish and German purchasing commissions for the Spanish insurgents; Rowak had Bernhardt at its head. It was disguised as a commercial firm and bought arms for them in Germany, Czechoslovakia and elsewhere.

"Canaris did not only organise arms supplies to Franco. He supplied them to the Spanish Republican Government, too."

This interjection came from Richard Protze of Abwehr III F, with whom I reviewed German participation in the Civil War.

"You won't find that in the documents, either," he said. "This is how it happened. Goering as Administrator of the Four Year Plan had charge of German arms deliveries and the release of foreign currency for the Civil War. Someone suggested at one of his conferences that Germany should attempt to provide weapons to the Spanish republicans as a means of sabotaging their war potential. Goering liked the idea and asked who could carry it out.

"'I can,' said Canaris, 'I've got the man for you.'

"There was a German arms dealer, Josef Veltjens, whom Canaris directed to buy up all the superannuated weapons from the First World War which Canaris had helped to sell abroad after the Treaty of Versailles. Rifles, carbines, ammunition and grenades were bought up in Czechoslovakia, Balkan countries and elsewhere. They were brought to

Germany, where S.S. armourers filed down the striking pins, doctored the ammunition, reduced the grenade charges or inserted instantaneous fuses. The consignments were then distributed to international arms dealers in Poland, Finland, Czechoslovakia and Holland and resold to the Spanish Government for cash payment in gold. Veltjens himself owned three cargo vessels which were used to ship the arms to Spain."

Canaris flew many times to and from the peninsula high over France by night in stripped-down Junkers transport aircraft sitting among the stores and the reserve petrol cans. Together with General Faupel, the military envoy to the Burgos government, he set up liaison headquarters with the Spanish Army that was to command and administer the German Condor Legion, an air corps with anti-aircraft batteries and observer units. The Condor Legion was highly specialised in air attack and air defence with fighter and bomber aircraft.

I remember meeting a Bavarian baron in the Luftwaffe, Sigismund von Gravenreuth, who had volunteered for Spain and earned Hitler's Spanish Cross for aerial combats. He was diffident about the decoration because he was still under oath of secrecy about operations in Spain. The Luftwaffe got valuable combat experience in Spain, he said. He was shot down in the Second World War by the R.A.F.

Britain and France were disturbed by the developments in Spain and the Popular Front saw itself, far from becoming a Pan-European party, being undermined by the Germans from both north and south. Communist and Republican arms and volunteers passed into Spain through the Pyrenean frontier and the Mediterranean ports.

As to German war supplies, a few telegrams went through Foreign Ministry channels to Canaris in the first months of the Civil War, asking for weapons; but the whole apparatus of German armed intervention was quickly transferred to the High Command and run by the Abwehr as a secret operation. Canaris had his correspondence on military aid and foreign intervention sent in Abwehr codes to his offices in Berlin. For three years he played a leading part in the Spanish affair as well as his general work of expanding the Abwehr and defending it against the increasing demands of the S.S. He succeeded in keeping the Condor Legion a top-secret unit, difficult to assess or penetrate even by the Spanish Army that worked with it. Meanwhile Colonel Baron Geyr von Schweppenburg, military attaché in London, had been appointed German member of the International Non-Intervention Committee and reported to Berlin that the British who held the key to the whole situation were evidently playing a waiting game.

"If you and France close the Pyrenees and enforce a proper blockade," the Burgos government's agents protested to the British, "the Civil War will be over in a few months." But the British were not certain that a speedy victory of Franco with German support would be to their advantage. There were lively sympathies between the British Labour Party and the Madrid and Barcelona Republicans. Mr. Clement Attlee, leader of the Opposition, made it plain to Mr. Chamberlain that if any favour were shown to the insurgents the go-slow among the engineering unions might well develop into strikes that would retard the vital rearmament of Britain herself. The Foreign Office comforted itself by saying that the forces of evil in Europe were bleeding themselves in Spain. A strong military government in Spain might well form military alliances with the Axis powers. Geyr von Schweppenburg reported to Berlin conversations with British military attachés whom, he said, casually asserted that Britain could best be served by a weak Spain. These arguments could be heard in London in 1937 and many responsible Englishmen were disturbed by them.

Admiral Canaris may have attributed a farseeing cunning to the British attitude on the Spanish Civil War. He never entirely understood the degree to which Great Britain was divided by its social-political disputes, and how, sitting half-way between *fainéance* and wisdom, the British Government had continually to defer to Socialist international opinion. Among his own people he had hard work to reconcile the conservative minds of the German Army to the Spanish adventure.

General von Fritsch, the Commander-in-Chief, and General Ludwig Beck, the Chief of the German General Staff, disliked it intensely. It was committing men and auxiliary weapons to a theatre of operations with no proper lines of communications, in face of superior naval power and hostile world opinion in a situation which might lead to a general war. Yet Canaris got his way and none of the strange leakages of information subsequently noticeable in German military planning marred the campaign in Spain. His own name did not even emerge, though he was the principal director infiltrating the Germans in by air and sea. A strict silence fell on all German personnel selected for the operation: it was related at the time that a few officers who had talked to their families about their destination were found guilty of treason and sentenced to death. The German aircraft flew over Spanish battlefields, the detectors and predictors were tried out, the A.A. guns of the Luftwaffe fought the Republican aircraft, Hitler's ordnance artificers toiled and sweated in Franco's service.

It needs an effort of memory today to recall how long the Spanish Civil War dragged on—until May 1939, within a month or two of the Second World War breaking out. I have met Spaniards who are equally vague about the latter date, and when you talk to them of the war assume that you mean their Civil War. When Madrid fell on March 28th, 1939, Canaris looked back on thirty-two months of intense work on the Spanish operation. *Germany and the Spanish Civil War* shows that he received some of the first reports on the confused fighting that broke out in July 1936, that General Mola on the Northern Front sent him urgent appeals for arms and that Hitler sent him to Franco in October 1936 to urge him to a more energetic prosecution of the war. He toured the front with Franco, heard his first tentative suggestions in April 1938 that the Condor Legion should be withdrawn from Spain, and in April 1939 was sent to persuade Franco to announce publicly that Spain had joined the Anti-Comintern Pact.

Abshagen relates from conversations with his staff that it was a constant exhilaration to Canaris to be quit of Germany and back in Spain, tearing about the ruinous Spanish roads in a fast car, dining at little wayside inns, whiling away an hour or so at Cartagena or Cadiz, savouring southern dishes and rough wine, chatting with his cronies of the Spanish Armada, looking across from Algeciras at the British warships at Gibraltar. The dry red hills of Spain, its worn Sierras and mud-built villages with their windowless churches, its beauties of Goya, Zurbaran and Murillo, how he was sad to leave them, and how his spirits rose when he was back in this land, joking with his head of Abwehr I, Colonel Piekenbrock, or his adjutant, and giving an exaggerated Nazi salute to a herd of sheep by the roadside.

"Who knows," he said with a wink to his adjutant as the car sped on. "There may be one of our high officials among them."

I do not suppose for a moment that the British Secret Service was not aware that a strange and important German was active in the peninsula. It could not know for certain at that time that German military aid to Spain, computed at 5,000,000,000 Reichsmarks, had been made unconditionally—described by Hitler to Ciano in 1940 as "an absolute gift" to Spain and that there was no secret military alliance between Hitler and Franco. When the Civil War was over, Germany had got Spain to become a signatory of the Anti-Comintern Pact and had certainly strengthened her influence openly and subversively—but the proud and independent Spanish character soon reasserted itself. When a law was passed restricting foreign control in Spanish mining interests, the German Ambassador hurried round to protest, but he was told by Count Jordana that it was not customary for Spain to consult foreign powers before passing her laws. It is noteworthy in view of what we shall learn of Canaris during the Munich crisis to see that his friend the Caudillo on September 28th, 1938, let it be known that Spain would remain neutral in the event of a general conflict over Czechoslovakia. Such were the beginnings of what can be called a policy of insubordination—in which Canaris played an important part. But in 1936, if his hand was seen in the peninsula at all, it was for the British the hand of a dangerous enemy, a man who was encouraging Adolf Hitler into foreign adventures.

CHAPTER IV

THE RUSSIAN KNOT

CANARIS HELD THEIR careers in his hand, the industrious, obedient General Staff and Abwehr officers who sat stiffly round the table at the Tirpitzufer for his daily conferences. They called him "Excellency", and when he laid a cigar on the table a dozen cigar cutters sprang from their pockets; he continued to talk on unseeing and then rapidly pierced it with his own. He half raised the cigar to his lips and the lucifers spluttered all round him. He laid it down again and went off into deep discussion for minutes together until their attentiveness tailed off, and then he was lighting his cigar in a twinkling before one of them could spring forward. That was a trait of his character, exacting, mistrustful, independent, and yet he inspired them. The spell of the Fuehrer and his automaton marshals and grand admirals faded out of the minds of Germans, but among those who worked under Admiral Canaris I had the strong feeling that they were still living in the past with their chief, obeying, quarrelling, doubting, and loyal despite everything. He disliked flattery, worked without ceasing, was abstemious and usually drank no more than a glass of red wine and water in the evening.

One of his many peculiarities was his demonstrative fondness for his rough-haired dachshunds. When he travelled they often went with him and slept on a second bed beside his own. He was a lover of horses, who rode regularly and well. In contrast to him, Hitler was never known to mount a horse or even travel with outriders. A few wolf-like Alsatian dogs prowled in his Berchtesgaden domain. He, too, was mistrustful, but he was harsh and disdained suffering, whereas Canaris was continually busy in some act of compassion. One of his many nicknames, used behind his back, was *Vater der Vertriebenen*, or father of the persecuted.

Yet despite their dissimilarities there was some sympathy

between Fuehrer and Intelligence Chief in the early days of office.

"He is reasonable and sees your point of view, if you point it out to him properly," Canaris repeated to his adjutant. "*Man kann mit ihm reden.*"

It was one of the silent obsessions of Hitler that his Army had never abandoned the policy of secret understanding with the Russian Army that had prevailed in the Weimar republic. Although he had denounced the secret training treaty of 1926 and argued his views with the retired Chief of General Staff, General von Seeckt, he was still not satisfied that illicit contacts did not exist. The two biggest armies in the world had been forcibly separated and arranged in opposite camps by Adolf Hitler. He and his internal system of tyranny thrived on the military tension between these two nations. Stalin, to judge by his subsequent behaviour, would have been willing enough to continue a policy of understanding and prolong the 1926 military agreement.

Suppose, then, that the German and Russian generals ever met each other secretly and complained: "We soldiers understand each other—it is these two political systems— Bolshevism and National Socialism that make our people enemies; if the regimes were destroyed the people would have peace."

This thought must have kept Hitler awake at nights. It will also have occurred to Stalin. So we come to the year 1936 in which Hitler resolved to have the unconditional obedience of the German Army.

Stalin was equally dissatisfied with some of his own generals. Marshal Tuchachewski, deputy chief of the Commissariat of Defence, had represented Russia at the funeral of King George V in February 1936, and subsequently he and General Putna, the Russian military attaché in London, had secretly met emissaries of General Miller and the White Russian émigrés of Paris. This much Stalin knew from his own spies. On his way back to Moscow, Tuchachewski had stopped in Berlin for talks with his military attaché, and there a German Communist agent named Blimiel had managed to slip into a small private meeting between the Marshal and some of the Russian émigrés in Germany. Blimiel reported the meeting to the Soviet Embassy in Berlin next morning. So when Tuchachewski arrived back in Moscow he walked into the shadow of suspicion.[1]

He was to have returned to London in May to the coronation of King George VI, but it was announced that the Marshal had a chill and would not go to London. He was transferred from the Commissariat for Defence to the Volga command, kept under secret observation for some months, and then arrested.

In the latter half of 1936 Heydrich went to the Tirpitzufer to ask Canaris for facsimiles of the expired German-Russian military training agreement with the signatures of the generals who had signed it, Tuchachewshi, Seeckt and Hammerstein. He asked, besides, for the loan of handwriting experts who would be able to forge these signatures, and he declared that the Fuehrer had given him charge of a most secret operation for which this material was required. It was intended to plant false information on the Russians. According to Abshagen, Canaris was on the defensive and tried to find out more about the operation. The Gestapo was touching delicate subjects that were outside its scope. He refused Abwehr co-operation, and there was an angry dispute with Heydrich.

On June 12th, 1937, it was announced in Moscow that Marshal Tuchachewski and seven other Russian generals had been shot for acts of high treason and espionage for a foreign state. The blood purge of the Russian officer corps followed and continued for the rest of 1937, thousands of suspect Russian officers perishing, many of them innocent. General Beck, writing an appreciation of the general military situation in the summer of 1938, gave it as his opinion that the Russian Army was not a factor to be reckoned with at that moment and that the blood purge had left it temporarily without morale, an inert machine.

Heydrich came back to the Tirpitzufer and related with gloating satisfaction that he found other means of forging secret correspondence between the German Army leaders and Marshal Tuchachewski that indicated intentions to overthrow the Soviet regime. He claimed that this was the idea of Hitler, that it had been planted first on the Czechoslovak General Staff and sent from Prague to Moscow. It was this ruse that had set

---

[1] I have the story of Blimiel from a German professor who shared his prison cell. My own attempts to trace Blimiel in Berlin have been without result.

the corpses rolling, he said, and the Russian Army would be exhausted by this blood-letting for years ahead.

It will probably never be known what these forgeries did to tip the scales against Tuchachewski. The details have been related in articles by Abwehr officers in the German press and in the book *I Chose the Gallows*. In several versions it is agreed that the papers were first passed to the Czechoslovak General Staff and President Benes is said to have been deceived by them and to have approved forwarding them to Stalin.

Hitler and Heydrich convinced themselves that some truth lay behind the forgery they had planted. On March 22nd, 1937, Heydrich arrested one of General von Sceckt's friends, Ernst Niekisch, who had helped to negotiate the 1926 training agreement. Niekisch was also a friend of the Russian journalist, Karl Radek, who had fallen from favour with Stalin, confessed deviation and been sentenced. Heydrich arrested nineteen other persons with Niekisch, some of whom had worked for the Army in liaison work with Russia.

Heydrich was bent on discovering whether the General Staff and the Abwehr still had forbidden contacts with the Russian General Staff. The investigation and the trial lasted till November 1938. One of Canaris's own agents was involved, and .the Admiral sat in the court to hear him give evidence. When that particular hearing was finished and the Gestapo learned nothing against him, Canaris walked forward in court, demonstratively shook his witness by the hand and asked him to let the office have a note of his expenses. This unusual example of civil courage was related to me years afterwards by Abwehr officers on whom it made a deep impression at the time. Canaris knew which were the moments when it was right to show some bravado. He had a solicitous care for his own people. Just before the trial began one of his confidence men (V-men) passed a report to the British press[1] with the comment that death sentences might be expected. This had some effect, as Niekisch told me afterwards. The President of the third senate of the Peoples' Court thundered at the accused: "The foreign press has forecast death sentences, lying again as usual. The court will pass sentences of imprisonment only."

The Gestapo attempts to discover a secret army policy were carried on in camera and neither side invited any publicity

[1] News Chronicle.

to this trial of wits, except when it was a matter of saving the
lives of the accused. I have been obliged to reconstruct the
sequence of events from the memory of Abwehr officers, from
the notes that I took at the time as a journalist and from contemporary press cuttings which passed without contradiction.
I may add that after sending reports on the Niekisch trial, my
Berlin flat was watched closely in November and December
1938 and one of my informants being followed away from it only
shook off pursuit by mingling with the crowd coming out of
a nearby cinema. The coincidence that a White Russian lived
next door to me led the Gestapo astray from my real informants
in subsequent investigations.

I met Ernst Niekisch nine years afterwards in 1946, a portly,
mild-mannered professor lecturing in Berlin University, still pur-
blind from his prison treatment, still also on friendly terms with
the Russians who had liberated him in 1945 after seven years
in Brandenburg gaol, where he happened to sit next to Blimiel,
the Communist agent who had shadowed Tuchachewski.
Blimiel had been arrested during the war for taking home a fuse
cap that was on the secret list from a Berlin munitions factory.
He had smuggled it out through the X-ray detection chamber in
a lunch-box lined with lead. Two other of these samples he
had taken to the Soviet Embassy in Berlin and forwarded to
Russia. His defence had been that he wanted "to use it as
a paper weight", which, since it was found lying openly on
his desk, answered wonderfully well. He escaped with a life
sentence.

The Niekisch cases were altogether too slow for Heydrich and
they were producing no revelations that would shake the Army.
Himmler and he could not wait to break the power of the
General Staff. They feared that it would otherwise break them
and act in a crisis against the Nazi regime. They therefore
prepared together with a living witness—he did not live for long
—a case of moral delinquency supported by perjured evidence against the Commander-in-Chief, General von Fritsch,
and ousted that upright and bewildered man from the key
position in the forces. Blomberg, the War Minister, who had
made an unfortunate marriage with a woman of bad reputation, was retired about that time, and on February 4th, 1938,
the General Staff was deprived of some of its most important

THE RUSSIAN KNOT

functions that passed to a new High Command under the direct control of Hitler.

"This was the time," nodded Richard Protze, "when Canaris began to turn from Hitler. He must have known more than us all about the extraordinary accusations of homosexuality that Heydrich concocted against the Commander-in-Chief. It is well known that Heydrich schooled a delinquent named Schmidt to swear that he had had perverse relations with General von Fritsch, whereas the other party to Schmidt was in fact a Captain von Frisch. The Admiral set me the difficult task at an hour's notice of taking a photograph of this Captain von Frisch being spirited away from his home by S.S. men who were afraid of the true version of the affair becoming known. I managed to get that photograph without knowledge of the S.S. and it was produced in court by the defence. The case collapsed, but Hitler never reinstated Fritsch. The S.S. murdered Schmidt and most probably Frisch, too. If you have to mark any one event as the crisis of loyalty between Canaris and Hitler, that is it."

The Fuehrer spoke what was in his mind in getting rid of General von Fritsch during a visit of inspection to a military parade at Gross Born in the summer of 1938. "I, too, would not recoil from destroying ten thousand officers," he told his listeners, in reference to the Russian purges, "if they opposed themselves to my will. What is that in a nation of eighty millions? I do not want men of intelligence. I want men of brutality."[1]

This was all a little too much for the Admiral, who stood in the midst of these affairs, a target for malice and suspicion. He had thought himself a master of secret weapons and the Great General Staff a force that could outride a period of national revolution. But now he saw from the Moscow trials and the Berlin intrigues that generals in the twentieth century were no more than puppets in uniform, helpless in face of the modern state and its apparatus of perverted justice and police rule. Early in 1939 the last restraint fell from Hitler and he began to form the S.S. into military divisions and equip them with the full scale of army weapons, so that he finally achieved his ambition of a well-equipped private army.

The General Staff selected several officers to work out the organisation and supply of these new formations, which was

[1] Contemporary report made to General Oster.

achieved only after bitter quarrels. Even so, there was no clear line for the Army to defend; for although most of them hated the idea of arming the S.S., some comforted themselves with the thought that the Waffen-S.S. (or S.S. Army) would then take its place in the battlefield and be bled with the rest. Unless the S.S. demands were resisted on principle, it was easy enough to find some reason good enough for not making an absolute stand against them.

While the S.S. helped themselves in the armoury, the Security Service, or S.D., bored its way into the counter-espionage trade. The S.D. men met the military intelligence officers at regular "comradely" beer parties between Army and Party and kept their ears open.

Colonel Bamler, the same man who studied Spain and deserted to the Russians in 1945, was Chief of Department III (military security) in the vital years 1934-8. He sold the pass to the Nazis. Bamler was an undistinguished character.

In his enthusiasm for counter-espionage work, he organised a team of some fifteen cabaret girls with linguistic and other cosmopolitan attainments in Berlin's Koenigin Bar, where they spied on the attachés and foreign visitors, while Bamler, like a ringmaster, or worse, sat nearby drinking champagne into the early hours at the expense of the Abwehr. I doubt whether "Colonel Bamler's Follies" learned anything from the attachés in that hectic red plush atmosphere; but while he fiddled in the Koenigin Bar, Heydrich and his henchmen were burrowing deeper into the mysteries of military counter-espionage.

CHAPTER V

OPERATION OTTO

HITLER HAD CASUALLY remarked in the course of a small conference held secretly on November 5th, 1937, that he intended to go to war sooner or later. The papers of General Beck, present as Chief of General Staff, give some account of this meeting. Hitler then said that after 1943 he would no longer have superiority in weapons. Lord Halifax, the Lord President, was sent out to Berlin and Berchtesgaden at this time. The open pretext given for his visit was the hunting exhibition organised by Reich Huntsmaster Goering in Berlin, but Halifax was really taking up the enquiries made previously of Hitler by Sir John Simon and Mr. Eden in 1936. Was an understanding between Britain and Germany possible? Hitler assured Lord Halifax that Germany intended to obtain a revision of her frontiers by peaceful means. He and Goering both declared that Austria and Germany could be united without a war, and the diffident and fair-minded Halifax admitted the force of their argument that it would be difficult in that case for the Western Allies to intervene. The American roving Ambassador, William Bullitt, was also in Berlin in November 1937, saw Goering, and wrote in a memorandum to the State Department; "I asked Goering if he meant that Germany was absolutely determined to annex Austria to the Reich. He replied that this was an absolute determination of the German Government. He was not pressing the matter because of certain momentary political considerations, notably relations with Italy. A union of Austria, Hungary and Czechoslovakia would be absolutely unacceptable to Germany—such an agreement would be an immediate *casus belli*." It was plain that what the Nazis most feared was a restoration of the Habsburg Monarchy.

Abshagen notes that in the winter of 1937–8 a secret metamorphosis was taking place in Admiral Canaris. He was in a better position than any to know what terrible conflicts lay ahead for Europe if Hitler persisted in his policy of war. His departmental chief of Abwehr I, Colonel Piekenbrock, brought him reports on Allied rearmament: it was proceeding slowly but evidently out of far greater resources than Germany commanded.

While Ribbentrop comforted himself with the thoughts that the British Fascists under Sir Oswald Mosley would achieve a national revolution in Britain, Canaris quietly asked an English visitor to Berlin what was expected of the British Fascists.

"We treat them as a joke," the visitor replied.

The Admiral demurred and then accepted the opinion.

General Ludwig Beck, the Chief of the General Staff, was disturbed at the thought of occupying Austria. It would not stop there, because it meant in fact a Balkan line, a southeastward thrust in German policy, assimilation of alien races, domination of Czechs, Hungarians, Rumanians, Bulgarians, and a clash with Turkey.

Canaris found himself in agreement with his service chiefs —a policy of annexation and expansion south-east was against all their ideas of security. He did not think that the attack on Austria could be prevented, but he began to collect around him, in the utmost stealth, such men as might be able to prevent Hitler from carrying out other plans. It was at this time that I had my first glimpses of his separate diplomacy, and first heard his name whispered.

Colonel Hans Oster, his deputy and Chief of the Central Section, was a more daring spirit in many repects than his chief. An elegant cavalry officer of the old school, handsome, gallant with the ladies and contemptuous of the National-Socialist leaders, he was all for striking when the iron was hot; but the Admiral had a more hesitant nature. Gradually his departmental chiefs, Piekenbrock, Groscurth and perhaps even Bamler—later, too, von Bentivegni and Lahousen—came to discern that their chief's heart was no longer in the business and that a depth of meaning lay behind his careless criticisms of the leaders of the Reich.

When Hitler, on February 4th, 1938, took over the post of War Minister himself and detached and formed the High Command of the Armed Forces under his direct control (known since as the O.K.W.), he appointed as Chief of the High Command General Wilhelm Keitel, who thus became the direct

chief of Admiral Canaris. Canaris must report to this big, stolid
soldier who was terribly ignorant of the world. The O.K.W.
took over prime responsibility for interpreting intelligence, planning and directing operations, for strategy and for higher command. The General Staff was left to organise, train and expand
the Army. Canaris now sent his reports to the O.K.W.

The next task that fell to him was to prepare plans for the
intimidation of Austria. Both Bullitt and Halifax had been so
negative in their reactions to German aims that Hitler saw the
Anschluss as a perfectly safe and reasonable operation.

The diary of General Jodl, the deputy chief of the High
Command, relates this phrase of the intelligence game. Jodl
declared in Nuremberg that he supplied the Admiral with full
information on German military dispositions in February 1938,
so that he could prepare a deception plan for "Case Otto".

The Reich Government had realised the adverse effect on
morale in the Army and on world opinion if German troops
were mobilised or moved to the Austrian frontier. Hitler decided
to feint instead.

Jodl wrote in his diary on February 12th:

"On the evening of 11th and on 13th February, General
Keitel with General von Reichenau and Air General Sperrle at
the Obersalzberg. Schuschnigg together with Guido Schmidt
are being put under heaviest political and military pressure.
At 23.00 hours Schuschnigg signs protocol.

"13th February: In the afternoon General K. (Keitel) asks
Admiral C. (Canaris) and myself to come to his apartment.
He tells us that the Fuehrer's order is to the effect that military
pressure, by shamming military action, should be kept up until
the 15th. Proposals for these deceptive manœuvres are drafted
and submitted to the Fuehrer by telephone for approval.

"14th February: At 2.40 o'clock the agreement of the Fuehrer
arrives. Canaris went to Munich to Abwehr Office VII and
initiated the different measures.

"The effect is rapid and strong. In Austria the impression is
created that Germany is undertaking serious military preparations."

A document submitted by General Keitel, who himself took
part in the deception scheme at Berchtesgaden, rattling off
fictitious troop movements to the Austrian statesmen, shows
these proposals of Canaris as approved by the Fuehrer.

(1) To take no real measures of preparation in the Army or
Luftwaffe. No troop movements or redeployments.

(2) To spread false but quite credible news which may give
the impression of military preparations against Austria:
(a) through V-men (*Vertrauensmänner* or agents);
(b) through German customs personnel at the frontier;
(c) through travelling agents.

(3) Such rumours could be
(a) stoppage of leave in the area of VII Army Corps;
(b) rolling-stock is concentrated in Munich, Augsburg
and Regensburg;
(c) Major-General Muff, the German military attaché
in Vienna, is recalled to Berlin for consultation
(this happened to be true);
(d) police reinforcements on the Austrian frontier;
(e) customs officials report Alpine troop movements
in the Freilassing, Reichenhall and Berchtesgaden area.

Both General Lahousen and Abshagen, first biographer of
Canaris, assure me that the Austrian Government was not
deceived and therefore presumably not intimidated by these
rumours put about by the Munich office of the Abwehr.
Nevertheless, President Miklas of Austria ratified the Berchtesgaden protocol with his signature and thus made the National-
Socialist Party legal again in Austria. They might wear
uniforms now and march the streets again.

Canaris—it was typical of his restless nature—would not
leave the deception plan to his departmental chief, Colonel
Groscurth, and himself flew to Munich to explain it to his
representative in Bavaria, Count Marogna-Redwitz.

Soon, at any rate, it must have become apparent to the
Austrians that their concessions had been wrung from them
by a bluff. But as they tried to reassert law and order against
the resurgent Nazis, it became obvious that clashes and bloodshed could be expected. Schuschnigg, who had been warned
by Hitler against a Customs Union with Czechoslovakia or a
restoration of the monarchy, suddenly announced on March
9th a plebiscite throughout Austria on the question of independence.

"The plebiscite should bring a strong majority for the Monarchists," noted Jodl in his diary. "The Fuehrer is determined not to tolerate it."

Hitler called together his military advisers and ordered the march into Austria for the day of the plebiscite. He wrote to break the news to Mussolini and told Ribbentrop to stay in London, where he sat firmly on the sofa in No. 10 Downing Street on the afternoon of the invasion telling his hosts that everything would be all right.

On March 10th General Keitel told Admiral Canaris of the decisions taken. There was now no need for a deception plan to intimidate the Austrians. The troops were concentrated, the rolling-stock really rolled, the police were reinforced. But now the Austrian Government was inclined not to believe their own intelligence reports. Schuschnigg thought that the game of bluff was still being played, until it was too late to mobilise the Austrian Army.

Canaris was in Vienna soon after the first German tanks to see what intelligence targets his men had captured. There were the files of the Austrian Intelligence Service to be perused. He had a special detachment out known as Force ZL, to lay hands on any documents relating to himself before the Austrian Nazis or the Reich S.S. should get them. One captured target he surveyed with satisfaction, Colonel Erwin Lahousen, the Austrian Chief of Intelligence, now became his personal property. The Abwehr promptly swallowed the Austrian Intelligence Service.

The Admiral, short of stature, looked up at the tall Lahousen when he reported to him, and asked with a mysterious frown:

"Why did you not shoot? You Austrians are to blame for everything."

Lahousen was a product of the Austrian Imperial Army. Obedience had become his second nature. Two men from the Reich were busy drawing others into their service, and while Himmler gathered the many Austrian brownshirts, Canaris carefully took his pick of the others. Lahousen served him with devotion to the end, and when they first discussed selection of Austrian intelligence officers for service in the Reich the Admiral fixed Lahousen with his keen eye and said softly:

"Bring me real Austrians. I don't want any Austrian Nazis."

Having given this second indication of his own opinions, Canaris set Lahousen to work spying out the Czechoslovak frontier fortifications and troop dispositions, and Lahousen set about it with zeal.

"I quite understand that you question my behaviour," he told me years later, as we sat and drank a glass of beer together in Munich. "I undertook this work because I was an officer of the Austrian Imperial Army. I had always regarded the Czechs as trouble-makers."

This was the time in which the Admiral's mind was filling with misgivings and Lahousen's analysis of his thoughts is interesting. He told me that Canaris was in favour of a union of Germany with Austria, but not on the basis of an invasion and National-Socialist supremacy. He hoped that the Austrians would take his deception plan seriously and mobilise, and he was obliged to admit afterwards that the Austrians, having failed to be taken in by the plan in February, deceived themselves into thinking that the real mobilisation in March was also a bluff.

Canaris made arrangements to absorb or dissolve the remnants of the Austrian Intelligence Service and returned to Berlin.

CHAPTER VI

THE CONSPIRACIES BEGIN

Everything had gone down before Hitler and his party: they were nearly as powerful in Germany as the Communist Party in Russia. There was nothing that Canaris could do but watch for some new means of curbing his master without revealing his own hand too far. So his regular service life went on undisturbed with a seven-day week in the office, a ride every morning in the Tiergarten Park, a small dinner party now and then in his new villa in the Dianastrasse that rarely exceeded two guests. During his working hours he and his deputy, Hans Oster, kept in touch with a small number of remarkable people, some of whom were taken into his organisation as soon as war broke out. Meanwhile he was careful to keep a meticulous diary of the events of his official life, first in his own hand and then dictated to his secretary and typed in two copies, one of which he kept himself, while the other was put in the safe within the department.

The National-Socialist system discouraged and forbade the free exchange of information between government officials. There was certain strictly organised liaison such as Heydrich maintained with Canaris in Gestapo policy matters and the Foreign Intelligence branch[1] maintained with the Foreign Ministry. Apart from that, Baron von Weiszäcker, the Permanent Under-Secretary of State in the Foreign Ministry, kept Canaris stealthily informed of events and political undercurrents in the Wilhelmstrasse. The Admiral could find out what was going on in the Reich Chancellery. Colonel Schmundt, Hitler's Senior Adjutant after the resignation of Colonel Hossbach, was in contact with Canaris. A suave, discreet, obedient soldier, he could tell of visitors, conferences and intrigues, though not always able to report these events quickly. I remember in 1938 hearing of some intimate details

[1] Of the Abwehr.

of happenings in the Chancellery that reached the Abwehr
through Schmundt.

In the same way there was a means of penetrating the
Gestapo activities through Senior Group Leader Arthur
Nebe, an old Berlin police type who had been transferred
from the criminal police to the secret police and hated it.

Then there were the men who had no official position, but
by reason of their standing and connections could gather and
disseminate information and opinions, politicians working in the
shadows because open opposition was impossible. The most
notable of these was Dr. Karl Goerdeler, former Lord Mayor
of Leipzig, who had been proposed to President von Hindenburg
by Chancellor Brüning as his successor. He was an influential
man, highly thought of in America, but his name, like that of
a host of eminent men in the 'thirties, fell out of public memory
and was forgotten.

Another associate of Canaris was the lawyer, Count Helmut
von Moltke of Kreisau, a man of high intellect and imposing
physique, intense and uncompromising in his principles.

There was Doctor Joseph Mueller, an able Bavarian lawyer
—known popularly as Ochsensepp—Sepp being short for
Joseph and his birthplace being Ochsenfurt. Mueller was in the
confidence of the Pope, who had entrusted him with missions
in Germany. Nicholas von Halem, a lawyer, had contacts with
the British press. Hans von Dohnanyi, a Reichsgerichtsrat,
or K.C., Canaris had met in sorting out the legal complications
of the Fritsch case.

Dohnanyi's brothers-in-law, the Bonhoeffers, had wide
connections with the Protestant Church and some contact
with the Church of England. There was also Ewald von
Kleist-Schmenzin, leader of the Old-Conservative faction,[1]
which, although it had been dissolved in 1934, was still in
being and represented the ideas of the powerful landowners of
Prussia. Kleist and the Admiral saw the future very much with
the same eye, the Admiral liked him and thought highly of
his political gifts; but the Prussian Junker had made himself
feared and shunned even by old friends through his frank and
caustic criticisms of the Reich Government. He was not often
in Berlin, but when he came the Nazi District officer at Belgard
near his country home used to report him absent and the

[1] A strongly monarchist group.

Gestapo Security Service in Berlin tried to pick up his trail and watch his activities. This was a man with whom Canaris could achieve something, but not one to have in the office too often.

Another German Conservative, a younger man, Fabian von Schlabrendorff, was in the confidence of Canaris and kept up contacts for him with the Prussian Conservatives. He also saw Hans Gisevius, political contact man to Dr. Schacht, whom occasionally he met personally. There came and went a host of others whose minds the Admiral fathomed and to whom he revealed his own in an infinity of degrees, according to his idea of their politics and their discretion. Even among themselves his collaborators had no idea of the several uses to which he was putting them; but the broad lines of their action were discussed in small conferences at the Tirpitzufer, when ordinary service work permitted.

"Don't forget!" His peculiar soft manner of speech was mimicked to me by Schlabrendorff, who described how the Admiral would drop his voice to a whisper when the conversations with his close intimates were over. "We have not talked treason—only discussed the safety of the Reich."

Logically Canaris and his confederates cast about for some new force against Hitler. The Civil Service had succumbed, the Army had made its peace in 1934, when a promise was extracted from Hitler not to arm the Brownshirts; the Protestant and Roman Catholic Churches had been squeezed out of public life; German industry had capitulated and German finance had been dominated by Nazi economists.

"Foreign allies—world opinion—the governments of such powers as Great Britain and America, must come to the aid of Germany if war was to be avoided."

Such were the views that I heard with some amazement during lengthy discussions in Berlin with two of the German Old-Conservative Party in the spring of 1938, Ewald von Kleist and Herbert von Bismarck: they represented Prussian Junker opinion, which has sometimes been wrongly associated with the aims of Hitler. We met one April day in the Casino Club in Berlin and there for the first time I heard spoken in a whisper the name of the man who was protecting them and furthering their efforts.

"Canaris!"

Kleist described to me the difficulty of dealing through the British Embassy, which, besides being accredited to the Reich Government, was not as critical of its methods as they could have wished. Also there was the danger of discovery. The diplomats sent messages in cipher, which could be intercepted and sometimes broken. These men wanted contacts of a political nature outside the world of diplomacy and outside the intelligence services. Schlabrendorff described to me a conversation with Canaris in which they had discussed the possibility of working with the British Secret Service against Hitler.

One of them had suggested that the British Secret Service might co-operate with them against Hitler even if this was not official British policy. They imagined the Secret Service much as the British thought of the Abwehr, as a machine of power under logical control that was capable of positive thought and action.

Here is the answer that Canaris gave, which I memorised as exactly as I could and quote in direct speech.

"I must warn you against the British Secret Service," he said, "for several reasons. Should you work for them it will most probably be brought to my notice, as I think I have penetrated it here and there. They will want to send messages about you in cipher and from time to time we can break a cipher. Your names would appear in files and registers. That is bad, too. It would be difficult to overlook such activities in the long run. It has also been my experience that the Secret Service will requite you badly—if it is a matter of money, let me tell you, they do not reward services well, and if they have the least suspicion, they will not hesitate to betray you to me or to my colleagues of the Reich Security Service."

So they knew then where they stood.

It became a business of searching out reliable men with good political connections who were not known to or suspected by the Nazis. Joseph Mueller possessed special contact with the Vatican that might be considered of a diplomatic nature. Ewald von Kleist let it be known that he had an English friend who could arrange direct contact with London politicians. Karl Goerdeler thought immediately of Brüning and thought that he would be able to explain to the British with his aid what the predicament of Germany was.

"Now we have come to the case of Czechoslovakia," the Admiral told Kleist in May. "I am not at all sure that Great Britain will not choose to fight, if the Fuehrer marches into Czechoslovakia."

They confessed that none of them had positive knowledge. The British were aloof, not easy to sound on such a hypothetical question. It was a difficult question to ask in its real form. Ribbentrop through his diplomatic and foreign party intelligence channels was repeatedly asking for the private opinions of Englishmen. "Would Britain fight to stop Sudeten Germans from joining the Reich?" he inquired. But that was not the real question that the General Staff wanted to put.

Canaris and Oster drew Kleist aside early in May 1938 and told him of the actual state of secret policy, which he repeated to me a few hours later.

There was to be no deception plan against Czechoslovakia, no false rumour of troop movements and, above all, no escapades on the frontiers by the Nazi Party. The High Command had explained to Hitler that with his western frontiers unfortified, in face of a French Army numerically nearly twice as strong as the German Army in the spring of 1938, no challenge by the Western Allies could be accepted in the near future.

"Hitler is vulnerable in the issue of Czechoslovakia," said Oster. "If the Allies were to warn him against aggressive or subversive action, he would be obliged to accept the warning and desist, even if it were given only through diplomatic channels."

Kleist pondered this interim situation. The Reich was not strong enough for war, yet could not recoil towards peace, unless some impulse were given. What could bring a swing of the pendulum? He fancied that he saw a way.

Canaris brought him to General Beck, and the Chief of the German General Staff confessed to him that he, too, needed foreign allies to overcome Hitler. He spoke with the quiet emphasis of the scholar and philosopher. It was evident that he was not growling for immediate action against the Nazis, and that he looked first to the Commander-in-Chief for a decision. He would, however, act independently, he said, in a certain situation of crisis.

"England must lend us a sea anchor," said the Admiral, "if we are to ride out this storm."

It was a foible of Canaris that he imagined Germany's great adversary was hampered by none of those imponderables that hold lesser nations helpless when they should be united and active. He did not take into his calculations the bureaucratic delays in Whitehall, the perplexity and ignorance. He imagined that the Foreign Office in London would easily read and comprehend Germany's dilemma. If Britain hesitated for reasons unknown to him, then it all seemed part of a clever and intricate pattern of policy. He saw the might and tradition of the nation whose Navy had hunted him in the cruiser *Dresden* years ago. Britain seemed unweakened by the social and political upheavals that had shaken Germany and Russia in the past twenty years. He could not think that the English would make capital mistakes or allow accident to rule their policy.

I said nothing of my conversations with Kleist for some days for the simple reason that I did not fully understand what I had memorised. Then something in the events of the day made things more comprehensible to me. I went to see Sir George Ogilvie-Forbes, then Counsellor of the British Embassy, who had a more open and receptive mind than most of his colleagues and seemed not to be wholly in sympathy with the line of appeasement that his Ambassador, Sir Nevile Henderson, was still actively pursuing. I repeated to Sir George my conversations with Kleist and how he said the matters lay. The Army had in fact vetoed any hasty action by the party among the Sudeten-Germans, because Germany was still vulnerable. Hitler had undertaken not to commit himself yet under any circumstances—consequently he was actually afraid of incidents at this moment which might harm his prestige if he had to stand by and watch them happen before he was strong enough to intervene. Sir George asked me a number of searching questions, then he composed a dispatch for London on what I had said.

Within about a week an extraordinary thing happened. Rumours from German and Czechoslovak sources in the third week of May attached importance to military exercises near the Czechoslovak frontier by the National Socialist Motor Car Corps and local movements of troops.

"On receipt of circumstantial reports from Prague and elsewhere on May 20th," wrote Sir Nevile Henderson, the British Ambassador in Berlin, "I immediately called on the

THE CONSPIRACIES BEGIN 57

Under-Secretary, Baron von Weizsäcker, and asked him to tell me whether there was any truth in these stories."[1]

Whitehall was now aware of the temporary weakness of Hitler's position. It seemed as if for a short time the British and German Intelligence Services were working together with one purpose—to squeeze Hitler out. Weizsäcker formally denied the reports to the British Ambassador, but Lord Halifax in London, with Vansittart at his elbow, felt sure that now was the time to press Hitler hard. Warnings were spoken freely upon the open wire between London and Berlin.

"I spent most of May 21st at the Ministry of Foreign Affairs registering protests," wrote Sir Nevile. It seems that Hitler had no intention even to cause civil disturbances in Czechoslovakia in the second half of May 1938. He knew the momentary weakness of his own position too well. There may have been plans in preparation for some dangerous action at a later date. Certainly Hitler wanted Czechoslovakia quickly— in 1938—and he did not want to have to mobilise to get it. He may still have played with the idea of an internal revolution in the Sudeten area as a means of gaining his ends. The warnings of May 21st put an end to such fancies.

Immediately after Sir Nevile Henderson's démarche and the angry denials of Hitler and Keitel, the European press published reports that suggested that Hitler had been obliged to "climb down". The effect on him was instantaneous. The stories of Hitler rolling on the floor and biting the carpet date from May 21st, 1938. "England, I will never forget this," he cried in paroxysms of rage. But he was not long inactive. He summoned his Commander-in-Chief, General von Brauchitsch, on May 28th and gave orders for the West Wall of Germany to be built immediately and for increases in the peacetime strength of the armed forces to be put into effect.

"A damned, disgraceful, awful show," exclaimed Sir Nevile Henderson to me privately of the diplomatic démarches of May 21st and the press reports that ensued. Upon reflection, he described the effect in his memoirs as "unfortunate".

Such are the facts that I was able to gather about the memorable May 21st, a minor setback for Hitler which might have started the swing of the pendulum against him. When he

[1] He was, in fact, instructed from London to make these enquiries.

had sufficiently thought it over, he decided to send his adjutant, Captain Fritz Wiedemann, to London, to discover whether Halifax had altered his outlook and methods since the visit to Berchtesgaden. I cannot say for certain how close the hand of Canaris lay behind this blow against Hitler in the vulnerable interim. Kleist was very close to Canaris at this time and warned his own wife, so she tells me: "Remember that you have never heard me mention the names Canaris and Oster." Kleist could be secretive, but it was not in his nature to dissemble his contempt for the Nazis in any company and therefore he could not be taken into the Abwehr like some of his less implacable associates when war broke out. I had to guess sometimes, as we sat in a quiet corner of the Casino Club in Berlin, from the accent and emphasis of Kleist's narrative whence his counsels came and I can do no more than tell the reader what my impressions were then, since no amount of research now will uncover what went on between these two. It seemed to me that Admiral Canaris was using every oblique means in his power to beset and confound the cocksure demagogue and that one of the highest officers in the state was Adolf Hitler's secret enemy.

CHAPTER VII

A GLIMPSE OF CANARIS

CANARIS WAS SOON informed of the brainstorms in the Wilhelmstrasse and the determination of Hitler to have his way over Czechoslovakia. He probed, listened and chatted with his chief, General Keitel, and went deeper into the risks ahead with General von Brauchitsch, General Beck and the Under Secretary, von Weizsäcker. Adjutant Schmundt helped to complete the picture. It is customary for intelligence services to try and place a man near the ruler, but the difficulties of ascertaining what Hitler thought and did should not be underrated. Kleist came to Berlin from his Pomeranian home soon after the turmoil had subsided and visited Canaris again.

"The situation has altered now," Kleist told me. "There will be an attack of some sort on Czechoslovakia this year unless Britain pledges herself openly to go to the aid of that state *whatever* the form of aggression against her. M. Blum's Foreign Minister, Yvon Delbos, spoke this word once— 'quelconque'—but M. Blum has been out of power since April. We cannot expect the French to master this situation."

We waited a few weeks, but there was no further reaction from the British and no fresh statement of policy in Westminster. The attitude remained that spoken by Mr. Neville Chamberlain in the House of Commons on March 24th—that a conflict would be unlikely to be limited to those powers who had treaty obligations to Czechoslovakia.

There was a German journalist in London, one Dr. Karl Heinz Abshagen,[1] who was sending private reports to Oster on the political situation. Oster showed them to the Admiral. Abshagen asserted that the British would fight if a general conflict arose over Czechoslovakia, but Ribbentrop was reporting that the Chamberlain government would on no account fight and would even restrain France from making a firm stand.

[1] Author of the German biography of Canaris.

Josef Goebbels was nervous. He read Abshagen's reports and told his editor: "Abshagen must continue to report quite frankly, whether or not his reports agree with those of the Embassy in London. But tell him to take care that his phrasing gives no offence, for they will be read by our Fuehrer in the original." Goebbels was learning to appreciate the good things of this life; his mansion at Schwanenwerder, his banquets and *bierabends*, his dancing girls and motor cars would vanish like smoke if the Third Reich made a blunder over Czechoslovakia.

The reports were studied in Canaris's Foreign Branch. This was the insoluble question that was fraying the nerves of General Beck and the Commander-in-Chief in July 1938.

"Do you believe that England will fight if we attack Czechoslovakia?" Kleist asked of me.

"I believe so," I answered. "Perhaps only by a blockade at the outset."

"I daresay it is true," said Kleist. "I believe the British will fight." Then he dropped his voice and whispered: "The Admiral wants someone to go to London and find out. We have an offer to make to the British and a warning to give them."

There seemed to be no secret between Canaris and his political friends that Hitler had ordered the High Command to prepare for a general mobilisation in the autumn.

As we sat and discussed the riddle of the British attitude, in the Bendlerstrasse opposite the General Staff were already working intensively on the planning of Case Grün, the invasion of Czechoslovakia, General von Brauchitsch had been notified by Hitler in the last days of July that a general mobilisation was to be prepared, with September 28th as zero day. It was now early August.

The Abwehr had its deception plan to cover these preparations, which would not fail to be noticed, as Reichsbahn staff received orders to assemble rolling-stock, and civil contractors sent forward stores and rations. The intelligence game went on according to the rules by which it was played. One of Canaris's V-men was sent to the British military attaché with the news that zero day would be August 15th, perhaps to test British reactions and perhaps to put them off the scent.

The Chamberlain cabinet did not like unpleasant news, and

it found this hard to digest. Colonel F. N. Mason Macfarlane was taken to task by the Cabinet. Sir John Simon cross-examined him from a cold height. August 15th came and went and there were no disturbances and not a sign of German troop movements.

"It is difficult to explain to people like that," Colonel Macfarlane complained afterwards, "that what did not happen yesterday may still occur a fortnight later."

The Cabinet was all the more inclined to disbelieve these many rumours and to agree with Sir Nevile Henderson that it was a matter of keeping calm and working for a peaceful solution that might indeed precede a general settlement with Germany. The ruse of the false date had some effect.

General Ludwig Beck had another order of mind than Canaris. A man with the forehead of a philosopher, thoughtful eyes and wide, sagacious mouth that drew down at the corners as his pessimism deepened, he knew by heart and quoted Clausewitz and Schlieffen, but his desire for knowledge reached beyond the military profession. He was at this time learning English and reading the English historians. As senior officer of the General Staff, his military lectures sounded sometimes like sermons, and moral and political lines of thought were inextricable from his appreciations of the strategic situation. Beck heard of a mission to London by Captain Wiedemann, one of the Fuehrer's adjutants, who had been Hitler's battalion commander in the First World War. Hitler had sent Wiedemann to sound Lord Halifax about Czechoslovakia and was satisfied with the impressions that Wiedemann brought back.

Beck noted in his diary: "I think it is a dangerous error to believe that Britain cannot wage a long war. The war effort of Britain has always been long-term, because her strength lies in the immeasurable resources of the Empire."

"I am convinced that Britain will decide to enter the war with France if Germany forces the Czech issue. She is forced to stand by France through thick and thin. But if she fights, it will not be so much to succour Czechoslovakia as to defeat the new Germany that has become a disturber of peace and a threat to the principles of statesmanship recognised by the British— 'Law, Christianity, Tolerance'."

Of Russia he wrote in cautious, weighing phrases in an appreciation of the situation in the summer of 1938:

"The Russian Army is to a great extent hampered in its efficiency by the shooting of its officers. Intervention of the Russian Army is not to be expected but we may reckon with immediate action by the Soviet Air Force. In the event of a long war the importance of Russia in all arms must be set very high indeed."

Beck had then in mind that the Commander-in-Chief, General von Brauchitsch, should at a critical moment declare to Hitler that he and his Army Group, Army and Corps Commanders were not prepared to take the responsibility for a war and would resign in a body. But when his proposals had been discussed at a meeting of the generals early in August, he had detected a wavering attitude in Brauchitsch, who was less resolute than his corps commanders. It was said of the despondent Brauchitsch that Hitler had bought his part allegiance with a gift of money that enabled him to meet a contract of divorce.

Hitler knew well what Beck's thoughts were. Still ringing in Beck's ears were the words of Hitler reported secretly to him that: "I will have to make war on Czechoslovakia with my old generals. When I fight Britain and France I will have a new set of commanders." If Brauchitsch would not take the lead, then he, Beck, must do so at the critical moment.

It was the Admiral's intention to undeceive the British in his own way. General Beck knew Kleist and trusted him and these three had a short and significant conversation in the Chief of the General Staff's office.

"Through yielding to Hitler," concluded Beck, "the British Government will lose its two main allies here, the German General Staff and the German people. If you can bring me from London positive proof that the British will make war if we invade Czechoslovakia I will make an end of this regime."

Kleist asked him what he would regard as proof.

"An open pledge to assist Czechoslovakia in the event of war."

Beck added that a letter from a member of the British Government defining its attitude would strengthen his hand with the generals. Such was the basis, Kleist told me on his return from London, for the secret mission which he undertook for Beck and Canaris.

Canaris was now perplexed as to how to get this dangerous man to London without being apprehended either by the Gestapo, who knew him to be an enemy of the regime, or by the British Intelligence Service, who might regard him simply as a German spy. The situation was all the more complicated because to protect him from the Gestapo, he would have to throw himself on the mercy of the British.

Kleist asked for a false passport. This was a stratagem in which the Admiral still delighted. He had an irreverent attitude towards the passport system. Though now staid and senior, he still travelled himself with a variety of documents, and had done so ever since he escaped from Chile in the First World War. A passport was prepared—perhaps two passports—and an issue of pound notes. Kleist walked over to the Cavalry Club and discussed with me the precautions he was taking to conceal his journey.

"I don't want to be mistaken for a Nazi agent or for a spy," he explained with a twinkle in his keen grey eyes. "If the British deported me, the German customs and currency control and the Gestapo would discover that I had left Germany, and the Admiral would be compromised. I am known to be an enemy of the regime. I would never get permission."

The Junkers 52 aircraft of the Hansa Airlines was standing at Tempelhof Aerodrome on August 17th with the civilian passengers checking through customs and currency control. Each patient German traveller was sponsored by some Ministry or official body, their allowances of foreign money approved by the Reichsbank and stamped in their passports. There were no bona fide tourists any more. It was a little like travel from England after the war had been won. Each had to show an invitation from kind foreign friends who would bear his or her expense abroad and each was noted in the Gestapo registers as having foreign friends and being either harmless or suspect, or vouched for by a government department with interests abroad.

As the aircraft was filling up, a military car drove onto the runway without making any detour towards Customs and Passport Control. A German general in uniform alighted and escorted a civilian to the air liner. There was no question of interference by Customs and Police. The civilian, a small man in a grey suit, was evidently in considerable nervousness until the aircraft took off, then sank back in his seat with a sigh of relief. The Junkers rose from the ground and droned over the roads of Berlin and the forests and lakes of Brandenburg. An English traveller who had watched the movements of Herr von Kleist with a certain interest from a seat behind him settled back comfortably, too. This was my friend and colleague, H. D. Harrison, who had promised to keep a watchful eye on him. The military escort, a kinsman, General von Kleist, got into his car and drove back from Tempelhof to the War Ministry.

There was the same nervous tension as the Junkers aircraft touched down at Croydon; but something of the informality impressed him. The Customs did not seem interested in his baggage, the Passport Officer hardly glanced at his passport. Before the London coach had left a telephone call informed the British Intelligence Service that a German visitor who might interest them had arrived on the afternoon plane.

"A visitor is here."

"Thank you, we know about him."

London in August 1938 was still unaware that the Czechoslovak crisis was imminent. Parliament had gone into recess as it was to go into recess a year later before Poland fell. Lord Runciman had gone on his mission to Prague. London was not as empty as it would have been in 1937. There were interesting men in town who had not gone to shoot grouse. Kleist looked at this immense and bustling city, which with its mercantile and political traditions had stood athwart German expansion for seventy years.

He had not been long at the Park Lane Hotel when Lord Lloyd of Dolobran arrived to whisk him away to dinner in a private room at Claridges. There was some similarity between these two men: Kleist the extremist of the German Conservatives shunned for his uncompromising views; George Lloyd, similarly shunned by Chamberlain and listened to reluctantly by his friend, Edward Halifax, who used his advice as an antidote to the more disastrous counsels of Sir Horace Wilson and Sir Nevile Henderson. Lloyd spoke no German and Kleist no English, and they managed the conversation in French.

"Everything is decided, Lord Lloyd," exclaimed Kleist. "The mobilisation plans are complete, zero day is fixed, the Army group commanders have their orders. All will run according to plan at the end of September, and no one can stop it unless Britain speaks an open warning to Herr Hitler." He added that it would be all the more effective if made jointly with France and Russia.

Then he related the state of power in Germany, the reluctance of the generals, the impotence of the civil service, the waverings of Brauchitsch, the bewilderment and fear of war among the people, the unpreparedness of the armed forces, which would not be at the height of their programme of rearmament until 1943. If Great Britain took a firm and positive stand with France and Russia and singled out Hitler for sole responsibility in an open declaration, there was good hope that the commanding generals would arrest him if he persisted in his war policy and make an end of the Nazi regime.

Lloyd, when their interview was ended, went to see Lord Halifax, and Kleist was given an appointment to meet Sir Robert Vansittart, former Permanent Under-Secretary and then Foreign Adviser in the Foreign Office. They went over the same ground again. From what I can gather Vansittart and Kleist found much common ground for discussion, but Vansittart was mistrustful. He suspected that this German was out for something and might want to do a deal.

"Of all the Germans I saw," Lord Vansittart told me years afterwards, "Kleist had the stuff in him for a revolution against Hitler. But he wanted the Polish corridor, wanted to do a deal." Kleist had sometimes emphasised to me that although Germany had no historical claims on Czechoslovakia, revision of frontiers with Poland was part of his policy. The brief reference to Kleist and his mission in the British official documents published since the war do not suggest that any discussion of Poland was part of his mission in 1938, nor did he ever mention that to me. Lord Vansittart's remarks did not seem to me to relate to the main problem.

Vansittart gave Kleist some hopes that Britain would stand firm. That was his own policy. He promised a display of British and French naval strength in the Mediterranean that would make Mussolini anxious to play the mediator's role.[1] He enquired into the aims and ideas of the secret opposition that Kleist represented. The Junker pressed for a declaration or a letter to the Great General Staff from the British Government.

[1] This suggestion came to nothing.

c

Kleist went from London down to Chartwell Manor, where he was received by Mr. Churchill with solemn precautions, and the same affairs of state were again discussed. He could see that although Churchill was not in the Government, he was in constant touch with Lord Halifax, and their views differed mainly in degree, emphasis and method. Here was the bulldog who would show his teeth when soft language failed. The Foreign Office and especially the Inner Cabinet demurred very much at the idea of sending an official letter to any one not in the acknowledged government of Germany; but Lord Halifax asked Winston Churchill to do so.

On August 24th Kleist slipped out of London as quietly as he had come. Two days later the British Government announced in a somewhat alarming communiqué that it had called Sir Nevile Henderson to London owing to "the serious nature of reports from Central Europe".

Mr. Chamberlain, Lord Halifax, Sir John Simon, Sir Robert Vansittart, Sir Horace Wilson and Sir Nevile Henderson debated the crisis that was only a month away. Sir Nevile was quite emphatic that there was no use in hoping for any opposition to Hitler. Instead, he suggested a careful approach on the part of the British Government that would not commit Hitler to a reckless line at the impending Congress of the Nazi Party at Nuremberg. The Inner Cabinet decided to ask Sir John Simon to make a speech at Lanark about the danger of the flames of war spreading, if once it started; but he took the British attitude no further in reality than Mr. Chamberlain had done on March 24th.

Kleist took his lunch at the Casino Club in Berlin on the day that the British Government announced "the serious nature of reports from Central Europe". He grimaced as he read the evening newspapers and pointed out the headlines to me. When he walked into Canaris's office in the Tirpitzufer he found several senior officers in the Admiral's room awaiting his report. Kleist usually knew what he wanted and got it.

"I will report to the Admiral alone," he said.

The room was cleared, he drew a deep breath.

"I have found nobody in London who wishes to take this opportunity to wage a preventive war," said Kleist. "I have the impression that they wish to avoid a war at almost any cost this year. Yet they may slip into it without wishing to.

They say that it is not possible under the British constitution to commit themselves on a situation that has not arisen."

He made his report and a few days later he laid on the Admiral's desk a letter to himself that Mr. Churchill had written after the visit to Chartwell. It foretold that Great Britain might well become involved in a war over Czechoslovakia, and that one thing was certain—that if this issue were forced by Germany, a war would become inevitable sooner or later in which after a long and hard struggle Germany would be utterly and terribly defeated. He, Kleist, might ponder these words with such patriotic Germans as he had come to represent.

One Englishman, at any rate, could speak in a language that the Germans understood.

Meanwhile Ribbentrop was working on the Hungarians and Poles. How it would perplex the British if suddenly the Hungarian Government presented similar claims in Prague on behalf of its minority in Moravia! Canaris got wind of these complications and was off to Budapest by air, relates Abshagen. Admiral Horthy, the regent, was an old friend of his.

"Canaris used to visit me every time he came to Budapest," Admiral Horthy told me in 1950, in retirement in Estoril. "We were both naval officers and apart from that our outlook was similar. He did not himself give me advice; but we were both agreed in 1939 that if America entered the war against Germany then Germany was finished."

Canaris and his companion, Colonel von Tippelskirch, warned the Hungarian Government early in September 1938 that Germany might soon find herself at war with Britain if Hitler persisted in his policy. Hungary should beware of fetching the chestnuts out of the fire for Hitler. Having quietly put a spoke in Ribbentrop's policy, Canaris flew back to Berlin again—perhaps to see what Lahousen might be able to tell him about the Czechoslovak defences, for although it was his private policy to prevent war, he was officially entrusted with preparing it.

The Admiral was still pondering as to how he would give best effect to the reports of Kleist when the Gestapo got in touch with Abwehr III, the Military Security Service.

"There has been somebody in London conducting treasonable conversations. Find out who it is! We are already at work."

Kleist sat about the Casino Club thinking up an alibi. He

was evidently extremely worried. Canaris called for the officer who had prepared the visit of Kleist to London.

"You are to take up this enquiry," he instructed him. " Explore every possibility. I have satisfied myself that there can be no question of our own man being involved. He is not to be mentioned. You must seek elsewhere."

The Soviet Foreign Minister, Litvinov, hurried to Geneva in the second week of September to see what could be done to save collective security. He saw Georges Bonnet, the French Foreign Minister, on the 11th, but Bonnet stayed only one day in Geneva and was not encouraging, and Lord Halifax did not come at all. The British and French Governments wanted to hold Russia out of this delicate situation. At Nuremberg the Party Congress was in full swing: the brown-shirts marched, the gauleiters shouted, the amplifiers blared out the speeches of Hermann Goering over the roofs of Albrecht Dürer's ancient home, the Army passed on parade. Among the foreign guests two psychiatrists from an English lunatic asylum, sent to Nuremberg by the British Government, sat and studied Hitler's reflexes.[1] *The Times* newspaper threw everyone into bewildered excitement by publishing a leading article on September 7th that first suggested that the Czechoslovak state might be better off if it made territorial concessions to Hitler. Hitler was not mollified by this. It gave him courage. He had brusquely rejected Lord Runciman's cantonal solution. He raged against Beneš.

The day after Kleist had returned from London General Beck had turned over his own duties to his deputy, General Franz Halder. The Chief of the General Staff had offered his resignation after Hitler announced in a speech to his generals at Juterbog in the middle of August that he intended to solve the Czech problem that autumn by force.

Now Canaris decided to show all the evidence he could that the British would fight if it came to fighting. Kleist went from one general to another urging them to act. The Admiral quoted to them the Churchill letter. Some were keen and excit-able, others dubious. But by September 14th General von Witzleben, Commander of the Berlin area, had made arrange-ments with General Halder and others to arrest Hitler as he returned from Berchtesgaden to the capital. Count Helldorf,

[1] Their secret report has yet to be published.

President of Berlin Police, was prepared to use his forces to arrest the party leaders. General Hoeppner, in command of the Third Panzer Division south of Berlin, would march on the capital at a signal from Witzleben. Beck would go back to his office in the Bendlerstrasse. "There can be no doubt of the existence of the plot at this moment and of serious measures to make it effective," wrote Mr. Churchill years later in *The Gathering Storm*. An awful calm hung that afternoon over the roofs of the Bendlerstrasse. Did Hitler, Himmler and Heydrich smell danger? The afternoon passed without incident and by dinnertime Admiral Canaris knew why.

He was sitting at table with Colonel Lahousen, Piekenbrock and Groscurth, when a message came to him from the War Ministry. Mr. Chamberlain intended to fly to Berchtesgaden to discuss a solution to the Czechoslovak situation.

Lahousen remembers how the Admiral laid down his knife and fork. He had quite lost his appetite.

"What he—visit that man!" He muttered the words blankly at first as if he scarcely understood. Then he repeated them to himself and got up from the table, walking about the room. He was utterly distracted and ate no more dinner. The tension was broken, half the world was in loud relief by midnight, and half was in deep gloom, and among those who sat in gloom was Hitler's intelligence chief. The Admiral excused himself to his heads of departments and went early to bed. Had he been mistaken in opening his hand to the British? Perhaps he had scared them in London into the Berchtesgaden policy. Maybe they had not believed that his advice was anything more than mischief or deceit.

CHAPTER VIII

BETWEEN PEACE AND WAR

SOME OF THE senior German generals were furious with
Canaris for leading them so far astray with his reports on
British determination to fight. The Intelligence Service should
not be entrusted to a naval officer, they said. Lahousen tells me
that he heard a senior German officer describe Canaris and his
friends as "the people who undermined the influence of the
General Staff" by opposing Hitler on the wrong issue. That was
one point of view. Colonel-General von Rundstedt had a brief
encounter with his old friend Kleist about September 25th and
his eye kindled with anger and annoyance when Kleist pursued
the idea of action against Hitler. It was as if the generals had
been hoaxed and Hitler right all along.

"The crisis is not yet over; we have still no solution," Canaris
pointed out. But they hardly doubted any more that a solution
was at hand. Brauchitsch would hear no more talk of a revolt,
the servile Keitel had been allowed to hear none from the
start; Halder despondently told General von Witzleben, the
most eager of the rebels, that he could not be answerable for
military action against Hitler if Mr. Chamberlain found a
peaceable solution to the Czechoslovak dispute. Kleist went
back to his estates in Pomerania, utterly disillusioned. There
seemed to be no end to the domination of Hitler.

His kinsman, General von Kleist, who had seen him to the
aircraft on his journey to London, remarked philosophically:
"Hitler may be a swine, but the swine is lucky."

Like many a lucky man, the Fuehrer did not seem to be able
to be contented with it. After Neville Chamberlain had visited
him in Berchtesgaden and worked out a draft settlement of the
Sudeten-German problem for the British Cabinet to approve
and submit to President Beneš, Ribbentrop was quickly at work
on the Hungarians.

"Do you not see that you will be too late to present your

claims if you do not make them now?" was the tenor of his argument in Budapest.

By the time that Chamberlain was in Bad Godesberg with the draft settlement accepted by his Cabinet and France, Hitler was in a surly mood and barely ready to be polite to the elder man.

"I am awfully sorry, but that's no more use," he exclaimed, indicating the Chamberlain plan, so Nevile Henderson relates. The subtle restraint that Canaris had put upon the Hungarians had broken down. They and the Poles had made Hitler the arbiter of their claims upon the narrow provinces of Czechoslovakia.

Down the Rhine Valley past the Hotel Petersberg where Chamberlain and his delegation sat out two September afternoons, the German troop trains ran at the top state of alert with light anti-aircraft defences mounted on open platforms at the front and rear of each train. The S.S. on the terrace, provided by Hitler as a bodyguard for Chamberlain, drank and sprawled in the autumn sunshine singing maudlin songs. When on duty their exaggerated sense of security conveyed no sense of politeness and hampered the delegation. Across the Rhine at the Hotel Dreesen, Hitler dictated a truculent answer to Chamberlain's letter of the 23rd asking whether the Reich Chancellor was willing to abide by his intention to seek an orderly settlement. The translator, Schmidt, took the letter and, as the hours lapsed, Hitler made a remark to his Chief of Staff of Storm Troopers, Viktor Lütze, which I heard about at the time and have seen nowhere else on record. He glanced at his watch, it was four p.m. on the 23rd.

"I know Mr. Chamberlain," he said. "He will give way. If he has not sent me an ultimatum by six o'clock, then the affair is won and he will get nothing at all."

Sir Horace Wilson and Sir Nevile Henderson crossed by the ferry at 5.40 p.m. and prepared a second conference at 10.30 p.m., which drew up proposals for dismembering Czechoslovakia. Chamberlain agreed to forward them to President Beneš, but said he could not recommend him to accept them. Then there was a desultory parting. Goering's Research Office had recorded telephone conversations between Godesberg and London and Paris and Prague that emboldened Hitler still further when reported to him. He made his ranting speech in the Berlin Sport Palace on September

26th, and I noticed that his voice was uncertain, with long blank periods, caused by the mental strain of the crisis. That evening the British Foreign Office issued a communiqué that suggested for the first time that:

"If in spite of all efforts a German attack is made upon Czechoslovakia, the immediate result must be that France will be bound to come to her assistance and Great Britain and Russia will certainly stand by France. . . ."

The following morning it was announced that the Home Fleet was to be mobilised and that had more effect than all the words they had hitherto spoken, but Hitler still raved and swore against the Czechs, until an urgent telephone call from his Excellency, Signor Attolico, on behalf of Mussolini, smoothed the way to Munich.

What of General Franco during this crisis? He has hardly been mentioned in early works on the Czech crisis, but the German documents on the Spanish Civil War published in 1950 showed that the Spanish Foreign Minister, Count Jordana, admitted to the German Ambassador on September 28th, 1938—the crucial date—that Franco had given Great Britain and France his assurance of Spanish neutrality in the event of a conflict. There was also a report, highly unpalatable to Ribbentrop and Hitler, that Franco had offered to intern the Condor Legion in Spain. I should think that this uncertainty went as far as Mussolini's attitude to prevent war at that moment.

These last turns of events were a stroke of good luck for Canaris. He had advised strong action by the British and Kleist had brought him Vansittart's hint of a fleet mobilisation in the Mediterranean. I daresay that the close friendship of Canaris with Franco and Jordana at this moment, as later, had some bearing on their attitude. They complained to the German Foreign Ministry in their explanations that they had not been kept officially informed of these critical developments of German policy. I do not suppose that Canaris left Franco more in the dark than he left Horthy, or that he counselled him to anything but a cautious attitude.

Canaris, therefore, persisted to say in defence of his reports that he was right in supposing that Great Britain might allow herself to be dragged into a conflict, unprepared as she was. Others still argued that it was the intention of Mr. Chamberlain to keep Great Britain out of a war in 1938 whatever happened and that argument will go on for years to come.

When the Munich conference was finished and Parliament set about debating the agreement, there was an uncomfortable revelation.

Lord Lloyd, in attacking the Government, was exasperated by the attitude of Lord Halifax that they had not known what crisis was upon them.

"I am sorry that my noble friend, the Secretary of State for Foreign Affairs, is not in his place at this moment," he said, "but he knows that I was able to inform him in the very early days of August of the whole German plan that worked out to the actual day. He knows where that counsel came from and that there was advice from that source that there should be an immediate declaration of solidarity with France and Russia."

Canaris might well have been worried at the openness of these words; but he was already on his guard and the words of Lloyd did him no particular harm. He was, after all, a master of embroidery and no doubt he pretended to ascribe Lloyd's intelligence to his old enemies of the British Secret Service.

It was on October 5th, when the ink of the Munich agreement was barely dry, that Ribbentrop produced fresh mischief. He showed Hitler a report from London that Russia had notified Britain and France on September 26th that she did not wish to send armed forces to take part in a European war. Within a short time I heard from one of Canaris's men that the Fuehrer had raged that he was "surrounded by cowards and incompetents. Had I received this report at the time this note was sent I should never have invited Chamberlain to Munich and by now we should be in the Balkans".

He had Keitel draw up a secret minute on October 21st, eleven days after the Munich settlement came into force, enjoining the armed forces to be prepared for surprise air attacks and to be ready to occupy Memel and the remainder of Czechoslovakia at short notice.

For a time Admiral Canaris eschewed high politics so that the dust might settle. No particular course of action was possible after the Munich conference. He had, besides, plenty to do organising his intelligence service for war. He was a man who, though he sometimes left important work to his deputies for months at a time, would suddenly concern himself with details; the very methods of gathering reports and spreading information were of interest to him.

The reader should not imagine that his sole interest lay in using his position to conspire against Hitler. "He was a man who was in perpetual motion, absorbing and disseminating information," so Schlabrendorff characterised him to me. "I tell them what they want to hear and what they can repeat."

Occasionally he would discuss the mechanics of intelligence with his associates. "Tapping telephones is of little value," he once told Schlabrendorff, indicating a pile of monitorings of telephone conversations that reached him daily from the Research Office. "Since nobody talks openly on the telephone in the Third Reich, they can read such records all day without learning anything."

"My Admiral was not entirely right in that observation," commented Richard Protze. "As a matter of fact, the Research Office had orders to watch his own telephone, but it abstracted records of his talks from the sets that were sent to the Abwehr. There is no doubt that the telephone told a great deal, if you knew what you were looking for. The Gestapo doubtless thought that Canaris's telephone conversations were worth listening to."

The Gestapo had been fixing microphones in the walls of that wing of the Hotel Adlon adjoining the British Embassy, but I do not suppose that much of vital interest was overheard. The Gestapo were intrigued to discover that one of the British diplomats was in the habit of inviting an actress to supper—but this kind of surveillance took up a lot of time and was not profitable in the end. Before long British engineers came out from London and located the microphones.

Ciphers? Both the Abwehr and the Gestapo had their deciphering branches. It was a high art. Sometimes the Foreign Ministry would deliver an important note to foreign embassies during a slack period at the week-end. Then the deciphering teams would wait for a cipher message to be handed in to the Reichspost. There was a possibility that an over-zealous secretary might transmit the note without paraphrasing, and that, with the original in their possession, gave the Abwehr a chance of deciphering a code. They found the British ciphers the hardest of all.

Apart from his system of regular agents in diplomatic, consular and commercial posts, the Admiral maintained a network of V-men or confidence men whose business was to transmit and gather strategic and tactical information. He was willing to pay highly for the services of deaf mutes, not, we might suppose, because they were more trustworthy with secrets, but because of their peculiar gift for lip reading. A deaf mute with a shorthand book in his lap sitting at the other side of a restaurant could bring him a pretty fair account of what the British diplomat had been telling his companion at dinner.

The German network in the United Kingdom was not large. It was directed from the German legation in Dublin, from Lisbon, Oslo and Hamburg, but there was a possibility of discovering British secrets through certain of the embassies and Dominion offices in London. Once in the period after Munich he showed a visitor a copy of a confidential report sent to London by the British Embassy in Berlin only a week previously. It dealt with the condition of the Reich railways and their potential in time of war. He often seemed careless in such conversations and soon the British were apprised that someone was photographing government documents for the Germans.

"I am told that Canaris believed he had penetrated the British Secret Service," I told Richard Protze. The old man nodded his white head. "Not everywhere, perhaps," he answered, "but more than you would easily suppose. It was quite simple in some cases. We had military intelligence agreements with the Baltic states before the war. We had merely to say: 'and we want to place agents of ours inside the British intelligence offices in Kovno, Reval and Tallin.' Then in The Hague during the early part of the war, I had a daily report of events inside the British intelligence office from an underpaid British agent. That kind of thing is quite usual."

Canaris was somewhat hampered in improving his services in Britain by a directive from Hitler. The military attaché in London was under strict orders not to take part in covert intelligence work, and General Geyr von Schweppenburg tells us in his memoirs that he quarrelled on this very subject with Canaris who wanted him to do more for the Abwehr. To the end of the war the number of German agents in Britain was small, their information unreliable and most of their communications under observation. The counter-espionage work of

M.I.5 was of a high order, and at times the German service operating from Dublin was bewildered by false information planted on it, and misled its own government.

Canaris insisted on seeing his agents personally when they came to Berlin and listened to their reports, nodding with visible interest, even if what they related was long since known to him. "Everything you are telling me is of the highest interest," he would exclaim.

There were four main intelligence centres in Germany that dealt with the gathering of intelligence from the world outside. The Abwehr office in Konigsberg worked into Russia, the office in Munich worked on the Balkans and Mediterranean countries, Cologne dealt with France, Hamburg with the British Isles, the Americas and Scandinavia.

It appears from subsequent events that Canaris fancied six of the capitals for developing his intelligence system—Madrid, Lisbon, Berne, Ankara, Oslo and Budapest. These were worth building up as a long-term policy because it seemed unlikely that any of them would be occupied by either side and that consequently the diplomatic courier would continue to pass and officials and business men come and go. He added to their number the Vatican, which had a sovereign status, its own ciphers and representatives all over the world. He listed as short term centres—Brussels, Warsaw, Sofia, Bucharest, The Hague, and Paris, which might be isolated or overrun when Germany made war, and would then be of no further use to him and perhaps a source of embarrassment. Although he considered them precarious footholds for an intelligence system, he nevertheless established vigorous groups in each for rapid tactical work in the event of German invasion. Both in Poland and France the Germans knew every move that was made in 1939 and 1940.

In recruiting his intelligence reserve he picked his men carefully among the German reserve officers and intelligentsia. It was not easy, because each name had to be screened by the Gestapo, and he did not want to be criticised in that quarter for employing enemies of the regime. His organisation, although it lost ground and consequently numbers to the Gestapo Security Service, was thirty thousand strong by 1943, of whom eight thousand were officers, and its expenditure budget for that year amounted to 31,000,000 Reichsmarks or £2,600,000.

Meanwhile the British were recruiting their intelligence reserve from much the same social strata—business men, gentlemen of leisure, bankers, stockbrokers, and dons, and they made mysterious reconnaissances of large English country houses, where they would be able to work undisturbed by bombing. The Germans had castles enough for the same purpose. There was to be in both camps some overlapping and jealousy in the spheres of responsibility between intelligence officers, "cloak and dagger men", and other secret appendages. At times the rivalries between the feudal establishments in England waxed so hot that they seemed to be in the Wars of the Roses with two dukedoms at odds rather than fighting the Second World War. General Lahousen, the senior survivor of the other side, assures me that the rivalries were intense within the German camp, too, quite apart from the perpetual feud with the Gestapo.

So these two vast intelligence services with their rival chiefs and their unlimited funds set about burrowing and countermining, even before the war had started. It was not to prove a healthy occupation for some, and it often happened that those who took part in it came away with warped minds, as great a handicap in settling down in an ordinary business life as the loss of a limb. The game, while it lasted, outdid anything that has been written in fiction.

"Nothing that you have read in novels can be compared with the real thing," a British diplomat from Ankara told me afterwards. "I am sure that the Germans had at least one agent in each of our embassies during the war and I daresay we had one in all theirs."

CHAPTER IX

THE GREAT MOBILISATION

PRAGUE HAD BEEN occupied in March 1939 and that
in itself meant war sooner or later. Lahousen remembers the
resigned attitude of Canaris at this time. As the German
columns rolled into Bohemia, he drove in behind them with
Colonel Longin and his adjutant to see what the intelligence
booty would be. He spoke his thoughts as they went: "My
goodness, the Czechs won't take this. They'll shoot, won't
they?" But the days when the Czechs would have fired their
cannon were gone with yesteryear. Then Memel was occupied
and the integrity of the Baltic states became the active concern
of Great Britain, Poland and Russia, though none of these
powers was able to identify its interests entirely with that of the
other two. The British gave their guarantee to Poland on
April 30th, 1939, and Europe had a momentary breathing
space; but it made it more certain that Poland would be
attacked next. Now that they had deserted their policy of friendship with Poland, the Germans set about rumours against
Colonel Joszef Beck, the Polish Foreign Minister, alleging that
he had long been in their pay. Having taken action, Chamberlain and Halifax hesitated, and from March 31st onwards until
August 26th the British guarantee of Poland remained in unratified form.

Canaris thought by June that it was now high time to send a
special agent to London again. He and Oster saw Kleist and
asked whether he would return on a second mission, but the
keen mind of Kleist foresaw no result from it.

"What have we to offer?" he asked. "I'm not going to
London with empty hands."

So a General Staff officer named Bohm-Tettelbach was
selected in his stead and went to meet the British under these
very altered circumstances. He was a pleasant-spoken, cultured
man, but there was less sense of reality about his mission. He
called secretly on Sir James Grigg and service chiefs and met

78

representative Englishmen, asking them for some sign that Great Britain would stand by Poland, and they plainly told him that she would, but they were not demonstrative of their feelings. Bohm-Tettelbach felt that he had nothing positive. Suppose Britain failed to conclude an agreement with Russia— the talks in Moscow dragged on. Was it to be supposed that the British would commit the madness of fighting for Poland if Germany and Russia, the two biggest military powers in the world, decided to partition her? Bohm-Tettelbach went back to Germany without having achieved anything. When the Rhine Army burst into Germany in 1945 it captured among others in the ruins round Dusseldorf Colonel Bohm-Tettelbach who disconsolately related to an incredulous British Major of the Public Relations Branch that General Halder had been ready to arrest Hitler in August 1939 if he had been convinced that the British were in earnest.

Such was the diversity of the British and German mentality that whereas nobody doubted in England any more that we would fight if Poland was attacked, nobody in the German Government believed it entirely and hardly anybody—even among the friends of Britain in Germany, felt perfectly certain of the British attitude. Now the instincts of Canaris were right, and when he discovered that mobilisation was finally settled, with August 26th as zero day, he insisted in his reports to the High Command that this time Great Britain would certainly fight. The generals objected that he had been very far wrong about the Munich crisis; nevertheless he held firmly to his opinion and it seemed early in August as if he might be right—if only the British would ratify their Polish guarantee and come to some understanding with Russia—then peace might be saved.

The Czechoslovak crisis had taught him that it was possible to sound the British on high secrets and at least agree to differ. I am inclined to ascribe to him or his deputy Oster two communications that were made to the British Intelligence Service in the second half of June 1939—that Ribbentrop was secretly negotiating for a pact with Russia and that Hitler would attack Poland soon after August 26th. I have been able to speak with one of the German visitors who carried these messages and was interested to hear him admit that he had been a close friend of Canaris. Baron Weizsäcker, involved in these very negotiations with Russia, also managed to send through Erich Kordt,

the German Chargé d'Affaires in London, a similar warning to
Sir Robert Vansittart. This was revealed during the trial of
Weizsäcker by the Allies. The General Staff sent General Count
Schwerin to London, a somewhat heavier gun than Bohm-
Tettelbach, but he, too, seemed to have gone there with no
definite proposals and returned empty-handed.

The preliminaries of the German negotiations with Russia
lasted from the middle of June with some interruptions until
August 15th, when Ribbentrop proposed that he should go
to Moscow to complete them. Molotov was evidently keen on
obtaining a non-aggression pact with Germany that would
give Russia a share of that territory which Hitler would otherwise conquer alone; but Molotov was also interested in making
perfectly sure that Germany did not intend to attack Russia
immediately afterwards. He therefore kept the British and
French negotiators in Moscow for the time being. Nobody could
really say in the third week of August for certain under what
conditions and in what alliance Germany would be fighting.

How ludicrous the Italians appeared in these days of confusion! They had signed a military alliance with Germany in
the spring—the pact of steel—on the understanding that there
would be no war for three years, and then Count Ciano consented to make approaches to Russia for Germany in June to
prepare that non-aggression pact that would, did he but know
it, make an immediate war possible for Hitler.

Ciano did not hear that war was imminent until the second
week in August when he hurried to Berchtesgaden. In fact the
British Intelligence Service knew it before him. Canaris happened to be at the Obersalzberg on August 10th and decided
to visit Castle Fuschl and see Ribbentrop. The Foreign Minister
regaled the Admiral at lunch with a version of the naval
war that would be fought in the Mediterranean. The Italians
would throw in a hundred submarines, he said, and close the
Mediterranean to the British Navy.

This was one of those conversations to which the Admiral
would simply listen and nod with apparent interest; but he
remarked dryly to his adjutant as they drove away from Castle
Fuschl:

"When the big battle starts in the Mediterranean you and I
will sit on a raft and just see how the roast-beefs bash the
Italianos."

A week later, in Berlin (the German-Russian pact was not yet concluded and general mobilisation would be complete in nine days), he had a significant discussion with General Keitel and saw that the simplicity of the Chief of the High Command was hardly less terrible than that of his master. Keitel, this solid, blond, pleasant-looking man with his light blue eyes and upright bearing, seemed bereft of all imagination.

Canaris noted this discussion in his diary—the famous lost diary for which the secret services of four powers have searched in vain. By chance the entry for August 17th, 1939, was copied and the copy kept by General Lahousen. It reads:

"Discussion with Colonel-General Keitel, 17. VIII. 1939.

"I report to Keitel my conversation with Jost (an S.S. officer). Keitel says that he cannot concern himself with this operation[1] as the Fuehrer has not informed him of it and has only told him to procure Polish uniforms for Heydrich. He agrees that I was right to inform the General Staff. He says that he does not think much of such operations, but that there's nothing else for it, if the Fuehrer orders them. It is not up to me, he says, to ask the Fuehrer how he imagines such an operation is to be carried out."

Such was indeed the attitude of Keitel towards Himmler's plan to dress German convicts in Polish uniforms (with film units standing by) and drive them into attacks on Reich territory so that it would appear that the hot-headed Poles had struck the first blow.

Canaris then reported to his chief that he had heard from General Roatta[2] of the unwillingness of Italy to be dragged into a war. The diary notes that Keitel replied "that he thinks it would be a good thing if Mussolini told the Fuehrer quite clearly that he would not fight. He, Keitel, believed that Italy would fight all the same. I replied that I considered that this would be out of the question and related to him the full gist of the Ciano-Ribbentrop meeting. Keitel replied that the Fuehrer told him the opposite. I told him also that Count Marogna[3] has learned that the King of Italy has said to King Alphonso of Spain that he will not sign if Mussolini lays a mobilisation order before him. Keitel remarks that it was interesting to see

[1] Secret operation "Himmler".
[2] His old colleague as Chief of the Italian Military Intelligence then military attaché in Berlin.
[3] Chief of the Abwehr Munich Office.

that even a nation ruled by a dictatorship could be quite temperamental when it came to war. How much more difficult it must be when it came to democratic countries! He was convinced that the British would not intervene. I try to refute this opinion and say that the British will immediately blockade us and destroy our merchant shipping. Keitel says that this will not be very important as we can get oil from Russia. I reply that this is not the decisive factor and that we cannot withstand a blockade in the long run. The British will fight against us with all means in their power if we use force against Poland and if it comes to bloodshed. I tell him that the British would have behaved in just the same way if there had been bloodshed when we marched into Czechoslovakia. I try to explain to Keitel the effect of economic warfare on Germany and tell him that we have only limited forces with which to fight back. I have just learned that we could put only ten U-boats into the Atlantic. Keitel says that it will be easy to force Rumania to deliver oil to us when Poland is defeated. I inform him of the precautions already taken by the British in the Balkans and tell him that they will have certainly prepared against that eventuality, too."

Hitler calculated on breaking the news to the commanding generals that he would make war on August 26th or soon afterwards before the announcement that the German-Soviet non-aggression pact had been concluded. The worst news first would have its sting drawn by the second, and the obedience of the generals would thus be ensured. He summoned them to Berchtesgaden on August 22nd and delivered his war speech after the adjutants had forbidden them to take any notes.

Hitler announced that he was going to make war on August 26th. He began by asserting that they would all have to realise that Germany was determined from the beginning to fight the Western Powers. The first task would be the destruction of Poland and the elimination of her manpower, not merely the reaching of a certain line of territory.

"I shall give a propaganda reason for starting the war, never mind whether it is plausible or not. Nobody will ask the victor afterwards whether he was speaking the truth."

So he ranted on, and Admiral Canaris, standing unobtrusively in the background, made his own notes the whole way through.

"We need not be afraid of a blockade. The East will supply us with grain, cattle, coal, lead and zinc. It is a big aim that demands great efforts. . . . I am only afraid that some Schweinhund will offer to mediate."

The following day the Soviet-German non-aggression pact was concluded and the Fuehrer spoke jubilantly to his Foreign Minister on the Moscow line, hailing him as a second Bismark; but the effect on the British was not what he had expected. Instead of allowing the still unratified guarantee to Poland to lapse, they ratified it on August 25th. Hitler then told Goering that he would postpone general mobilisation by a few days, while Goering tried through a Swedish mediator, Birger Dahlerus, to dissuade Chamberlain from fulfilling British obligations; but it was obvious that whereas a day or two was welcome to the movements and transportation officers to bring delayed dispositions into line, this terrible monster, a general mobilisation, could not be held back for long. Even when Mussolini sent Hitler a message that Italy definitely could not enter the war Hitler was not discouraged.

He gave his final order on August 31st, Himmler's convicts in Polish uniform carried out their futile propaganda attack on Gleiwitz radio station, were shot down and subsequently photographed. German troops emerged from merchant ships in Danzig where they had lain for a week under hatches and stormed the Westerplatte fort; the Panzer spearheads that Guderian had built penetrated the Polish corridor.

On September 2nd Sir Nevile Henderson delivered the British ultimatum through Ribbentrop. It declared that Britain and Germany would be at war next day unless Germany suspended hostilities against Poland. The face of Goering waddling in the antechamber fell when he heard this news. " It was like a blow with a club to us soldiers of the First World War," commented General Jodl, the Deputy Chief of the High Command. What else did they expect?

Canaris had meanwhile sent out to Stockholm the man through whom he hoped to keep alive his stealthy contacts with the British; but Kleist sat about for a few days in the Park Hotel and achieved nothing. I received a last letter from him. Before the last threads snapped, the Abwehr attempted one final kindness to its old rivals of the Intelligence Service. A junior officer was sent on September 2nd to warn the British military attaché, Colonel Denis Daly, that a blitz daylight attack was intended for 11 a.m. next day. A report was accordingly sent in cipher to London. "I am convinced that there was no intention to deceive us in this matter," Colonel Daly told me after the war. "The man who came to bring me that message was certainly taking considerable risks."

General Halder was subsequently able to dissuade Hitler from this isolated attack which would have no lasting military effect, but by then it was no longer possible to advise the British that it was cancelled. The state of alert in London was such that the sirens were sounded at 11.15 a.m., just after Mr. Chamberlain had finished speaking in the House of Commons. It was explained afterwards that an unidentified French aircraft in the Thames estuary had occasioned this alert. British Government departments were meanwhile taking up their prepared war quarters. The British felt that a war without mercy lay ahead and from now on they might expect no more help from Admiral Canaris. Meanwhile at the Tirpitzufer the Admiral, who had read out to members of his own office extracts of Hitler's speech of August 22nd, declared to them that the defeat of Germany would be terrible, but that a victory of Hitler would be more terrible still! He considered that nothing should be omitted that would shorten the war.[1]

Walking that morning in the Tiergarten he saw the Spanish military attaché driving past and waved to him to stop.

"Naturally," said the Spaniard, "Germany has calculated out this war to the last detail of ultimate victory."

"Calculated nothing at all," answered Canaris.

·

[1] K. H. Abshagen, *Canaris*.

CHAPTER X

THE ADMIRAL HELPS A LADY

OUR FUEHRER WAS delighted with the progress that his armies were making. All along the front from the Baltic through the Polish Corridor, Posnan, Silesia and Galicia, the fifty-six German divisions, led by all nine Panzer divisions, had burst through thirty divisions of the Polish Army, which was still only partially mobilised and too far forward to retreat in good order. The Luftwaffe had bombed lines of communication, and the German minority in Poland, guided by Canaris's K.O. or war organisation and Heydrich's Security Service, had supported the offensive with acts of sabotage. The Admiral caught up with Hitler on September 12th when the Fuehrer's special train lay at Ilnau in Silesia with Generals Keitel and Jodl and Joachim von Ribbentrop in attendance. The Polish divisions, such as had not been destroyed or surrounded near the frontiers, had fallen back into the valley of the Vistula round Warsaw, were encircled north of Lodz and at Radom, or were being chased over the River San, past unpronounceable Przemysl towards Lemberg and the frontiers of Rumania.

It was now a question of bombarding the capital or laying siege to it. The Fuehrer was in a gloating, destructive mood and ordered the former. M. Molotov would soon inform M. Gryzbowski, the Ambassador of Poland in Warsaw, that "Russia was moving forward to take into her protection the kindred peoples of Poland". It was evident that Hitler must act quickly if he wished to achieve the glory of maximum destruction without the aid of his treaty partner.

Canaris had come furnished with information reports on the movements of the French Army which was probing the German defences in the Saar basin. If it went ill with Germany in the East and France could seize the Saar, German war potential would suffer considerably.

There was a map room in the train, and Canaris, taking the lanky Lahousen with him, found himself first listening to Ribbentrop.

"Immediately after we had entered," he noted in his diary, "Foreign Minister von Ribbentrop expounded his ideas to me as to how the German-Polish war might be ended politically. In subsequent discussions in Keitel's coach, these solutions were summarised as follows:

Solution 1: The fourth partition of Poland takes place, and Germany declares herself disinterested in territory east of the Narev-Vistula-San line in favour of the Soviet Union.

Solution 2: The remnants of Poland are made into an independent state, a solution that would commend itself to the Fuehrer, as he could then negotiate with the Polish Government on the manner of establishing peace in the east.

Solution 3: The remains of Poland are dismembered.
   (a) Lithuania is offered the Vilna region.
   (b) Galicia and the Polish Ukraine become independent (provided that this is agreeable to the Soviet Union).

"I would have to arrange in Solution 3b for a revolution organised by Melynyk's Independent Ukraine Movement to annihilate Jews and Poles in the Ukraine. This movement would have to be prevented from spreading to the Russian Ukraine (Great Ukraine Movement)."

After discussing the role of the propaganda companies in "re-educating" the Polish proletariat while the S.S. were exterminating the Polish intelligentsia, clergy and nobility, Canaris tackled Keitel on the question of atrocities. This was the first of a series of "lectures to the generals on the facts of life", as he described them to Lahousen.

"I told Keitel that I was aware of extensive executions planned in Poland, and that the nobility and the clergy particularly were to be exterminated. The world would in the final reckoning hold the Wehrmacht responsible for these deeds that would be committed under our noses.

"Keitel replied that the Fuehrer had already decided this matter. He had made it plain to the Commander-in-Chief that if the Army was not prepared to take charge, the S.S. and Gestapo would take over. A civil governor would be nominated for every district as well as the military governor. The former would be given the task of racial extermination."

Reading over his version of the day's conference, the Admiral made a marginal note in pencil: "Political spring-cleaning."

Canaris then protested that the bombardment of Warsaw would have a damaging effect on German prestige in the world.

"Keitel answered that such matters were definitely decided by the Fuehrer and Marshal Goering. The Fuehrer had frequent telephone conversations with Goering."

"Sometimes they keep me informed," Keitel explained, "but not always."

Then Hitler suddenly appeared in the coach and asked what news Canaris brought from the Western Front.

"I answered that the information to hand indicated that the French were assembling troops and artillery to prepare a systematic and methodical offensive in the Saarbrücken area. I had taken measures to inform him shortly of the locality and direction in which this offensive would be launched.

"'I can't imagine that the French will attack in the Saarbrücken area,' remarked Hitler. 'Our defences are the strongest there with A-fortifications and the French will find a second and third line of prepared positions, if anything still stronger than the first. I consider the Bien forest and the Palatinate forest as our weakest spots. Although the other side object that it is useless to attack in a wooded area, I think otherwise.

"'They may risk an adventure by crossing the Rhine, although we are prepared there, too. I do not consider an attack through Holland and Belgium to be likely. It would be a breach of neutrality. In any case, time is required before they can launch a big offensive against the West Wall.'

"Keitel and Jodl agree with the Fuehrer. Jodl adds that France will need at least three or four weeks for artillery preparations before an offensive can be made on a large scale, so that an attack could not take place before October.

"'Yes, and October is pretty cold,' continued Hitler. 'Our men will be in protected concrete works, while the French must lie in the open and attack. But even if the Frenchmen could reach one of the weakest spots in the West Wall, we will be able to bring up something in the meantime that will baste him in such a manner that he will lose both sight and hearing.

"'Therefore the way through Holland and Belgium is all that remains. I don't believe it, but it is not impossible, so we must be vigilant.'"

This was nothing if not lucid, and though we have laughed since at the hideous blunders of Hitler's intuition, it was not a faulty guide in the military calendar of 1939. Canaris was regarded as a cautious pessimist by Hitler and Keitel in these days. They suspected no more than that. The conference prepared for an independent Polish Ukraine on the basis of Solution 3 and Ribbentrop approved broadcasts in the Ukrainian language emphasising that the Wehrmacht had "no quarrel with the Ukrainian people". These broadcasts were of course heard by Moscow, and small wonder if when Ribbentrop returned to Moscow on September 26th to sign the Soviet-German treaty of friendship that consolidated the month-old non-aggression pact, he found Molotov insistent on Solution 1— a complete partition. Russia wanted no little Ukraines.

Canaris left this ghoulish company at Ilnau, after Hitler had solemnly enjoined him to exert the utmost vigilance in neutral countries. Then he returned to Berlin. Herr von Hassell[1] noted in his diary that Canaris was overcome and exhausted by the horrors that he had seen in Poland. Then the Admiral was off again, this time to Posnan in a train of his own to hear more reports from Poland and to examine some of the more interesting intelligence targets captured.

I supposed that by now all the threads between Britain and Germany had been broken, that there was no personal link left between him and his old enemy. I met a Polish diplomat, an old friend from the days in Berlin, and consulted him. "I think I can find an answer to that for you," he said. "Would you like to meet Madame J? She knew Canaris in those days." We drove out to a small house in Surrey, where a Polish family had settled after the war and my friend introduced me to the lady of the house, a grave woman with black hair and dark steady eyes, who for a short while laid aside the busy duty of looking after a home to tell us her story. First she gave us tea and when I had asked her whether she had known Canaris she ran on from memory.

[1] The German ambassador in Rome until 1938, when he quarrelled with Ribbentrop over Axis policy.

"If I ask you not to mention my name or to tell anything that would identify me, it is because I do not often tell this story and would prefer to tell it once and then have done with it. My husband and I lived in Berlin before the war. We knew the Polish colony there and we had some contact with the Germans. I remember meeting some of the German generals in the house of our military attaché. There were Luftwaffe generals, too, and I remembered this Admiral Canaris, because he was a singular man, not stiff and hard-voiced like some of the others—the opposite in fact, soft-voiced and friendly. Of course, I had no idea then who he was, nor do I think did anyone else.

"When the war broke out I was in South Poland with my children near Lublin at the home of my family. The Ukrainians plundered us and stole my handbag which contained my identity card and money. Soon afterwards we heard that the Russians were advancing, so I said to my family that we had best go westwards towards the Germans rather than stay where we were and be killed. The first German officers we met wanted to know who we were, and when I claimed diplomatic immunity they wanted me to give them the names of Germans as references. I mentioned the names of an army general and a general of the Luftwaffe whom I had met in Berlin. Then I remembered the friendly little naval officer and added: 'And Admiral Canaris.'

"I noticed that the German officer found it hard to conceal his astonishment when I uttered this name. His whole tone and bearing altered. He told me that he could not give me a pass to go westwards, but he ordered a military vehicle to take me on its way to Posnan."

There Madame J found herself among a great many other fugitives awaiting identification, but she did not have to wait long. One of the Admiral's staff officers singled her out and asked her to go with him to the railway coach.

"Can he not identify me here?" she asked proudly, not willing to enter a German train.

"It will be difficult for him to talk to you among these people."

When she had mounted the Admiral's coach it became gradually clear to her that he was in some high command with special powers. She had managed to keep her composure until that moment, but as she encountered him again in these altered circumstances and contrasted them with remembrance of old days she wept. The fate of the Polish armies was uppermost in her thoughts.

"Our armies have been routed," she exclaimed; "I fear they have not stood and fought."

"Do not distress yourself," the Admiral answered gently. "The Polish armies have fought well and bravely. They were simply out-mechanised by our armies and could do nothing against such a weight of material. You have perhaps seen the survivors retreating in the south-east, but you need not be ashamed of the stand that they made here in the north and west."

He asked her what he might do to help her, and she asked him to send her and her children to her parents in Warsaw.

Canaris frowned and shook his head. "I would not go to Warsaw," he suggested.

He seemed to be sorting out the future for her, and wherever he looked at the map he frowned.

"Switzerland," he said, "that is the best place."

It took a week or so before clearance could be obtained for Madame J and her children. Then she was sent out by train and managed to find an apartment not far from Berne. Her parents, whom she had wished to join, remained in Warsaw, but the Admiral promised that all letters she might send would be immediately forwarded and that if they forwarded their letters to him he would in turn pass them on. In this manner Canaris saved an old acquaintance from the dangers of Hitler's "Eastern" policy and protected her parents, too, for he could well say that while he held his hand over them, he retained his influence with her, even if she had been able to rejoin the Polish Government in Western exile, and similarly while she was abroad they could not be molested.

Madame J reported to the Polish Legation in Berne when she arrived in Switzerland and was registered as one of the Free Polish Movement. She told the strange story of her release through the good offices of Admiral Canaris whom she had once known in Berlin. When she mentioned this name again, the Poles showed immediate interest and the British reacted, too. They wanted to hear more about him. Madame J stayed in Switzerland.

"That's a well-known trick for securing an agent," commented a British diplomat to whom I related this ruse of Canaris. It seemed to justify the boast of Canaris to Bamler that he kept a special intelligence service of his own. I recalled the unsubstantiated stories that Canaris in Spain had made use of Mata Hari in Paris during the First World War.

But when I asked Madame J whether Canaris had attempted to draw her into espionage work, she shook her head and continued the story.

"The Admiral never asked me to find out anything for him about the Allies, although he must have known that I was in touch with my own countrymen in Berne and, through them, with the British.

"Not long after I had arrived in Switzerland he made a visit to Berne. That was in the winter of 1939. He took the opportunity of calling to see whether we were settled and whether he could do anything for my parents. Once he spoke of sending out his second daughter to Switzerland as she had become depressed by the atmosphere of war in Germany. During his first visit I could not be sure that Switzerland was not going to be invaded next, so I asked him whether I should go on to France.

"No, not France, that is an uncertain place."

I asked him whether he thought Italy was safe.

"'Italy, madam, yes, I think so, until the spring of next year, then Switzerland is better.'

"I don't suppose you could call Admiral Canaris an indiscreet man or he would not have held that high position in Germany for so long. But he could be very outspoken. He told me that winter of 1940 that Germany would certainly make war on her treaty partner Russia sooner or later. Next spring he was in Berne again, and when I asked him whether the troop movements in the Balkans were aimed against Turkey, he simply replied, 'No, Russia perhaps.' During the first stages of the Russian campaign he visited me again—that would have been in October 1941—and said that the German front had run fast and bogged down in Russia and that it would never reach its objectives. But he was most interesting when he was talking about the tension within German and the conspiracy that was gathering against Hitler. By then I was asked to relate our conversations to the British only—I don't suppose that it could otherwise have remained secret as long as it did."

"Do you suppose that he knew of your connection with the British?"

"There was not much that Admiral Canaris did not know, but then he could talk very impulsively. All his conversations were in the sphere of high politics; but you could sense from them what was imminent. He would not have told me of purely military matters—small treason such as agents deal in. When he spoke it was of the Reich and Russia and Great Britain and America. At times the tension in him affected me deeply when he spoke of their aims against Hitler. I asked the British sometimes—'Shall I tell him to go ahead'; the British were very correct in such matters and said nothing. But the British Secret Service could keep secrets, and throughout the war this link was undiscovered."

Months later, after seeing many friends and officers of Canaris, some of whom remembered Madame J, I went over her story again with her. It seemed to fit the pattern of Canaris's calculated indiscretions in conversation.

"He never once tried to find out anything about the Allies through me," she repeated. She was silent for a while and then added:

"And you should make it plain too that he did not give away ordinary military secrets—otherwise the Germans will say that he was a British spy."

CHAPTER XI

THE DOUBLE DUTCHMAN

W HAT WAS THERE about the flat Dutch landscape
that so perturbed Admiral Canaris? He had warned his chosen
friends who were conspiring against Hitler that they should
not venture into Holland. "I think I have penetrated the
British Secret Service," he had said. "I might receive embarrassing reports from that quarter."

"Not Holland!" said the friends of Canaris to me in 1938
when we spoke of possible meeting-places abroad; but they
could not give more precise reasons for their anxiety. As
years have passed, the true grounds have become apparent.
Agents of all sorts came and went in the Lowlands, and one
of them in the late 'thirties slipped into a position from which
he could watch the activities of many others. This was the
Dutchman, Walbach.

A man was skulking in a quiet avenue of one of the suburbs
of The Hague one summer evening, glancing at a pleasant
Dutch villa set back from the road. He was there the next day
and stumped out of the shadows, hardly taking the precaution
to conceal himself. Two men inside the villa watched him and
returned from time to time to the windows. He was always
there!

On the third day a man walked out of the villa and straight
up to the stranger.

"If you don't clear off I will fetch the police and charge you
with loitering!"

"I have no particular wish to loiter here." The Dutchman,
Walbach, sullenly returned the searching gaze of the German
agent. "It's hardly worth the money that Svert gives me. I
have a family to keep."

"Come inside!"

Walbach the loafer soon found himself in the presence of a

short, thickset man with a massive white head and a penetrating stare. The Chief of German counter-espionage in Holland, Richard Protze, shook his finger at the Dutchman.

"Don't you meddle with us, my lad. It will do you no good. What do the others pay you?"

"Seven hundred guilders a month."

"If you get results, you shall have eight hundred a month from me—and more! Your job will be to work your way into the British Secret Service."

The loafer Walbach stumped off through The Hague, armed with information as bait to catch bigger fish than himself. His activities in the last years of peace and the first months of the war were a nightmare to the Allies up and down the Lowlands, as Allied agents ceased to return from Germany, as operations went awry and secret information leaked out to the enemy. The agent Walbach is always in the shadows of the Dutch landscape, diligent, dissembling, undetected, while his victims walk away to prison and death.

During the war months of 1939 everything in the West seemed peaceful and flat as the landscape. Except for reconnaissances the French and British remained quietly behind the Maginot Line. There was no shelling of cities and not much aerial combat. Only at sea the U-boats and cruisers ranged and struck at British shipping. The American newspaper correspondents, who could see both sides, began to say that this was a "phoney war". Some aspects of the war were difficult to explain to onlookers. The British were cautious of using their unmustered strength. There was intense winter activity in the German High Command, with Hitler ordering weather forecasts and astrological reports and pushing ahead with preparations for a general offensive in the West while his generals entreated him to postpone it, at least until the spring.

Reinhard Heydrich was meanwhile unsatisfied with the balance of power in the Reich. He had lost some face over the Fritsch affair when Goering, resplendent in the uniform of a Reich Marshal, had risen in court, overawed Heydrich's witness and torn the prosecution case to threads. At the outbreak of war Hitler had proclaimed himself "first soldier of the Reich" and confided his person to an army bodyguard battalion led by Major-General Erwin Rommel, instead of relying on the S.S. who had protected him throughout the years of struggle between party and state. It was only after the mysterious death of General von Fritsch in the field not far from Warsaw that Hitler began to think of an S.S. bodyguard again.

Heydrich had never got to the bottom of the intrigues of the Army in London during 1938. He knew that some military opponents of the regime had warned the British against Hitler. The Heydrich Security Service had since been extending its activities abroad in the field of surveillance; but Heydrich had found no positive trace of conspiracies against the Reich Government. Then his lieutenant, Schellenberg, suggested to him that if such plots existed and could not be detected, Hitler might equally well be convinced by an invented plot. It would also have a deterrent effect on the generals if what they were contemplating was actually disclosed in another form. So two operations were planned in outline at the Prinz Albrechtstrasse—more or less simultaneously, though not at first directly related to each other. One was for a mock attempt on the life of the Fuehrer on November 8th, 1939, in the Burgerbräu beer cellar in Munich during a reunion of founder members of the party. The other was to kidnap two of the principal British agents in Western Europe.

The first was fairly easily arranged by means of a convict, just as the sham Polish attack on Gleiwitz had been carried out by German convicts in Polish uniform, who were either shot on the spot or slaughtered afterwards. A Communist named Georg Elser, under long sentence of internment in Dachau, was promised his liberty by S.S. agents if he would construct a hiding-place for a time bomb in one of the pillars of the beer cellar, put an infernal machine inside and then replace the woodwork so as to hide all trace of it. As far as the management of the beer cellar were concerned it would be easy to inform them that a microphone had to be installed in the hall. At any rate the job was done by Georg Elser, who was evidently, like van der Lubbe, a man of subnormal mentality. Captain Payne Best, who had snatches of conversation with him in the concentration camp, relates his story fully in *The Venloo Incident*. Elser was afterwards given a large sum of foreign currency and offered the chance to escape. The bomb, connected by a wire to a detonating point outside the hall, was exploded about ten minutes after Hitler had left the reunion and killed several of the founder members of the party who were sitting on and drinking beer together. This lent colour to the incident and made it seem more realistic. Elser was "recaptured" the following day at the Swiss frontier where he was naïvely trying to cross without a passport at a Customs station.

The business of capturing these particular British agents appears to have been a little more difficult. Heydrich believed that the principal agency of the British Intelligence Service for watching Germany was situated in The Hague. Walbach had by now burrowed deep into the British Intelligence system and asserted that its Chief was Major R. H. Stevens, an official attached to the British Consulate in The Hague. Heydrich took Stevens to be the Chief of British Intelligence for northern Germany.

So it came about that after the Polish campaign was over the S.S. Security Officer Schellenberg, who had been watching an agent called Franz who went to and fro between Germany and The Hague, used him to carry the idea to Major Stevens and his associate, Captain S. Payne Best, that a group of army officers plotting against Hitler were anxious to establish contact with the British Secret Service. There was excitement in high Foreign Office circles in London.

Stevens and Best were ordered to probe the offers that might be made on the spot. A cautious game of cat and mouse went on for some time in the flat Dutch landscape at frontier villages between Arnhem and Venloo. The British agents grew bolder, even careless, and gave a wireless set and a code to Schellenberg, who was posing as an army officer under the pseudonym of Schaemmel and declared in solemn secrecy that he was in the confidence of General von Rundstedt. Lord Halifax was kept informed of the progress made, and the British agents were instructed from London not to commit themselves or to make any propositions in writing but to listen to what might be proposed to them. These two German "emissaries" showed a strange reluctance to venture far over the frontier, though German business men were going to The Hague and Amsterdam every day. The ninth of November was the day of evil omen. The Germans came to Venloo to talk, said that their general was on the way to a frontier café, the Café Backus near Venloo, but they contrived to keep the British so late that Stevens and Best drove to the rendezvous at the café without waiting for the Dutch bicycle patrol that was to have been their bodyguard. At the Café Backus there was no general and no peace proposals; instead a car loaded with an armed Commando of Germans in plain clothes roared through Tom Tiddler's ground, seized these unfortunate men, and shot the Dutch conducting officer, Captain Dirk Klop, who gallantly drew his pistol and tried to prevent the car driving off. Within a few seconds Stevens and Best were riding under heavily armed escort into the Reich.

"Have you a hand in this? Where is Major Stevens?" Canaris fired this question at Richard Protze whom he had ordered to report to him personally in Dusseldorf.

"Stevens is in Holland," answered Protze.

"He is not! He is in Germany!" shouted the Admiral. "If you have a hand in this there will be the devil to pay."

"I know nothing at all about this affair," replied Protze, quivering with apprehension.

"Ask Abwehr II," hissed the Admiral, but none of his branches could tell him anything about it.

Protze quickly put his beagle Walbach on to the trail in The Hague and received the dry answer from the British: "The Germans know better than we do where Stevens is."

"Canaris was not informed in advance of the S.D. action at Venloo," General Lahousen assured me. "Nor were the Commanders-in-Chief, and they were more than a little perturbed. The Admiral had a horror that the Gestapo might extort from Stevens and Best something about the opposition in Germany." Canaris took soundings with Heydrich as to whether any German intelligence officers were compromised by the affair. Heydrich answered that there were no Abwehr officers involved, but it seemed that the loyalty of some senior generals was questionable.

The German newspapers were full of the details of the "bomb plot" in Munich and on the following day the Venloo kidnapping. Schaemmel, alias Schellenberg, sent one last sarcastic message over the British wireless set and then let it be photographed by the Propaganda Ministry as a piece of evidence. One Professor de Crinis, an S.S. doctor, who later became head of the Psychiatric Clinic of the Berlin Charite Hospital, had the brilliant idea of linking the Venloo incident with the Munich beer-cellar "plot" and suggested this to

D

Heydrich. Stevens and Best were paraded where Elser could see them and learn to identify them without hesitation; he was briefed in the second phase of the deception; but although German newspapers asserted that the British agents were behind the plot on the life of Hitler, details of the two incidents were not entirely easy to reconcile and eventually the idea of a grand state trial was dropped. Heydrich had nevertheless achieved two stage effects. He had invested his Fuehrer with the aura of a charmed life and recalled the ebbing sympathies of the common people. He had also made it appear that there were traitors in Germany with whom the British wanted to get in touch. He established his case for an S.S. bodyguard beyond all doubt, and Hitler never again confided his person to the Army.

Canaris had meanwhile transferred his political intelligence work, which was a forbidden field for him, to the safer precincts of the Vatican.

Dr. Josef Mueller, his Roman Catholic friend, was a deep and crafty mind and a man who could dissemble with almost the artistry of his chief. Short, paunchy, with the bland face of a bon viveur, nobody would have believed that this lieutenant of the reserve would quietly carry on negotiations of high treason at this time when the shadow of Heydrich had fallen across their secret contacts with England.

Mueller was attached to the Munich office of the Abwehr which worked into Italy. He had an old friend in the Vatican, a German Jesuit from Freiburg in Breisgau, Father Laiber, who was secretary to the Pope. Pope Pius XII himself, as Cardinal Pacelli, had made a particular study of Germany before his election to the throne of St. Peter in March 1939. He had spent many years in Berlin as Papal Nuncio, had seen the struggle between the pagan Nazis and Mother Church and met the leaders of the German opposition. Mueller was given his passports by Canaris's office and set off to Rome in the middle of November. He soon made progress at the Vatican. Francis D'Arcy Osborne, the British Minister, sent home to London for instructions and permission was given for discussions to be held with Mueller on a basis for peace which would be acceptable to both Britain and a Germany that had purged itself of the Nazi regime.

His object, Mueller tells me, was to work out a draft of

peace terms that would convince the German generals that they might make a reasonable peace with the Allies.

Mueller was under the impression that these negotiations were sufficiently advanced for Lord Halifax to fly to Rome and visit his Holiness in the Vatican. D'Arcy Osborne has told me that there was no question of a visit to Rome by the Foreign Secretary at this time. It is probable that the most the British did was to send out a specialist to Rome to prepare a personal report. We shall see, however, from his speeches at the time that Lord Halifax was kept informed of these peace discussions.

The risks that Mueller ran were great indeed. After a prolonged visit to Rome, it was decided to set forth the basis of negotiations, and the Vatican undertook the draft.

"I had considerable difficulties in my discussions," Mueller told me. "The British keep their word, and they were not ready to promise anything that might be unacceptable later."

The draft was written out on Vatican notepaper. One copy was sent to the Foreign Office in London, and the copy that Mueller took back to Berlin with him had attached to it the visiting card of the Pope's secretary. Father Laiber wrote on the visiting card:

"Dr. Josef Mueller, the bearer of these proposals, enjoys the full confidence of His Holiness."

When Mueller reached Berlin he put his letter in the hands of Dohnanyi in the office of Canaris. The Admiral, who did not want to appear to know about this business, glanced at a report known as the "X-report" which was based on the Mueller negotiations before it was passed on to General Halder, the Chief of the General Staff. The X-report was prepared by General Thomas, Chief of the Economic Department of the War Ministry.

The conditions which it outlined as a basis for a peace settlement, as Mueller remembers them, were that

(1) Germany must rid herself of all Nazis in the government and make an end of their political system.
(2) A German government must take over that is able and willing to adhere to its obligations.
(3) A settlement could then be reached which would leave Germany in possession of Austria and the Sudeten area.

Lord Halifax gave some weight to these views during a public speech on January 20th, 1940.

"The only reason why peace cannot be made tomorrow," he said, "is that the German Government has as yet given no evidence of their readiness to repair the damage that they have wrought upon their neighbours or of their capacity to convince the world that any pledge they may subscribe to is worth more than the paper on which it is written."

This was a clue which the German General Staff could compare with its secret report.

General Halder examined the basic terms of peace with General Beck, who, though retired, still maintained close contact with his former deputy. The Vatican documents were locked away in the safe of a Colonel Schrader, a trustworthy staff officer at Army High Command H.Q. in Zossen. General Thomas, the Wehrmacht Economic Chief, had combined his knowledge that Germany could not wage a long war with the political appreciation that Mueller had brought home and drawn the conclusion that they must make peace. When the X-report was shown to the Commander-in-Chief, General von Brauchitsch said that the Fuehrer was invested with the glory of his Polish victories; the younger officers and the troops could not be relied upon for action against the Fuehrer. Germany was involved in a struggle of ideologies which would have to be fought out to the end.

During his visits to Rome Mueller discussed fully with Laiber such matters as the Vatican methods of conducting its diplomacy and the security that must be taken in their negotiations. Again the anxiety of Canaris about ciphers was discussed. He lived day and night in peril of being mentioned by name in the codes of the Allies and neutral powers.

"The Vatican ciphers are perfectly safe," declared Father Laiber.

Mueller demurred and advised him to be cautious.

"So he says that the Vatican ciphers are safe," Admiral Canaris nodded, as Mueller related his conversations in Rome. "Show him this."

He held out a deciphered copy of a Vatican secret dispatch to the Nuncio in Portugal. Laiber blenched when Mueller showed it to him.

Mueller returned many times between 1939 and 1943, when a peculiar mishap interrupted this contact with the British. By then, of the two copies of the protocol that had been worked out between him and Osborne, the British had destroyed their copy.

"We asked them to take that precaution in 1940," said Mueller, "when it seemed that England might be invaded before the Foreign Office had time to destroy its records."

Although the German Commander-in-Chief was despondent and thought that perhaps Hitler must first get a bloody nose on the Maginot Line before he could be overthrown, the Chief of the General Staff, General Halder, played with the idea that Canaris might plan the murder of Hitler and so provide a solution to the dilemma.

There was a force at his disposal, the Brandenburg Regiment, a mixed commando unit for attacking or capturing special intelligence targets. It was under his command in the same way as the little Commando Force of Admiral Lord Keyes was held for special duties. But the Brandenburg Regiment was not politically reliable for an attack against Hitler.

Besides, there were disturbing voices on the ether. Quite early in the war the B.B.C. German service broadcasting an impulsive attack on the Nazi leaders, added:

"The only decent fellow among them is Admiral Canaris."

His friends remembered distinctly the shock of hearing this broadcast, and worse was to follow when an American magazine carried a gossip paragraph about Admiral Canaris as the "man who would lead a revolution against Hitler".

By chance I received a letter from a remote country rectory which confirms the mischief that some of these unguarded reports must have done.

The Rector of Wraxhall, the Rev. H. S. Briggs, told me that he clearly remembered that similar reports in a small gossip periodical alarmed him at the time.

"During the war . . . even I in a Somerset village had divined from what I had read in a British newspaper that Canaris was working in Berlin against Hitler."

At least twice in the five years of his war service such rumours attached themselves to his name, and though he encountered his two colleagues, the Reichsfuehrer S.S. and Heydrich, shortly afterwards with the pleasant observation:

"It seems from the foreign press that I am to start a revolution in Germany"—who could tell from the cold stare of Himmler and their exchange of glances whether he had outfaced their suspicions.

Events pelted so fast in these six months of false calm on the edge of 1940 that some awkward moments were submerged though not forgotten. The men in black uniform and the men in field grey had to work together for all their mutual suspicions of each other. The military situation in the West held their attention. That winter and spring Holland grew more and more important to both sides. Abwehr I and III collected information on Allied activities in the Low Countries —Hitler had asked for the sharpest surveillance, and many of their reports were selected by the Foreign Ministry to embody in a white book accusing the Allies of violating the neutrality of Belgium and Holland. Both Keitel and Canaris agreed that they would not sign the White Book when they saw the proofs ready for publication, especially when the German Foreign Ministry commented that Canaris's reports were not conclusive in proving Allied violations of Belgian and Dutch neutrality and might have to be "touched up a little".

There was a disturbing incident when Abwehr II, the sabotage branch, was instructed to procure Belgian and Dutch Customs and gendarmerie uniforms, because they were wanted for use by shock units of the German Army. It would have seemed more logical to get a German master tailor to pay a visit to Belgium and size up the cut and colour of these uniforms, because they need not be genuine, and could only be wanted for momentary surprise—the seizing of Maas and Meuse bridges before they could be demolished. As it was, the thefts were noticed and reported in the Dutch and Belgian press. A Dutch newspaper published a caricature of Goering in a Dutch tram-driver's uniform.

Abwehr II was also laying a network of inactive agents for special use when D-day came in the West. This explains why there was such a sudden burst of undetected activities when the lull of the "phoney war" was over and the Germans marched in. Bridges and road blocks were seized and held by civilians or men in Allied uniform and curious acts of sabotage disrupted the defence, its supplies, transport and telephone communications.

It was the task of the British Secret Service in the lull to detect and report these agents wherever they were planted. It watched the activities of the Abwehr and the Dutch Nazis, and a hectic race began, each side working day and night to demolish the net that the other side was building up. Walbach, the stolid Walbach, slipped in and out of the German intelligence offices in The Hague and Amsterdam bringing vital news from the inward parts of the British Secret Service. "Klemmer is a British agent! The British know that Schramm is a German agent." The Abwehr struck here and there at a harmless-looking business man or a peasant at the frontier. Walbach turned in one name after another. He reported also to Commander Protze the names of those men whom the British had discovered to be working for Germany. One after another, the names of the German agents rolled out. As fast as the Abwehr built up, the British knew it. Protze's nerves grew taut.

"The British know that Admiral Canaris has been to Holland," reported Walbach. Here and there Walbach brought in the names of German intelligence officers as men who were working with the British! Protze could not sleep at night. Nightmares of hidden traitors filled his brain, names sprang up at him. The German spies from France had to pass through Holland to reach Germany. The British seemed to know their names, too, Walbach reported. Protze sat down and tried to cool off and form his own conclusions. There must be a highly placed Allied agent within the German Intelligence Service.

"The British are watching for a man with a limp coming from France to The Hague, taking the evening express for Cologne tomorrow evening!"

So one catastrophe after another was reported by Walbach.

Then the bomb fell.

"There is an agent of the Allies highly placed in the German Legation in The Hague!"

Protze sprang to his feet. He was within an hour in the study of Count Zech, the German Minister, and whispered his news.

"Whom do you suspect?" asked the Count guardedly.

Protze uttered a name.

"Quite impossible, my dear Commander. I know him well. .
He comes of a very good family."

The minister drew out of his desk a list of security suspects.

"I think there are some British agents listed here," he
said. "Let's see if one of them could have penetrated your
service." But Protze thought he knew his man. He would
wait to get him. At the end of the discussion he pledged the
Minister to secrecy and withdrew to set his snares about the
victim.

Count Zech was asked to a security conference with
German intelligence officers in Amsterdam. He mentioned it
thoughtfully to one of his secretaries on his return to The
Hague.

"They tell me," he mused, "that there is an Allied agent in
my Legation."

The man addressed gave an imperceptible start, smiled
and nodded vacuously. But within twenty-four hours the
Minister noticed that the secretary had vanished. He made
enquiries of the Dutch police and the German intelligence
offices in Cologne. They could tell him nothing. "Perhaps he
has gone to join his regiment," suggested the Minister; "he
was always asking to."

The old sleuth, Richard Protze, was soon back in his
study, with a sorrowful expression,

"Excellency, our man has flown. He is in London. Did you
talk, Excellency?"

Admiral Canaris heard the whole story with the utmost
calm in his offices in Berlin. Richard Protze sat at his elbow.
Count Zech was not present, but over his head there hung a
charge of breach of official secrets regulations. Yet oddly
enough in this case, as in so many others, Canaris was not
moved by rancour either against the Count, who had lost him
his prey, or the enormous treason of the vanished man himself. Protze was astonished to find that Canaris was only
anxious to hush up the whole affair. I met the elusive secretary
in London years later.

"Canaris would have hanged me had he caught me," he
said with an uneasy laugh.

I think that he spoke the truth there, except that it would
have been Heydrich who did the job.

When the full force of the German offensive broke in the West on May 10th, 1940, the affair of the renegade secretary had already been buried. Walbach had somehow escaped the suspicion of the British and even risked leaving Holland with the other Allied fugitives who took boat for the white cliffs. Walbach swam unnoticed with the shoal.

CHAPTER XII

NORWAY

HITHERTO EVERYTHING AGGRESSIVE that Hitler had planned after the seizure of Austria had been reported to Great Britain by the German opposition within the Abwehr, with what degree of complicity on the part of the Admiral the reader will doubtless decide in the course of this narrative. I had myself seen how the mobilisations against Czechoslovakia and Poland were imparted in outline with dates and subsequent changes of dates sometimes as much as two months ahead of D-day. The shortest warning of all had preceded the march into Prague, because on this occasion Hitler had needed relatively few divisions and had given Keitel orders that they were to be kept at twenty-four hours' notice at the frontier to advance before any follow-up troops had been moved. It remained to be seen whether the Abwehr chiefs would continue to seek to identify their interests with those of the British in wartime. Would they communicate to the enemy information that might lead to the loss of thousands of German lives, even if it meant spoiling the pattern of aggression, too?

"Your friends will now have to serve their country," an intelligence officer suggested to me shortly before the war. There seemed to be a certain staid readiness in the minds of the Foreign Office to abandon contact with the enemies of Hitler. Of Canaris, I am inclined to think that such on our side as could observe something of his activities had not yet fully grasped his motives and identified him still with the aims of his department—the Intelligence Service of the Wehrmacht. I had been induced before the war to abandon journalism and join the Foreign Office—not, as I supposed at the time, to utilise the contacts that I had already made, but in order to eliminate an unorthodox channel of communication. The reports that had come out of the Tirpitzufer in the two previous years had mystified and disturbed the British conception of German unity of purpose and had contributed to the sudden and energetic decision to give the Polish guarantee in March 1939. It was a few weeks later, after some discussion in the Foreign Office on my activities, I was invited to join that department and spent several months with them until the outbreak of war. There I practically lost sight of Canaris and his friends and often wondered whether they had found new contacts with us and renewed understanding. These months revealed to me the groping and hesitant fashion in which big departments work slowly forward on the preconceived lines of national policy—like big ships at sea with helm hard over to avoid collision that is inevitable miles ahead.

At times advance intelligence had seemed of little use—while we were still weak and while our vital interests did not seem to be threatened. Now, if ever, in the spring of 1940, knowledge of enemy intentions would be perhaps decisive. The land forces involved were numerically nearly equal, the Luftwaffe preponderant on the one hand and the Royal Navy on the other. Everything depended on surprise and speed, everything—immediate success, the extent and length of the war, the fate of the belligerent nations and that of Europe itself.

Hitler started to talk of invading Norway during a conference with Grand Admiral Raeder on October 10th—fifty days before Russia invaded Finland. The threat of British and French military aid to Finland through occupying Narvik did not exist at the time. Jodl was initiated to the secret in the middle of November; by December 14th Hitler decided to mount the operation—it was called "Weser-Exercise"—and on February 20th he appointed his military commander, General von Falkenhorst, after being enraged and alarmed by the action of February 15th when Captain Philip Vian with H.M.S. *Cossack* seized the *Altmark* in Norwegian waters and rescued three hundred British sailors captured in South Atlantic waters by German raiders.

Accordingly Canaris must have been apprised of Operation Weser-Exercise in December, at the planning stage. His reports on the dispositions of the Royal Navy will have been necessary, as well as Abwehr reconnaissance of the harbours, fiords and batteries of the Norwegian coast. According to the pattern, his K.O. or war organisation would have to tackle special targets on D-day. The secret now lay in his hands.

"It was a terribly weighty decision to occupy Norway," said Jodl. "To put it shortly, it meant gambling with the entire German fleet. . . . The Fuehrer said in those days—'To carry out a decision of this kind I must have absolutely reliable information with which I can justify that decision before the world and prove that it was necessary. I cannot say that I heard this and that from Herr Quisling.' And for this reason he kept the Intelligence Service, in particular, very busy at this time in order to get even more precise information."

Canaris reported in the middle of March that the Home Fleet had moved from Western Approaches to Scapa Flow—the nearest base to the Norwegian Coast. Here the British could move either to the Skagerrak or athwart the iron routes from Narvik to Germany.

"The Fuehrer's decision was made on April 2nd," said Jodl, "on reports from the Navy of repeated firing on German merchant ships in Norwegian and Danish territorial waters. Secondly, a report came from Canaris that British troops and transports were lying in a state of readiness on the north-east coast of England." The British Cabinet had decided on March 12th to revive plans previously discussed for occupation of Narvik and Trondheim, and later Stavanger and Bergen. Thus under the pretext of helping the Finns by securing our supply route to them, a German operation to seize Narvik could have been forestalled and all her northern approaches sealed.

Falkenhorst's troops, embarking at Hamburg and Bremen, Stettin and Danzig, were battened under hatches, divisions in South Sleswig were made ready to march into Denmark, and the entire German Navy assembled in the several task forces required for convoy duties or bombardment. German merchantmen set out first for Narvik with several thousand troops below decks. They would lie there as long as was necessary like the assault troops that stormed the Westerplatte in the previous year.

Now there were six days left in which the Admiral might be able to prevent this mad operation taking place. He was not convinced that the British intended to land in Norway, but he was sure that they were prepared to act if Hitler did so, and the Royal Navy was even stronger in comparison to the German fleet than in the days when he had served in the *Dresden*. It was likely enough, if the British were met in the Skagerrak again, that the Battle of Jutland would be refought twenty-four years after and the German Navy destroyed in such a manner as the French and Spanish Fleet at Trafalgar, but with the additional carnage—that the corpses of tens of thousands of German soldiers from the transports would be weltering in the Sounds. Beyond that the discomfiture would be such for Hitler, his prestige so shaken, that the Army could be prevailed upon to make an end of him and propose terms of peace. Had Canaris not bestowed in the safe in Zossen the terms that had been worked out in Rome through the mediation of the Pope? An end to the massacre of the Poles, the nightly murders in the concentration camps, the sickly and hysterical perversion of a great nation to worship a madman. As he discussed these doubts and fears with General Oster on April 2nd, it seemed that this might well be the turning point of the war.

Oster found his way next day to the Dutch military attaché, Colonel J. Sas, and told him that the invasion of Norway was imminent. Sas passed on this information to the Norwegian Legation in Berlin, but the diplomat who received it thought the report too incredible to be forwarded. It is my belief that Canaris, too, did not miss this opportunity to bring about the crisis that he desired.

"The shortest way to defeat will be the most merciful," one of his friends, Ewald von Kleist, had told me a year previously. Abshagen hastens to say that "the many assertions that Canaris warned the Scandinavian governments a few days before Weser-Exercise began . . . are absolutely untrue". He bases his opinion on that of an Abwehr officer—probably Lahousen or Liedig—"who never heard even a hint of the idea of warning the Allies or the threatened countries during the early April conferences of the Abwehr directorate". But the Admiral was not so rash as to discuss in his office what he intended to do—perhaps not even with Oster! It was interesting to me to find that Lahousen, for years his assistant and Chief of Abwehr II, never heard from Canaris of the London negotiations of 1938. We have precedent, according to Gisevius, in the Abwehr planting information about atrocities in Poland in foreign newspapers in order to create an impression on Hitler. In this case, the Swedish press was full of reports for several days before Weser-Exercise of German troops embarking in Baltic ports.

Abshagen finds it necessary to mention—and discount—the possibility that Canaris had special contact with the Swedish Legation in Berlin and that it served his purpose in warning the Allies. Captain Franz Liedig, his intelligence officer attached to Army Command XXI that planned Weser-Exercise in detail from the O.K.W. outline plan, remembers the Admiral saying to him that Hitler had always recoiled when he sensed his opponent to be stronger and that if the British Navy showed the flag in Norwegian waters Hitler would abandon the operation. Liedig was convinced that the shipping concentrations could not have escaped the notice of the British, whose intelligence service in Sweden was active.

"We felt absolutely certain," Lahousen told me, "that the Allies had at least forty-eight hours' notice of Weser-Exercise. Foreign Consuls had reported the movements of German shipping and Abwehr had records of their telephone conversation."

"Of course, we had full reports days ahead," a British intelligence officer told me. "We had all the movements of shipping as they occurred. But they did not know what to make of them in London."

It is certain that a British official in Oslo received a firm report on April 7th that invasion was intended, and this was then communicated first to London, though the British naval attaché in Oslo was not immediately informed—one reason for the unpreparedness of the Norwegian fleet. An air reconnaissance on the following day—the same day as British mines were laid in Norwegian waters south of Narvik—showed a force of German warships and transports steaming up the coast off Norway and H.M. submarine *Trident* sank one of them, the *Rio de Janeiro*. It was only on the afternoon of April 8th when the three hundred survivors of the *Rio de Janeiro*, mostly soldiers in battle order, had been interrogated that the Norwegian Government realised that invasion was imminent. Opinion prevailed in Whitehall that the Germans were intent on capturing Narvik—not until April 9th did it become apparent that they meant to occupy the whole country. I have no doubt at all that German intentions were correctly reported by one source or other. The Norwegian Government had put the Oslo coastal batteries and air defences at a state of prolonged alert in the second half of March, but there were so many agencies, missions and departments receiving, reporting or collating intelligence that it was exceedingly difficult for the correct appreciation to prevail.

Mr. Chamberlain complained afterwards of the bewildering diversity of reports. Mr. Churchill, then still First Lord of the Admiralty, argued that the Home Fleet could not always be patrolling close to the enemy routes in all weathers, easy targets for U-boats. If in fact Admiral Canaris asked through neutral channels, as I suspect he did, for a demonstration of British naval strength in the days before Weser-Exercise, he must have been overestimating the insight of the enemy into his own mind and underestimating the power of the machine of intelligence and deception, his own Abwehr, that was carrying him against his will, whither he would not go.

There is little doubt from what Abwehr officers relate that Canaris hoped for a sharp defeat in the Norwegian adventure that would bring a swing in public opinion against Hitler. In point of fact, it was his own K.O. or war organisation in Oslo that had to lead in the German warships, and the German naval attachés who gathered the Quisling ministers and officers together and set the German legation in a state of defence. Although the bravery of the Norwegian Navy foiled the German warships, and airborne landing was necessary to capture Oslo, much of the credit went to Canaris for German success in Norway—and he was promoted from Vice-Admiral to his final rank of full Admiral.

Lest it be imagined that Canaris was squeamish or stood aside from the attempts to thwart Hitler, let us turn the clock on one month from April 1st to May 1st; Operation Gelb (Yellow) was about to take place with breach of Dutch and Belgian neutrality—the grand offensive against the Low Countries and France. The act itself was not more flagrant than the attack in Norway; but the precautions that General Oster initiated were two-fold. The case of Norway had shown how far astray British intelligence could be in its final appreciations—a failing that the German intelligence developed in measure as the situation of Germany worsened.

The persistent Dr. Josef Mueller had been served with his passport once more and ordered to Rome on pretext of an Abwehr mission in the last days of April. By now most of the German Navy had been sunk piecemeal in vivid and desperate actions with units of the Home Fleet and submarines—without the effect hoped for by the Admiral, a repulse of the German invasion. The extent of German naval losses was being hushed up, the extent of their gains on land given full publicity in Wehrmacht communiqués. Now General Beck abjured Mueller to tell the Allies unmistakably what was impending on the Western Front. He named the date of May 10th when the attack in the West would be launched, irrespective of the fortunes of XXI Army in Norway. This extraordinary stroke of backroom statesmanship was necessary, he argued, if the Allies were not to destroy Germany utterly when she was defeated. She must prove that the forces of good were still alive in her and working for the ultimate salvation of Europe.

Mueller did not stop long in Rome; but he met a senior Belgian diplomat and reported to him that Germany would attack in the West, violating Dutch and Belgian neutrality on or about May 10th.

This time the message went home as it was intended—but by cipher telegram. How the Admiral hated ciphers! Mueller made his way back to Berlin quickly. He found time before leaving Italy to ask the Italian frontier officials to insert an omitted entry stamp in his passport. He gave the date as May 1st—the place of entry was Venice, where he had landed by air. The good-natured frontier control official, so he tells me, was willing to stamp whatever date he suggested. It is foolish for intelligence officers and police to imagine that a passport contains an exact record of movements. Pick up your own passport and see if you can read out of it your own travels over a year or so. This horseplay with rubber stamps was the salvation of Josef Mueller; for when he arrived back in Berlin and reported in the Tirpitzufer the Admiral said quietly:

"Look here! The Fuehrer is foaming about this."

He held out a report of a deciphered telegram forwarded by the Security Service to the Abwehr with the request to investigate it and discover the name of the officer concerned: Mueller memorised the telegram that might be his death warrant in approximately these terms:

From H.E. THE BELGIAN MINISTER
THE HOLY SEE
To FOREIGN MINISTRY, BRUSSELS.

May 1st 1940.

An officer of the German General Staff visiting Rome today, reports that invasion of Belgium and Holland may be expected with certainty on or soon after May 10th.

As he held the deciphered intercept, his blood ran cold. The Gestapo had the keys of the Belgian diplomatic code.

CHAPTER XIII

THE ABWEHR IN ENGLAND

B ETWEEN M AY I ST and May 7th a mysterious message went out also to Switzerland through a contact known as "the Viking line", a still secret channel of communication between Admiral Canaris and the Swiss General Staff. It warned the Swiss to mobilise against an imminent threat of invasion. The Swiss did, in fact, mobilise, but this storm passed westwards. Did Canaris suspect that if Hitler could not penetrate through Belgium he would thrust his left flank through Switzerland and the Belfort gap? Or did Canaris simply make this feint to alarm the French and lead them to tie down strong forces unused in the Belfort area, that might be badly needed elsewhere. The Swiss have been puzzling about it ever since.

Nine days of calm in May! Rumours had thickened fast since the Belgian Minister had sent his dispatch from the Vatican. The British and French would have gladly taken Belgium into full alliance and linked the Meuse defensive system with the Maginot Line: but King Leopold had been firm that Belgium must remain neutral until she was attacked. Signs multiplied that the Germans were concentrating for an attack in the West. The Falkenhorst army was by now advancing north from Trondheim and the Allies had re-embarked at Namsos though they landed a Polish force at Narvik a day later; there had been a heated debate in the House of Commons on the 7th and 8th and the authority of Neville Chamberlain was tottering. The Dutch increased their frontier precautions, the Belgians suspended traffic on the Albert Canal. Nothing was certain yet, but the Western Powers and the neutral states sensed something in that unholy calm beyond the Rhine.

General Oster left the Tirpitzufer on the evening of May 9th for an appointment to dinner with his old friend, Colonel G. J. Sas, the Dutch military attaché. This time there was no doubt about it. He told Sas quite openly that he could expect an attack on Belgium and the Netherlands at first light on the following day.

Sas managed to get a telephone connection to The Hague before midnight and dictated a message to the duty officer.

"The surgeon has decided to operate at 4 a.m. in the morning."

He waited, appalled and helpless at his own foreknowledge of what was apparently only a few hours distant.

About midnight the telephone rang again. It was a senior officer in The Hague wanting to know if Sas was positive that this meant an attack on May 10th.

Colonel Sas was aware that the Gestapo was listening with especial attention to all foreign telephone calls at this moment. A cold perspiration broke out as he shaped his answers to give the clearest indication without prompting the German Security Service to break the connection. He succeeded in doing this; but the secret was now out to the enemy that he had been informed. The Dutch Government tried to get in touch with Sas again in the early hours of the morning. This time all telephone communications were cut, and invasion came soon afterwards. The Abwehr war organisations in France and the Lowlands sprang into activity, Germans in Allied uniforms seized bridges and strong points, Rommel's phantom division stormed over the Meuse on the 13th and the Fourth Army streamed after it. If Germany had lost tactical surprise to the Allied Intelligence Services, it was not enough to make any difference to the fortunes of the field. They had crossed the Maas in Holland on D-day and by May 15th the Dutch Army, cut off from its Allies, was forced to capitulate. King Leopold offered capitulation on May 27th; by June 5th the Germans had entered Dunkirk and crossed the Somme; four days later all hostilities in Norway ceased, and on June 10th, a month after D-day, Italy entered the war.

It is obvious that Hitler, strutting in exultation and soon to take the surrender of France in his railway coach at Compiègne, will have forgotten his ill-humour at the Security Service reports on the betrayal of his plans. Not so the Gestapo itself! Canaris received a report on the telephone talks with The Hague on D-day: somebody remarked at a diplomatic reception in Berlin that General Oster was a close friend of Sas. It seemed that the Gestapo were on the verge of a discovery.

"You had better investigate this leakage in Rome," Canaris whispered to Josef Mueller, and Mueller went with a feeling of confidence that his chief would protect him. He did a wonderful job of work. He called first on the German liaison officer with the Italian Intelligence Service, Colonel Helferrich. In the course of conversation he made it plain that he, Mueller, was not a General Staff officer, simply a Lieutenant of the Reserve. The incriminating intercept had referred to a "General Staff officer". He was himself in Venice on May 1st (as his passport showed) and he knew of no General Staff officer who would have been in Rome on that day. Of course, Colonel Helferrich was a General Staff officer, but suspicion of him was out of the question! Had they not better consider other possibilities? The Crown Princess of Italy was a Belgian princess. Ciano had been on friendly footing with the Crown Prince and Crown Princess. The German Foreign Ministry had the closest contact with Count Ciano. Was it not likely that the leakage had occurred through those channels? Within a few days Mueller had so thoroughly tangled the investigations in Rome that on his return to Berlin Oster remarked to him with a rueful smile:

"You have done so well in Rome that they have dropped that line of enquiry, and are working on this end."

But Canaris covered Oster's tracks.

Mueller remained free to come and go into Italy, though Colonel Helferrich made a private mental note to himself that his own guess still was that Mueller had given away the secret.

The British showed themselves more receptive now to Mueller's opinions. The last of the B.E.F. had been withdrawn from France by June 17th, and by June 27th the German Army had reached the Spanish frontier on the Atlantic coast at Hendaye. The British were evacuating the Channel Islands, and Hitler was considering the idea of a direct invasion of Great Britain. It was now that the opportunities of deception on the British side were considerable. The whole issue hung on a fine balance of air power with neither side able to gain the supremacy for some months at any rate. The British may have hinted through obscure diplomatic channels that they would not prolong the struggle indefinitely—Hitler wanted to hear such suggestions, for he was not entirely enthusiastic about Operation Sealion.

Mueller suggested that the British might soon abandon the

unequal combat when he was lunching with Canaris one summer day of 1940 in a Munich hotel. The fortunes of the Third Reich had never stood so high.

"I think you will find that the British will not go on," he exclaimed to test his chief.

The good humour of Canaris faded in an instant. He pushed his plate away.

"Of course they will go on," he exclaimed angrily, as if his best friend had been insulted, and Mueller had some difficulty in calming him down. German army officers, exulting in their easy victories to Canaris, found him sceptical and out of humour. "What a strange fellow we have as Chief of Intelligence!" they remarked.

Hitler gave Keitel orders on July 2nd for the outline plan of Operation Sealion to be sent forward for detailed planning. Preparations were to be complete by the middle of August. Mueller slipped down to Rome and passed this information to the British. He also asked for the written drafts of the peace agreement to be destroyed, in case the invasion should succeed and the archives of the Foreign Office captured.

Grand-Admiral Raeder, the driving force behind the invasion of Norway, had prepared an outline plan for invasion of the British Isles in November 1939, even before Hitler had asked for it. The Fuehrer declared in a conference at Wolfschacht on June 20th, 1940, that all bases on the Atlantic coast must be completely at the disposal of the Germany Navy for warfare against Britain. Raeder made a report on the types of shipping and barges available and the areas where it was proposed to land the troops. He asked for air supremacy as indispensable to the operation and requested the Army to work out a light scale of equipment for the assault divisions. Hitler was at this time confident and expansive, talking about demobilising the forces and settling down to a new order in Europe, but he let the naval staff go on planning.

"The German Navy plan, of which I had some inkling in June . . ." wrote Mr. Churchill in *Their Finest Hour*—in other words, before the outline plan had gone forward to the Commander-in-Chief for detailed planning! "Our excellent intelligence confirmed that Operation Sealion had been definitely ordered by Hitler and was in active preparation. . . ." He writes a few pages later of the second half of July: "The front to be attacked was altogether different from or additional to the east coast on which the Chiefs of Staff, the Admiralty and I, in full agreement, still laid the major emphasis."

This intelligence evidently did not come from air reconnaissance or ground observers: for at the time that it was received, the German forces were still in the champagne stage of their victory over France. It could only have come from some person in close contact with the German naval staff or the chiefs of the High Command—outside a dozen or so German senior officers, nobody in Germany knew what Mr. Churchill knew in June. As to the July planning of Operation Sealion, it confirmed that "the landing operation must be a surprise crossing on a broad front extending approximately from Ramsgate to a point west of the Isle of Wight". The hand of Mr. Churchill seems to have been guided at this time by somebody to whom the innermost counsels of Hitler were revealed.

And when the great speeches of Britain's wartime leader thundered across the Straits of Dover "let us therefore brace ourselves so that if the British Commonwealth and Empire last for a thousand years men will still say 'This was their finest hour' . . ." Canaris took home the forbidden monitorings of the full text of his speeches and read them in the evenings to his wife.

The Admiral found something at last that he had looked for in England for a long time; but he could not rejoice in so late a discovery. As he laid down one of the verbatim reports of a Churchill speech, he said despondently to Erika Canaris:

"They are lucky over there to have a statesman to lead them, we have only a guttersnipe here who bawls across the fence."

"I cannot believe that Canaris took home monitorings of Churchill's speeches with him," exclaimed his adjutant, Lieutenant Jenke, when I told him of this incident.

"Why?"

"The Admiral was always dinning it into us. Don't discuss service matters with your wives."

I produced the letter from Frau Erika Canaris in which she told me of his reading evenings and was interested to see how astonished Jenke was. Everybody had his own vivid picture of Canaris and was surprised to discover that so many others existed.

"Canaris admired your Churchill," Richard Protze told me.

"He had the same initials and would refer to him as 'the great W.C.'.

" 'I am only the little W.C.' he used to say at his daily conference when some big stroke of British statesmanship turned the screw a little harder on Germany. 'What can *I* do against the great W.C.?' "

Meanwhile the three German service chiefs were plying the Abwehr for information about their target—England.

The Navy wanted beach and port data and the probable strength of coastal defences; the Army wanted to know how many divisions there were in the British Isles.

Keitel had issued a top-secret instruction to the three Commanders-in-Chief on July 2nd:

"THE WAR AGAINST ENGLAND

"The Fuehrer and Supreme Commander has decided:

" 1. That a landing in England is possible, provided that air superiority can be attained and certain other necessary conditions fulfilled. The date of commencement is still undecided. All preparations are to be begun immediately.

" 2. The Commands of the three Services are to supply the following information:

" (*a*)   Army

  (1)   Estimates of the strength of the British forces, of losses, and of the extent to which the British Army will have been re-equipped a month or so hence.

  (2)   An appreciation of the operational strength of our coastal batteries, and their capacity to provide additional protection for our shipping against British naval forces.

" (*b*)   Navy

  (1)   Survey of possible landing points for strong Army forces (25–40 divisions), and estimated strength of English coastal defences.

  (2)   Indication of sea routes over which our forces can be transported with the maximum safety. In selecting landing areas, it must be remembered that landing on a broad front will facilitate subsequent deep penetration.

  (3)   Data of shipping available, with probable date on which this could be ready.

"(c)   Air Force

An estimate of the chances of attaining air supremacy, and figures showing the relative strengths of the Luftwaffe and R.A.F.

To what extent can the landing be supported by a parachute attack? (Highest priority to be given to the production of transport aircraft.)

"3.   The Commands of the three Services should co-operate in evolving a plan for the transport of the maximum number of troops with the minimum of shipping and aircraft space.

"The invading force must be highly mechanised and numerically superior to the opposing armies.

"4.   All preparations must be undertaken on the basis that the invasion is still only a plan and has not yet been decided upon. Knowledge of preparations must be restricted to those immediately concerned.

                                        (*signed*) KEITEL."

I have questioned Abwehr officers as to how they imagine the British to have been so well informed about Operation Sealion. Was it treason at the top? Perhaps not solely that. The underground headquarters had been built at Margival, General Speidel tells us, and fitted out for Operation Sealion. That could not have happened without some talk. Infantry Regiment 9, which bore the traditions of the Prussian Guard, had been selected for the assault task at Hastings—and that will have occasioned some gossip in the regiment. For a time everybody talked of Operation Sealion, and when it was no longer contemplated it became Hitler's policy to have it still talked about.

It was evident to the German naval staff that the British were fully aware of what was afoot. The German Navy's war diary on July 3rd noted that "the whole foreign press, in particular the English press, comments that a major German attack is expected". The reports that reached them from Canaris indicated that a strong defence could be expected, and as July wore on Raeder reported to his Fuehrer that there would have to be postponement. Preparations could not be completed by the middle of August, indeed it would not be possible to fix D-day until after air supremacy had been gained; then the Army and Navy fell to quarrelling on the advantages and drawbacks of a broad and narrow landing front. More time was lost, and on August 15th the operation had to be postponed to September 15th. The Army had won its arguments for a broad front, but it seems that the Navy might well reverse the decision at the last moment, in which case the Brighton area had been selected for the narrow front invasion. Now began the mounting Luftwaffe offensive on S.E. England. Keitel issued a top secret directive on September 3rd naming September 20th as the earliest day for sailing. Four days later General Paget issued to Home Forces the code word "Cromwell"—invasion imminent. The Luftwaffe attacks increased and so did their losses, and still the R.A.F. held fast.

The Canaris reports from England were tinged by a strange unrealism—they vastly overestimated the strength of the British defence forces, suggesting that there might be as many as thirty-nine divisions, though only twenty might be completely operational. In fact, there were by September no more than sixteen to defend the invasion area.

An odd report on the British defences was forwarded to the German Navy by the Abwehr Foreign Intelligence:

"Foreign Intelligence Department.

Berlin
5/9/1940

To: Supreme Command, Navy,
       Naval War Staff, Section 3.

Re: England. Fortifications on the South Coast.

A secret agent reported on 2 September:

"The area Tunbridge Wells to Beachy Head (especially the small town of Rye, where there are large sandhills) and also St. Leonards is distinguished by a special labyrinth of defences. These defences, however, are so well camouflaged, that a superficial observer on the sandhills, bathing spots and fields, would not discover anything extraordinary. This area is extremely well guarded, so that it is almost impossible to reach it without a special pass.

"In Hastings, on the other hand, most of the defences can be recognised quite plainly. In the town there are troops of every kind. The presence of numerous small and heavy tanks is most striking.

"Numerous armoured cars were also seen in St. Leonards and in a small locality where there is a famous golf-course, probably St. Joseph.

"War Organization (Espionage) Appendix:

"The agent was not able to give a clearer account of the number of armoured cars in the different localities, or of the regiments he saw there.

"From the position of Beachy Head (west of Hastings) and Rye (east of Hastings), it can be deduced that the place in question near St. Leonards was the western villa-suburb of Hastings. Tunbridge, which lies on the railway line from Hastings to London, according to the sense of the report, ought to lie on the coast, as in the case of St. Joseph; this cannot be confirmed from the maps in our possession."

The Admiral himself, had he given it a moment of his attention, would probably have admitted that there was a strange smell about this report. It may have been a hoax; the people of Tunbridge Wells and St. Leonards will find it hard to recognise their landscape in it. But what if it smelled? It was just such damping reports that suited the mood of the Fuehrer at this moment. The Luftwaffe was failing in its spearhead mission; Hitler was squinting over his shoulder at his frontiers in Poland and his Soviet friends; he was also casting meaning glances southwards at the Pyrenees and easier victories.

The Germans could put a few feathers in their caps when smuggled copies of some of Churchill's dispatches to Roosevelt had been passed to the Italian Embassy in London during the early months of the war by a dishonest cipher clerk in the American Embassy. Towards the end of the war the Abwehr could pick up and decipher or unscramble some of the wireless cipher messages between London and Washington and some of the "scrambled" telephone conversations between Prime Minister and President; for all that, the Abwehr foothold in Britain itself was precarious and unreal.

"There was no Abwehr K.O. or war organisation in England," Lahousen tells me. "The Abwehr worked on the British Isles from Norway, Holland and Portugal." There was an Abwehr foothold in Ireland, too, which was maintained by and helped to maintain German U-boats.

I have discussed his British service with Commander Herbert Wichmann, the senior surviving intelligence officer of Canaris's branch in Hamburg, which operated to the British Isles and the Americas. He showed a marked reluctance to discuss episodes which might compromise such of his agents as had not yet been caught—but he did claim to have known a good deal about the movements of Churchill during the war—a subject to which we shall return in examining the attempts to assassinate the Prime Minister. Wichmann also claimed to have had advance intelligence of the landings in North Africa, the invasion of Normandy, and to have employed a spy similar to "Cicero" who apparently also had the enviable position of working in the British Embassy in Ankara between 1939 and 1941.

The rivals of Canaris in German intelligence—Heydrich, Himmler and Ribbentrop, with their assistants, Schellenberg and Kaltenbrunner—began to say that the Admiral's show was inefficient and that their own organisations must be strengthened. In London, too, where the Abwehr was being closely studied from a professional and unpolitical point of view, some experts were of the opinion that the Admiral was not worth his salt. He had failed to report the terrible weakness of the British Isles in June 1940, and even later had reported us as stronger than we were.

Hence the word went round, and those who hoped for more from him echoed it fervently: "Don't do anything to upset Canaris. His outfit is so bad that it is an asset to us."

Serious minds in England were concerned with thoughts of closer contact with the German Chief of Intelligence.

CHAPTER XIV

THE HENDAYE TAPESTRY

ON THE WHITE cliffs of Dover, the sands of El Alamein, and
the banks of the Volga at Stalingrad there are monuments to
three turning points of the Second World War, where the flood
of Hitler's fire and steel was stemmed and turned back. But if
our grandchildren ask why it was that Hitler stopped at the
Pyrenees and how Spain remained neutral against all historical
likelihood, there is no simple answer that we can give them.
The fourth and most enigmatic turning point of the war is
practically forgotten. The English bathers at St. Jean-de-Luz,
the Americans at Biarritz, the Frenchmen lounging under the
palm trees of Hendaye, where the white façade of the Spanish
Consulate with its pretentious wrought-iron doors (nearly
always shut) faces the Atlantic rollers, none of these gives a
thought today to the memorable October 23rd, 1940, when the
German Chief of State travelled along this coast to meet the
Spanish Caudillo at the foot of the Pyrenees. No stone will be
raised to mark what is dimly remembered as the Hendaye
Conference.

When painters and weavers were historians, they often
conveniently put several incidents of the same story on to one
canvas or tapestry. The monarchs advanced on their steeds;
the cloth of gold, the carcanets gleamed; the thickness of
spears, heads, legs and spurs lent a thronged importance to their
meeting. Another moment of time was caught in the background, the vanquished lying slaughtered in an olive grove or
hurtling from a cliff, the traitor hanging incongruously from a
gibbet.

Here, then, are the figures that fill the centre of my tapestry
of Hendaye: the German conqueror in uniform with peaked
cap, bulging eyes set snakelike on the small plump Caudillo;
with them all their chivalry in grey and scarlet; the meeting
place a railway coach, the Fuehrer's own, at the end of the long

124

THE HENDAYE TAPESTRY 125

railway from Paris and Bordeaux between the Pyrenees and the Atlantic.

Ribbentrop is with the Fuehrer in pseudo-military uniform, designed by himself; Marshal Keitel, Chief of the High Command; Marshal von Brauchitsch, Commander-in-Chief of the Army; Colonel-General Dollman and Lieutenant-General Bodenschatz. There is the tall figure of Dr. von Stohrer, German Ambassador in Madrid; Schmidt the interpreter; General Espinosa de los Monteros, the Spanish Ambassador in Berlin; and Ramon Serrano Suner, brother-in-law of the Caudillo, newly made Spanish Foreign Minister, attending his master with translators and secretaries, A.D.C.s and staff officers.

The German infantry band at Hendaye station—it soon created a diplomatic incident by venturing into San Sebastian—struck up military music as the two trains pulled in. The game for high stakes began in what the official United States documents describe as "Hitler's Parlour Car". Will you walk into my parlour? . . .

In drawing up the frontiers of Vichy France, Hitler had left himself this coastal strip of holiday resorts, the Côte d'Or, connecting with Spain. He wanted to end the neutrality of Spain and make more use of her possessions in Africa, Spanish Morocco and Rio de Oro and the Spanish bases in the Canaries from which German submarines could attack British convoys. The game in the military coach was for the pillars of Hercules—Ceuta and Gibraltar—and Melilla. How well Rommel might have fared if the Straits of Gibraltar had been closed by German siege guns and Stukas in 1941!

Plans for a march into Spain and an attack on Gibraltar existed. General Jodl explained at Nuremberg that these outline plans were there for every contingency, though they would not be put into detailed preparation until the political omens were favourable.

The communiqués of October 23rd did not even say where the Chiefs of State met. Accounts of the Hendaye Conference are sparse. Serrano Suner, now retired from politics, has not been allowed by the Caudillo to publish a chapter about Hendaye in his book *Between the Pyrenees and Gibraltar*. The official German documents published by the United States Department of State in 1946 break off their records of the parlour-car conversations unfinished with the note that "the record of this conversation is incomplete". Yet we do know that Hitler travelled all the way to the Pyrenees to try and get beyond them; what we have to find out is why he failed. Even Schmidt, the interpreter, does not tell us that.

Who arranged this meeting?

Serrano Suner, brother-in-law of General Franco, and a man with distinct leanings towards the Nazis, was sent to visit Berlin as Minister of the Interior a month previously. He relates in *Between the Pyrenees and Gibraltar* something of his preliminary conversations with Hitler and Ribbentrop in Berlin. He speaks of affable talks conducted in the vaguest terms, during which he mentioned the need for artillery if Spain were to undertake the siege of Gibraltar; but he is shown by the captured German documents[1] to have reaffirmed an official Spanish assurance given in strictest secrecy in Berlin in June 1940 that Spain would in her own time cease to be neutral and enter the war on the side of the Axis powers as arms and grain supplies from Germany enabled her to defy the British blockade.

Suner continued that an attack on Gibraltar had been discussed with German military experts and that Spain would need ten fifteen-inch (38-cm.) guns to reduce the Rock. It is curious that a Minister of the Interior should have been authorised to go into such details at that stage of discussing an "eventual entry of Spain into the war"; but we shall see later a possible explanation for this. It is interesting to divine from their talk, when they moved over to the map table, that Hitler was insistent that Stukas were far more devastating against fortifications. Obviously he was anxious to establish his Luftwaffe staff on the airfields of Spain. Once he had given artillery to Spain he could no longer control its use; but even if Gibraltar could not be taken with Stukas, the aircraft would be able to attack British convoys in the Straits and would remain a German weapon. Suner, who spoke for Franco, wanted the guns, but he was less enthusiastic about the aircraft. Finally Hitler was obliged to state that "it would not be possible to provide the fifteen-inch guns". This was probably true. When we read German reports on the lack of heavy coastal artillery on the Atlantic Wall four years later, we are tempted to suppose that there was some inevitable bottleneck in casting German heavy ordnance and that Franco had touched upon a weak

---

[1] *The Spanish Government and the Axis*, U.S. Dept. of State, 1946.

spot. Suner is convinced now that his own conciliatory firmness helped to dupe the Hun. He writes: "I held it to be self-evident to avoid categorical refusals to Hitler, lest he should seize them as an excuse for violating Spanish neutrality."

No doubt many influences were working upon Franco, many incoherent stresses were pulling him this way and that, when he heard that the Fuehrer was going all the way to Hendaye to meet him. If he thought of the fate of Rotterdam and Eben Emael, no doubt he also remembered the destruction of the French Fleet at Oran, just three months earlier.

The grimness of the British war leader may have had a steadying influence: the thought that, harassed and stretched as it was, the Royal Navy with its famous system of Navicerts still sailed between him and his American wheat and petrol. Even so, with Britain alone and beleaguered by bombers and U-boats, with Operation Sealion not yet cancelled, it was not entirely easy to decide to postpone the blow at Gibraltar.

A Chief of State like Francisco Franco, a practical man and no fanatic, will have sized up first his country's needs and decided that neutrality was best for Spain, still exhausted from her own terrible civil war. Secondly, he will have attempted to divine the intentions of his German opponent and the exact meaning of Wehrmacht troop concentrations near the coastal road towards Hendaye. Then an old friend came quietly to his aid, Admiral Wilhelm Canaris.

Canaris is mentioned by the pro-Nazi Suner in describing his Berlin conversations with Hitler in September as spreading "confused ideas on Spanish problems".

It has taken some years to unravel the discreet allusions of Suner. When Ramon the Zealot left Berlin, he hastened to Rome to see what Ciano thought about the determination of Hitler to drag Spain into the war. While he was on his way, Canaris had discovered what was afoot and was afraid that Hitler would bluff a way into Spain.

It was my first idea that Canaris must have warned General Vigon, the Chief of Spanish Military Intelligence, that Hitler would do no more than bluff and that Franco must resist him. But General Lahousen tells me that the wires to Spain at this time were so loaded with inter-staff preparations for a military alliance and the attack on Gibraltar that General Vigon would not have understood a divergent political message—if indeed Canaris had been so rash as to commit his views to cipher. No, there was another means. Up popped the resourceful Josef Mueller in Rome while Suner was still there and said to him:

"The Admiral asks you to tell the Caudillo to hold Spain out of this game at all costs. It may seem to you now that our position is the stronger—it is in reality desperate, and we have little hope of winning this war. The Caudillo may be assured that Hitler will not use the force of arms to enter Spain."

This was a disconcerting message for Suner to carry, for he read history with a different eye. Nevertheless I have no doubt that he delivered Mueller's message. There were other mysterious channels through which the Admiral could ascertain whether he had fulfilled his request.

When Hitler exclaimed to Suner in Berlin on September 17th that "It would be a matter primarily of taking Gibraltar with extraordinary speed and protecting the Straits", the perplexed mind of Suner turned to the activities and opinions of Admiral Canaris. "With extraordinary speed?" The Admiral had not been so sanguine of success as his Fuehrer. Who had advised Franco to ask for ten fifteen-inch guns for the Gibraltar undertaking, which he was now told could not be provided? The Admiral and General von Richthofen had been the principal German officers of the military commission that examined the Gibraltar undertaking. They should have known that the guns were not available. "I perceived in Berlin that anything to do with Spanish affairs was utterly confused," wrote Suner in his memoirs. "One of the reasons for this confusion was the somewhat singular role played by Admiral Canaris who had relations in Spain with persons other than the Ministry of Foreign Affairs."

Aloud and to Hitler at the time Suner said that the report on the vulnerability of Gibraltar given by the German experts in Spain "had not brought their views clearly to the surface". Strangely, no suspicion even then dawned on the mind of Hitler. He insisted that "on the basis of the impressions of the German military commission that had gone to Spain to examine the question on the spot, as well as on reports formerly obtained or sent recently by Admiral Canaris, they had come to the conclusion that Gibraltar could be conquered by a modern attack with relatively modest means".

Suner begged him to put these views in writing to Franco, as if the Caudillo had been told something quite different. So Hitler set about softening Franco himself. He decided that he would have to go and see him to be sure of being properly understood in future. He complied with the suggestion of Suner, committed to writing his views on the vulnerability of Gibraltar and other military problems connected with the spreading of war to Spain, and asked for the Hendaye meeting.

"I received your letter, my dear Fuehrer," replied Franco on September 22nd, "with your views and those of your General Staff . . . which, with the exception of small details, match my thoughts and those of my General Staff."

The letter that Hitler had written was insistent on the Spanish affair. He had discovered that England could hardly be defeated by direct assaults, though he did not reveal that. Spain offered the most obvious and immediate opportunity for a secondary success.

It was on October 23rd at Hendaye that Hitler made his formal demand for military passage through Spain to attack the Rock, though he may have first mentioned his target date, January 10th, when Suner visited him in Berchtesgaden in November.

Canaris, this fluent subtle man so passionately conversant with the affairs of the peninsula, was the very person who might have been expected to accompany his Fuehrer in the parlour car and help to persuade Franco to a comradeship in arms. Yet he was not there. His diminutive figure, white of head with intense blue eyes and an expression of silent nervous concentration, stands apart from the flamboyant personages of the tapestry.

"Ribbentrop did not trust his influence and did not want him to be there," said General Lahousen. "They knew that he took a separate line on the Spanish problem."

The mesmeric powers of Hitler were abnormal, the bulging eyes beneath his peaked cap as he seized the Caudillo's hand gave forth every symptom of hypnotic effort. He sought to overbear the Caudillo, and during the next nine hours there was that suffocating flow of language with which he habitually stupefied his victim, like a boa-constrictor covering his prey with saliva before devouring it. But the Caudillo showed extraordinary toughness and resilience, and took his wonted leisure after the repast. The Fuehrer complained that he was being kept waiting for above an hour, but the Caudillo excused himself with a message that he must invariably have his siesta.

Hitler described the bombing of London and the U-boat war in the Atlantic, and he totted up his two hundred and thirty divisions. The Caudillo was affable, dignified, quite un-cowed and at moments even detached; and when he mounted his own railway coach again to cross the Bidassoa and climb the Pyrenees, he was fending off an insistent Fuehrer's:

"I must have your answer now."

"I will think about it. I will write to you."

There was indeed correspondence, and a to and fro of ministers, ambassadors and generals. Hitler wrote on February 6th—after his target date had come and passed—and Franco left his letter unanswered until February 26th, when he replied: "Your letter of the 6th makes me wish to reply very promptly. . . ."

At Hendaye the brusque methods of Hitler against smaller men than himself had failed for the first time, because Franco had gone to Hendaye armed with certain knowledge. Indeed he had vital information that deciphered the views of Hitler and his General Staff as set forth in the Fuehrer's September letter. The Admiral had given him the clue that while they would welcome Spanish participation in the war, Hitler, his High Command and his Army General Staff were agreed that, with Russia unconquered in their rear, there could be no question of entering Spain by force if the Spaniard resisted. The prospect of guerilla war along the roads and railways from the Pyrenees to Gibraltar had sobered them; they were daunted—and no wonder—by the thought of having to use and maintain the Spanish railways; they thought of the necessity, once in, for conquering Portugal, too, if Britain were to be kept out of the Peninsula, and the immense addition of coastline there would be to defend. There were only the coastal road and railway to carry their military transport into Spain, and the German Ambassador had reported in a dispatch of the previous August: "For long stretches between Bayonne and San Sebastian, they can be observed and fired upon from the sea." The alternative road over the Pyrenees through St. Jean Pied-de-Port had been reconnoitred by a German general and found unsuitable.

When Hitler got over the first discomfiture of Hendaye—"I

would rather have four teeth out than go through it again," he told Mussolini in Florence—he sent Admiral Canaris—what better man!—to see Franco in Madrid and urge him to enter the war and give German troops the right to attack Gibraltar. Perhaps friendly persuasion would succeed where hypnotics and bullying had failed. Canaris saw Franco alone with General Vigon, Chief of Spanish Military Intelligence. Suner was not present!

"Canaris had subsequently to attempt to secure Spanish intervention several times," suggests Dr. Abshagen, his German biographer. "He hardly expected Franco to yield as the German position grew steadily worse"—but who kept Franco informed of the worsening German position but the Admiral himself, and his good friend the Chief of Spanish Military Intelligence, General Vigon, with whom Canaris played an open hand? "It probably never entered Hitler's head at that time," comments Abshagen, "that if he wished to intervene in Spain any of his own officers should oppose it."

Canaris was discreet in his indications. Just that sarcastic inflexion of the voice during an audience was maybe enough to tell his Spanish intimates what were his inward thoughts. His adjutant, Lt. Colonel Jenke, tells me that Canaris found it appropriate to discuss the real situation of Germany and the interests of Spain with General Martinez Campos, the Spanish Chief of General Staff, and that "he was quite frank in advising that Spain should remain neutral and defend her neutrality".

"Ask our Fuehrer for fifteen-inch guns," I can imagine the Admiral's whispered counsel to Vigon or Franco at the time when Gibraltar seemed a most tempting prize and German pressure almost irresistible, "*die kann er nicht hergeben*".

When this quaint story of medieval guile is told in full and the ornate border of the tapestry filled out with all the symbols of war and peace, it will no doubt surprise another in the remote background, Lord Templewood, the Ambassador in Madrid, who was filled with anxiety by the frequent visits of the Admiral to Spain. Upon the face of General Sir F. N. Mason-Macfarlane ("Mason-Mac"), who took over the Rock from Lord Gort, and had some knowledge of Canaris from his days as military attaché in Berlin, I fancy I see a wry smile.

The border of the Hendaye tapestry is peopled with small and busy agents (like ants, bees and crickets among the grapes,

oranges and olive branches of Spain); the British and Germans
watching each other; the Germans observing fleet movements
from Algeciras and La Linea; the Germans watching Spanish
troop movements both near the Pyrenees and near Gibraltar,
to discern the measure of Franco's aspirations and fears. The
high game was played over their heads. The Abwehr found no
signs of a Spanish assault force gathering against Gibraltar, but
they did notice a movement of troops towards the Pyrenees.

So the immediate danger passed and the Fuehrer swerved in
his purpose from a southward bending strategy that might have
rolled up in the Middle East through Morocco and Persia, if he
had been willing to accept the Red Army as the eastern claw
of the pincers. It seems that for a short time the secret diplomacy of Canaris passed unnoticed in the Reich Chancellery;
but General Munoz Grande, who led the Spanish Blue Division
to fight for Hitler on the Russian front, said openly that Canaris
had persuaded Franco that it was not in his interest to enter the
war on the side of Germany. This came to the ears of the
Gestapo, and S.S. Group Chief Walther Huppenkothen of the
Reich Security Office noted it in a long report on Canaris for
Himmler—the affable silence of General Franco deprived the
accusation of some of its weight, but the suspicion remained.

Canaris still came and went to Spain as he pleased until late
in 1943, when it was pressure from the British that held him out
of the peninsula on one occasion for reasons that I cannot
properly guess. By then Ribbentrop and Himmler had organised
two foreign intelligence organisations that overshadowed and
absorbed some of the Abwehr service and intensified the struggle
with the Allies, who could never be certain which organisation
of the three was pitted against them.

It was not only with Franco that the Admiral pursued his
singular designs. Another old friend was Don Daniel de Araos,
Baron de Sacrelirio, a shipping magnate and a retired officer of
the Spanish armada. The Baroness de Sacrelirio was well
known in Madrid for her Anglophile sentiments. Canaris
regarded these friends as part of his personal intelligence circle.
Now Don Daniel was also well acquainted with the British
naval attachés in Madrid, and when the Navicerts squeezed his
cargo ships, as they often did, he would put on his uniform and
the cloak of an Armada officer and call ceremoniously at the
British Embassy. Strangely, it may seem, the British allowed

Don Daniel more Navicerts than some of his compatriots considered fair, and they were loud in their complaints.

"Here is Don Daniel," they said, "friend of the German arch spy Canaris, being given favourable treatment by the British when others are refused Navicerts!" What a conundrum for the Gestapo!

I cannot pretend to have discovered all the contacts in Spain and Portugal through whom it was possible for Canaris to try and influence the British, nor would it have been possible always to decide which indiscretions were intentional. But since this book was first published I have been told of another link by one of the British Intelligence Officers who were in Tangiers during the war. Otto Krüger, an Abwehr officer in Tangiers, went over to the British in 1943 and after the war he asserted that there had been links between Canaris and the British during the war in the island of Majorca. Krüger, like Don Daniel, is dead. The link that was in Majorca may still be there.

So the Admiral continued to come and go to the peninsula, and every time his visit was reported to the British Ambassador, Lord Templewood was seized with malaise, and no doubt the German Ambassador groaned, too. . . . Templewood no doubt thought of him as the Abwehr Chief whose agents nearly succeeded in inserting a microphone in his embassy desk telephone and set women to debauch his servants. As for Canaris, it was with a sense of relief that he turned his back on the maniacs of the north and flew southwards. So much of what he had schemed between London and Ankara had gone astray; but in Spain he had achieved something lasting. He had saved this mysterious land from prolonged torture. As his aircraft left captive France behind, he was happy to think of the dark confidences of Madrid and sunned himself in the dazzling smile of the Pyrenees.

CHAPTER XV

IN THE BALKANS

If Canaris helped to thwart Hitler in Spain, where Germany could expect much advantage from commanding the Straits, it seemed to me that he might pursue the same policy elsewhere. I thought of the Balkans, where German interests were not greatly furthered by Bulgaria and lukewarm Hungary in her unhappy position across the marches of Europe. Did Canaris pursue a separate policy in these countries, too? I can recollect the pained astonishment on the faces of some of his subordinates, who evidently revered him deeply, when I suggested that the Admiral did in fact pursue his own grand policy with such weapons as he could. Some found it a terrible suggestion that he could differ with his government in wartime and perhaps undermine it. We read with enthusiasm in history books of the doings of Henry the Lion against his emperor, of Wallenstein and Warwick; but in our times the independent line is regarded simply as treason against the state.

King Boris of Bulgaria, with whom Canaris was familiar, seemed to be in a similar position to Franco at the other end of Europe.

Hitler's brain was teeming with ideas of wresting away from the Balkans their precarious neutral status and striking a terrible blow at Russia. He had directed Keitel to give the Central Army Group at Borisov the task of outlining a plan of attack on Russia as a staff exercise. Oddly enough, by a stealthy selection of staff officers, a military group hostile to him was being collected in Central Army Group Headquarters, and they saw with amusement and wonder that Molotov was sent to Berlin in November 1940 to prolong Russo-German collaboration. Hitler and Ribbentrop spoke to him of a crusade against the British Empire and promised him warm water ports in Asia; but Molotov insisted on talking about the situation in Eastern Europe and Finland, and in the Balkans. The

R.A.F. interrupted their conferences at one of the most heated
moments and forced them to descend to the air-raid shelter.
Hitler waited a month after Molotov had gone home, and then
on December 18th ordered that Operation Barbarossa against
Soviet Russia should go forward for detailed planning and
organisation. In the meantime he had called King Boris to
come and see him and dispatched German troops into Rumania.

Boris, an intelligent head and a sensitive face, dark, oval, and
high of forehead, a linguist and savant, who liked to study
botany and entomology in the solitude of nature, stood between
two counsellors: Wilhelm Canaris, an old friend, and George
Earle, the American Minister in Sofia, President Roosevelt's
personal watchman in the Balkans. Ambassador Earle, a former
Governor of Pennsylvania and at one time in the running for
the Democratic nomination for the Presidency, had stood down
for his old friend Roosevelt, and Roosevelt remembered it,
sending him first as U.S. Minister to Austria and then to Sofia,
where it was hoped that his friendship for King Boris would
keep Bulgaria out of the war. Hitler was perhaps fighting the
influence of two secret advisers when he declared at Berchtesgaden that Bulgaria must become the ally of Germany—but he
had on his side the Bulgarian General Staff, traditionally pro-
German—and the national fear of Russia and Turkey.

Rumania, the smiling land of the Danube delta with its
wealth of oil in Ploesti, was falling into his hand. Canaris had
flown to Venice early in September for a conference with the
Rumanian Chief of Secret Police, Morusov. They agreed upon
infiltration of German agents into Ploesti, to guard the oil
wells against sabotage by the British Secret Service. The danger
was not acute from that quarter—in fact, the derricks, wells and
refineries of Ploesti were the main source of wealth that
Rumania possessed, and it was about as likely that she would
neglect their security or destroy them to deny them to an
aggressor as for the French to lay waste their vineyards. But
Hitler was anxious about the oil wells and Canaris would make
the most prestige he could of his success in placing his men in
Ploesti.

Hitler required Bulgaria, not for any resources, but for its
strategic position. Boris wavered. He could have got no backing
either at home or in Ankara for a policy of armed neutrality
with his neighbour and traditional enemy, Turkey. He had

visited London and seen Chamberlain in 1938, but what help could Britain give him now? So he consented on March 1st 1941 that his government should join the Axis. Thus Hitler had a small ally on the south-eastern border of Europe who would conveniently help him if Turkey should march through the Balkans; his first use of Boris was to attack Greece and Yugoslavia in the flank after the revolt against Prince Paul's regency brought in a pro-British government in Belgrade. Hitler angrily postponed his zero-day of May 15th against Russia and turned the fury of the Luftwaffe on Belgrade within ten days of the national revolution. Joszef Lipski tells me that as Hitler was ordering the annihilating attack on the Yugoslav capital, Canaris, who had learned of his intentions, passed a warning to the Yugoslav Government, which on April 3rd declared Belgrade an open city.[1] They were of little avail, either the warning or the declaration. The German bombers appeared over Belgrade at 5.15 a.m. on the 6th and flew in relays from airfields in Rumania. "From rooftop height without fear of resistance," Mr. Churchill paints the lurid picture in his memoirs, "they blasted the city without mercy. This was called Operation Punishment. When silence came at last on April 8th, over seventeen thousand citizens of Belgrade lay dead in the streets or under the debris. Out of the nightmare of smoke and fire came the maddened animals released from their shattered cages in the Zoological Gardens. A stricken stork hobbled past the main hotel which was a mass of flames. A bear, dazed and uncomprehending, shuffled through the inferno with slow and awkward gait down towards the Danube."

Canaris, as if in expiation of his powerlessness to alter the destructive will of his master, flew to Belgrade. He spent a day apparently investigating intelligence targets and wandering round the agonised city. Towards evening he returned to the billet found for him in a suburb and collapsed in prostration at the horrors he had seen.

"I can't see any more of this," he cried. "We will leave tomorrow."

"Tomorrow? Where for?" asked his adjutant.

"Spain."

[1] This was hardly likely to have been invented by a Pole about a German; the Ambassador assured me that the Yugoslav General Staff was fully aware of Canaris's warning.

He could, so it appears, fly whither he would. The extra-ordinary extent to which he did travel abroad during the war excited no unfavourable comment "simply because nobody in the German Government really had any idea how an intelligence service works," Lt.-Colonel Viktor von Schweinitz suggested to me. The High Command did not require him to seek permission for travel abroad, and when he wanted he could turn his aircraft towards Spain or Portugal and find solace in these distant and ancient realms. Whether on this occasion his solace consisted in relating to Don Daniel how the Fuehrer had raved at the Serbs when he had been obliged to postpone his summer offensive proper against Russia, I cannot say.

He flew in all weathers, with an utter indifference to his safety, resigned and philosophical in his outlook. Even those who were his close friends cannot remember the bewildering pattern his aircraft wove over Europe, Africa and Asia Minor in these months. Lahousen remembers that he visited Rommel at his desert headquarters west of Derna probably to acquaint him with the impending revolt of Rashid Ali in Iraq and the intention of the German High Command to support Rashid Ali with arms and aircraft, using French Syria as a stepping stone. Dr. Paul Leverkuehn[1] found Canaris sceptical of this revolt behind Wavell's back, and told me that the German Minister in Baghdad, Dr. Grobba, was really the moving spirit.

When the Rashid Ali rebellion broke out in May 1941 there were pitched battles for the British air base of Habbaniyah, but the Iraqi air force was largely destroyed and before German assistance could reach the Iraqi rebels through Syria Wavell had sent up a force against General Dentz that compelled him to surrender after hard fighting.

Canaris in the oasis produced his secret dossier of Abwehr reports on the S.S. atrocities in Europe and gave Rommel "a lesson on the facts of life" as he described it.

"You, Rommel, of the Army, will one day be held responsible for what is happening behind the lines."

He found Rommel hardly sympathetic and so keen on his desert war that he had no time to be shocked.

"That's not behind my front—not my concern at all," was his attitude. "I'm a fighting man."

Canaris visited Turkey twice during the war, though Asia

[1] One of the German intelligence officers in Istanbul.

Minor was not a territory he understood well. He had paid a
fleeting visit to Baghdad before the war on the pretext of sizing
up intelligence requirements. It was a comic episode that did
not enhance his reputation as a spy. The political influence of
Great Britain in Iraq was strong. She maintained air bases
there by treaty rights and had transit facilities for her armed
forces. The Admiral therefore chose to travel with false passports, taking with him his head of Abwehr II, Colonel Groscurth
—responsible for subversive activities in enemy territory and
abroad. It was like something in a Marx Brothers farce in
Baghdad. First Groscurth wrote his real name in the hotel
register; then Canaris, after angrily rebuking him, gave up a
large parcel of his linen for laundering. It came back with a
bill made out to W. Canaris from the name tabs in his shirts
and the story goes that the package was "paged" round the
hotel by the mystified staff. A few hours later a curt message
came to him from the British Secret Service that he was to
leave Iraq forthwith.

It was odd that a man of such cunning and perspicacity
should neglect such elementary details of his profession as a
laundry mark, but carelessness often goes with high rank.

In the early spring of 1941 he was in Berne, too. Europe was
disquieted by German troop movement eastwards and south-
eastwards. He seemed indiscreet to the point of ignoring
security altogether.

"Will Germany attack Turkey?" asked Madame J after
Allied intelligence reports had showed a trend of German
armour to the south-east, as if towards Asia Minor.

"No, we won't attack Turkey," said the Admiral; "Russia
perhaps."

Mr. Churchill felt certain enough about the intentions of
Hitler by April 3rd to send Sir Stafford Cripps to Moscow
with a personal message for Stalin that Germany had begun
to move three divisions of armour from Rumania to Southern
Poland—opposite Russia. The movement had indeed been
countermanded when the Yugoslavs rose against the Axis—but
it was nevertheless significant.

Josef Mueller of the Abwehr appeared once more in the
Vatican city and tells me that he told the British of the planned
date of invasion of Russia. Reliable neutral diplomats in
Berlin were getting thin on the ground as country after country

was invaded. There was, however, an Abwehr agent going to Moscow as a business man in advance of the invasion, Nicholas von Halem, of the Admiral's personal staff. He knew a British resident there, but was not sure that he could safely meet him. His own pretext for travel was simple: business men were going from Berlin to Moscow daily to promote the economic and political co-operation that continued between Germany and Russia, until June 21st, but he could not risk the N.K.V.D. seeing him approach an Englishman's office. He searched about his Moscow hotel till he found a postcard photograph of it, which he marked with a cross on his bedroom window and wrote, "I am here for a day or so and hope to have the opportunity of seeing you." He signed himself "Keats". The postcard went through internal postal censorship without arousing suspicion.

"Keats" had been his nickname since early youth and it served well. He did not have to wait long for his visitor, who walked up to his room next day. On his way back to Berlin von Halem related this to a friend in Central Army Group which was waiting at Borisov for the great attack.

Russia herself was not warned by the Germans—neither by Herr von der Schulenberg, the German Ambassador in Moscow, whose hand Stalin seized at a reception three days before the day of the attack, asking him with a searching stare, "I hope that our treaty of friendship will remain honoured"; nor apparently by Canaris, who preferred that the political knowledge should be laid in the hands of the British. He himself had for years considered the Bolshevik regime to be the worst misfortune under which the world suffered; but Hitler's attack on Russia did not hearten him or win his approval. He knew that his own political ideas of an independent Ukraine and an alliance with the Russian people against their masters had no place in the minds of Hitler, Ribbentrop and Rosenberg. Calculated extermination would be their policy even before the campaign had even been decided; fertilisation of the soil with the blood of the vanquished; the Commissars were to be shot as soon as captured, the S.S. were to drive the Jews, dead and dying, into mass graves. Towns and villages were to be razed—and yet allegedly the object in attacking Russia was to seize a productive hinterland for the prolonged struggle with the British Empire. Worst of all, most of the generals

accepted Operation Barbarossa with resignation and professional élan. Now they would see how whole army groups
could be pushed forward on a wide front. They would have
freedom to manoeuvre and they could put into practice all
the theories of Cannae that they had ever studied—so they
thought. Soon after midnight on June 22nd, 1941, the attack
on Russia began and the Soviet air force in forward areas was
surprised and destroyed on the ground.

Great Britain was planning military aid to Russia in the
autumn of 1941; but the Germans had got so close to Moscow
in such a rapid march that it seemed that these arms, that could
ill be spared, would come too late. The British service ministries
were loath to see them go. There was panic in Moscow as the
Germans approached, and it appeared that the capital was
about to fall. The Soviet Government and the diplomatic
missions moved four days' journey into Central Russia.

I am told that the British Intelligence Service picked up
indications that Canaris was far forward when the German
Army was thrusting at Moscow and that he was warning the
High Command that they would not reach Moscow—"and
never will reach Moscow," a British officer quoted to me from
memory one of the Canaris reports of which we hold copies.
"He went up in exactly the same way before the Caucasus
offensive in the following year and foretold that they would not
reach their objective. But they did not believe him."

This account fits in with information from another source.
Canaris returned from the Russian front in the autumn of 1941
and went from Berlin to Berne, where he arrived at the moment
when the German lines were stretched to the utmost and the
Moscow panic at its height.

"If the Russian Army is disorganised and exhausted," he
told Madame J "so are we, too. We have outrun our supplies;
our resources in transport are wholly inadequate to maintain
such large formations so far forward. If the situation of Russia
is bad, it can hardly be worse than ours."

After the Caucasus offensive had failed in 1942, came the
winter campaign of Stalingrad, and Boris must have shivered
when he heard the news. If I leap on in time here, it is to
finish the mysterious story of the king whom Hitler summoned
to Berchtesgaden on March 31st, 1943, to obtain his assurance
that Bulgaria would resist a march of the Allies through Turkey.

Boris returned to Sofia and stealthily took up negotiations with Turkey in May through his Minister in Ankara. His idea then was a pact of armed neutrality between Turkey and Bulgaria which would at once draw his own country out of the war and offer Germany the apparent compensation of ensuring against an Allied thrust from Asia Minor. These negotiations were conducted by the Bulgarian Minister in Ankara with the Turkish Foreign Minister, M. Menemenjoglu; but when the Bulgarian minister went back to Sofia to discuss progress, Herr Delius, the German Area Intelligence Chief, obtained a complete record of his verbal report from a microphone which his agents had managed to install in the Foreign Ministry.

"How is that possible?" I asked Dr. Leverkuehn, the Abwehr agent in Turkey who related the incident.

"It would only be possible in Bulgaria," he replied with a smile, "but I had a similar report from Istanbul. The Turkish generals had discussed the idea of a Turco-Bulgarian pact and spoke against it. I reported that to Herr von Papen and he forwarded my report to Berlin."

Walther Huppenkothen of the Gestapo, in his subsequent investigation on Canaris and Abwehr political activities, mentions that the Admiral saw Boris in August a week before the king died; but he infers nothing from it. It appears that Hitler had invited Boris to return to Germany to stiffen him further in August and that Boris actually went a second time despite rumours at the time that he declined to go. General Antonescu was also invited to Germany to discuss the attitude of Rumania.

The summons to Boris and Antonescu, the stamping boot on their attempts to extricate themselves from unholy alliance, may well have been the sequel to an intelligence report sent by the worthy Dr. Leverkuehn from the talkative city of Istanbul. He had some contacts on political matters with George Earle and this gave him a chance to observe the other activities of the American Secret Service man and special emissary. Just after Earle had completed a laborious intrigue with Bulgaria, Leverkuehn nullified it with one stroke.

"Opinions (that he was a dilettante) have changed in the British and American embassies about George Earle," he wrote in a dispatch of May 1943 to Herr von Papen and Colonel Hansen, his superior officers in the Abwehr. "It is reported that he has succeeded in reaching an agreement between the United States and Bulgaria. The negotiations took place in Istanbul but mainly through men of Earle's in Sofia. The basis for the agreement is that it should be recognised that Bulgaria has acted under compulsion in her present policy and will return to full neutrality as soon as such compulsion no longer exists. Bulgaria would evacuate all Greek territory that she has occupied. The American military attaché says that this agreement is due entirely to the skill of Earle who has been in direct contact with Roosevelt. A letter from the President to 'My dear George' has caused a stir in the American Embassy. It has not yet been decided who will sign for Bulgaria—the king and his government are hesitating and casting about for a suitable person. There are similar reports about Rumania."

Small wonder, then, that Hitler should invite Boris and Antonescu to Germany. Walther Huppenkothen of the S.S. in his painstaking account of Abwehr activities relates that Canaris visited Boris in Sofia shortly before the last illness of the king. Huppenkothen adds nothing—he evidently suspected political talks which were strictly forbidden to Canaris. I find it credible that Canaris would have advised Boris to make his peace with the Allies as and when he could, and Leverkuehn hesitantly agreed with me that this was not out of the question. But Boris fell suddenly ill in the third week of August. His brother, Prince Cyril, made a brief allegation before a war crimes court in 1945 that the king had been poisoned by the S.S. through a defective oxygen mask used on his return flight from Berchtesgaden; but Cyril could offer no detail of evidence, even circumstantial, to support this. Dr. Leverkuehn in Istanbul, who knew his Abwehr colleagues of Sofia well, disbelieves the story of murder and tells me that Bulgarian doctors diagnosed an embolism that mounted to the heart, and that he was found dying one morning in his bath. Either the hypnotic influence of Hitler was still strong, or the king sensed that the walls of his palace were hollow, too, and that the Abwehr men were close about him; for as he lay helpless on his deathbed he murmured that he still had a faith in the final victory of Adolf Hitler. His words were noted and duly reported to Berlin; they stuck in the memory of Leverkuehn, who repeated them to me seven years afterwards.

King Boris died on August 28th, 1943, aged forty-nine, and Hitler sent a message to Queen Giovanna that "the overpowering news of the death of His Majesty the King has moved me deeply". On what evidence is available, I am inclined to think that King Boris died, by accident, a natural death. His son, King Simeon, aged six, reigned in his stead, under the regency of Prince Cyril.

Two months after this an emissary of Hungary signed a secret declaration of surrender in Sir Hugh Knatchbull-Huguessen's yacht off Istanbul: but it was to profit Hungary as little as Earle's scheme helped Bulgaria.

CHAPTER XVI

HOW THE ADMIRAL GOT HIS BAD NAME

"THIS IS THE paint that the Germans paint their tanks with."

Lieutenant-Colonel A. D. Wintle of the First Royal Dragoons told me how he met an excited intelligence officer in the marble corridors of the War Office shortly before the war broke out.

"What are you going to do with it?" asked the Colonel, fixing his monocle in his eye and regarding pot and officer with a glassy stare.

"I am going to have it analysed."

"Why?"

"We shall then know what their camouflage mixture is."

"My dear fellow, and then?" the Colonel summed up with devastating logic. "When you have discovered how much oil, what binding colour and spirit, and what-not gives it that dull finish, what will you do then?"

There was a slow hiss of escaping enthusiasm.

"If," said the Colonel, "you people would make it your business to discover what date Hitler has selected to make war, as I have done, you would be doing the duties proper to an intelligence officer."

In every intelligence service there was drudgery and a certain amount of unnecessary work, while the vital operations lay in a few hands only.

By 1942 the British Intelligence Services had multiplied in strength many times in several departments, ancient and modern, within the service ministries and in new ministries formed during the war. There were practical men, shrewd men, political men, theorists and paintpot analysts. Business men, dons, artists, scientists, men of letters, retired officers and gentlemen of leisure, they took up the game with alacrity and often with overlapping terms of reference. Certainly the best work was not begun until long after Dunkirk. When France was collapsing Wintle had the idea of dropping in at French airfields to see what French airmen could be persuaded to throw in their lot with ours; but his idea did not at all appeal to his senior officer and there was a sharp quarrel, after which Wintle was committed to a brief sojourn in the Tower of London on charges of threatening a senior officer. He soon emerged after conducting his own defence with some success in a court martial and served with distinction in the Middle East. These were the teething troubles of the new intelligence outfits, in times when it was still easier to be committed to the Tower for wanting to do too much than for doing too little. The French Section of the War Office within S.O.2 (Special Operation 2) began its work with the French Resistance, the planners of Special Operations launched saboteurs into Norway to wreck the power stations which had been harnessed to produce heavy water for the German atom-bomb research organisation. The cloak and dagger men ran their small boats into the Gironde and sank German shipping there; they inflicted pinpricks on the enemy all along three thousand miles of coast. There was intense rivalry between intelligence and operations staffs, because the latter was apt to stir up the hornets' nest of the Gestapo by blowing bridges, burning factories or sinking shipping, whereas the former came and went stealthily, leaving no sign. The one game spoiled the other. The rivalry and dislike was so keen that at one time neither "show" would inform the other what its activities were; once both landed agents in the same spot on the Norway coast within three days of each other. The S.O. or "Cloak and Dagger" men landed first with sub-machine guns and explosive charges and left smoke and debris behind them. The I-men came in stealthily afterwards into an apparently placid fishing village and ran straight into the arms of the German Field Police. No wonder that officers blanched, groaned and ground their teeth at mention of the rival "show". It was policy to keep the Boche alert and nervous on the seaboard of Europe and in occupied countries and "tie down" his garrisons; but it made the work of the intelligence officers far more difficult. Sabotage was the enemy of intelligence, and yet the enslaved peoples of Europe upon whom we depended for intelligence expected some action, too. So did the War Cabinet.

Canaris had laid his intelligence organisation ahead of the Army in the countries to be overrun. Britain prepared no organisation to be left behind as she retreated. It was no use improvising. Almost everything had to be built up after the Battle of Britain. There was a desperate series of small-boat sorties and parachute descents that helped to establish the British Secret Service again in its proper place in Europe— adventures like those of Captain Peter Churchill and Odette Sansom among the Maquis which Jerrard Tickell tells so vividly. The nation which had hesitated so long before intro- ducing conscription, which had neglected its secret service during peace, when war became earnest, did not scruple to drop women behind the enemy lines, where as likely as not Gestapo torture awaited them and ultimately death in the furnaces of concentration camps.

It was oppressive to think of these valiant efforts to dint the iron breastplate of Germany while we neglected the Achilles heel. Within the subdued but independent brain of the German General Staff, the Abwehr, moved similar thoughts to those that guided the Directors of Intelligence and Operations in London—Germany could not win in the end. There would be not total Sieg, there could not even be stalemate, there could only be defeat. Some German officers, thinking for their troops, suspected as much. The Abwehr knew it.

I found myself attached for a short time in 1941 to a War Office branch that was broadcasting in German to the Wehrmacht: when I proposed that some of our talks should be directed towards the officers and that it was useless to try and incite the German private soldier to mutiny or disaffection, my Brigadier replied that although he himself preferred that line of approach it was forbidden in his directives.

By 1942 it seemed that unless we were to have a long war decided simply by weight and numbers, it was high time for this secret weapon against Hitler, the German opposition, to come into play. There must be somewhere in London an officer of standing and power who would appreciate the opportunity that lay at hand.

The War Office was otherwise occupied. The War Office diagrams showed the field-grey uniform, the silver wings and swastika emblems: "Know Your Enemy!" The Admiralty posters showed the silhouettes of German warships and their badges of rank. The Air Ministry issued its models of the enemy aircraft and identification posters of the bombers that were raiding London. It was an all-time job keeping this Wehrmacht at bay—"Know Your Enemy!". The night bombers flew over London and dropped their loads till the glare of burning houses was as bright as sunset. The Japanese took Singapore, Burma and Java. Rommel stood at Alamein and glowered towards the Delta. The war was all action and ebb and flow.

At length I came upon two intelligence officers who had heard of Admiral Canaris. I remember well one autumn day of 1942, chatting with an elderly Colonel in a Whitehall office.

"Ah, you have ideas. You were in Germany before the war?"

I ventured to turn the subject of conversation to the Abwehr.

"The mentality of Admiral Canaris is singular," I suggested.

"The man is a Greek," barked the Colonel. He took no delight, evidently, in a study of the unusual; it was his profession to do so, but here at least was an office, reticent and unpretentious among many that seemed far busier, in which this name raised more than a glimmer of interest. Here it seemed that the motion and pulses of the European capitals were registered, and the moves of the game were understood.

The second British officer I met in wartime who evidently knew all about the Abwehr had a more imaginative approach to the enigma of Admiral Canaris. He was a small man with soft, expressive hands and a quiet, sad smile. Intuitive gifts, training, a constant flow of knowledge, secrecy and a dispassionate temperament all made him an exceptional intelligence officer.

"I can imagine so well what the Admiral is thinking," he exclaimed with a movement of his small hands. "I think I know exactly what is in his mind."

We talked of the states of Europe and the policies of nations, of the Reich itself and its terrible destiny. He seemed to understand the movements of history when it was still not set in the mould, when several great alternative vistas were open to us.

Once he startled me by saying:

"Would you like to meet Canaris?"

There was something in this question that took a great weight off my mind. The Admiral had evidently flown his signal.

A few weeks later, in September 1942, I again met the man with the soft voice and expressive hands. He was saddened and depressed by a sensational report in an American newspaper that the Admiral had been plotting against Hitler and the Nazi regime.

"Every time we build something up," he said, "something like this happens and destroys what we have built."

I suggested to him that the position of Admiral Canaris might not be shaken by this report. It might be regarded as a malicious attempt to sow discord between the Wehrmacht and Party. If a violent attack were now made on the Admiral by a British newspaper that might work to his advantage. My acquaintance smiled a wan smile, as if he thought that it might just be worth while.

"I could do it myself," I said; but at that time I was a serving officer in the Royal Marines, out of touch with newspapers, and hardly ever saw members of the intelligence services. Someone else, I think, was soon encouraged to write about the Admiral in the sense I had suggested, though I thought the tone of the subsequent articles somewhat more violent than was really necessary. I record them here for two reasons: firstly, to undeceive those English readers who may have been given a false impression of the Admiral by what they read in contemporary newspapers, and secondly, to convince some of his German friends, highly indignant at the time, that there were good intentions behind a façade of wild and impalpable abuse.

Specimen obituary notice sent to British newspapers in December 1942:

ADMIRAL WILHELM CANARIS Germany's Master Spy, Evil Genius of the Reich.

"Implacable enemy of Britain, the evil genius of Hitler's Reich, Germany's master spy and cold-blooded assassin of all who stood in his path, are but a few of the epitaphs that can be applied to Admiral Wilhelm Canaris, the man who did much to bring the Fuehrer to power, and who, in time wondered whether he ought to regard the man as much as foe as an ally."

This script then credits Canaris with the assassination of General von Schleicher (whom Goering and Himmler had murdered), and with the killing of General von Fritsch, his old friend (who purposely walked into a beaten zone seeking death during the advance on Warsaw).

Other and similar articles published before and afterwards pointed out Canaris as the trainer of Heydrich and Himmler in the arts of murder, the lover and employer of Mata Hari and a recruiter of Quislings all over Europe. "The world will be a cleaner and purer place without him," two commentaries concluded.

I thought at the time that the report of Canaris plotting against Hitler might have been politically inspired to embarrass him. As it became better known that there was deep opposition to Hitler in the German General Staff, uneasiness seized some of the men in Britain's wartime propaganda services—a revolt from above did not accord at all with their ideas of the future of Socialist Europe. It would be fair to say also that the idea was forming in more serious minds at this moment that the General Staff of Germany must not be allowed to shuffle off its joint responsibility with Hitler for the wrongs which it had been instrumental in preparing and carrying out.

"You may understand the Admiral's mind," I thought, as I took leave of the man who had grasped the essentials of things. "You and he could work out a short way out of this prolonged ruin and misery, but the machinery of your service and his service will keep each of you in your place until the one machine or the other is broken."

I have related these memories of 1942, at the risk of digressing, because they show how the Admiral got his bad name.

CHAPTER XVII

EXIT HEYDRICH

HIMMLER AND HEYDRICH were not satisfied that the Abwehr was prosecuting the war whole-heartedly. It seemed to want to treat Commando troops as ordinary prisoners of war, whereas the Fuehrer's orders were that they should be killed on the spot. Canaris had objected to racial policy, to executions and assassination, as if this war was to be fought on the same footing as previous wars, with the survivors sitting down together afterwards to make peace. The Reichsfuehrer wanted every German to fight as if there was to be no survival for the vanquished.

Schellenberg called on Admiral Canaris in August 1941 at the Tirpitzufer and took along with him Dr. Walther Huppenkothen, a young lawyer who had specialised in police matters and risen to become S.S. departmental chief in the Reich Security. So Canaris met the man who was to become his executioner. Huppenkothen, one of these precise and polished Germans to whom cleanliness is above godliness, eyed the Admiral, noticed that his hair was white, that he looked worn and hard-worked and that he was somewhat untidy in his dress. He noted the soft voice that spoke in whispers, and wrote in a memorandum: "Not the Prussian officer type!"

Then they all went to Horchers together for one of the fortnightly lunches that Heydrich and Canaris took together. S.S. Chief Group-Leader Mueller (Gestapo Mueller) joined them, Colonel von Bentivegni, the departmental chief of Abwehr III (Security), Canaris's deputy, Admiral Bürckner and Colonel Lahousen.

Horcher's food was excellent, brought in from Denmark, and his French wines were bought with occupation francs at controlled prices. The intimate little restaurant in West Berlin, where Himmler and Ribbentrop had entertained the Duke of Windsor in 1937, had been abandoned for a safer villa in Wannsee suburb standing among trees on a sand ridge above the lake. Here Colonel Piekenbrock, Chief of Military Intelligence I, joined the party. The manager, Herr Haeckh, whose solicitude and art in the cuisine I well remember, the placid and faithful Haeckh, smiled and bowed to his important guests. Canaris had helped Horchers to open their famous restaurant in Madrid, where perhaps his deaf mutes watched the conversations of the diplomats. He was a powerful patron. Heydrich was another important customer.

The gentlemen chatted so openly with each other, though the needles in their words probed at vital secrets and closely guarded departmental privileges. Here was "Piecki", grand seigneur, being so friendly with the black butchers of whom he said in his own circle:

"Keitel must eventually tell his Herr Hitler that the military Abwehr is not an organisation of murderers like the S.S. and S.D."

Huppenkothen noticed how friendly Canaris and Heydrich were ; but he remembered that Reinhard Heydrich had warned him beforehand: "Canaris is an old fox and not to be trusted." As for the old fox, he had written in his diary of Heydrich when he first met him: "It will hardly be possible for me to work closely with Heydrich, because he is a brutal fanatic." There was nothing to be seen of such antipathy during the Horcher repast.

Hupenkothen met Canaris again in Heydrich's villa in Schlachtensee and then at the Canaris villa. They seemed on very good terms. He went to the Abwehr mess in the Army High Command Headquarters at Zossen, south of Berlin, and then they met in Horcher's again.

The division of responsibility that left Canaris the field of intelligence and counter-espionage did not answer to Gestapo requirements, Huppenkothen discovered as he looked back.

"In practice it was obvious time and again that the terms of reference must be revised. The question of counter-espionage especially had to be cleared up."

It irked Himmler and Heydrich that the Wehrmacht should run security in northern France and Belgium. Towards the end of 1941 Heydrich wrote to General Jodl and explained that relations between Wehrmacht Intelligence and Security Police must be adjusted. As a matter of course the letter was passed on to Canaris and a conference was held—Canaris, Heydrich, S.S. Mueller, Colonel von Bentivegni and Huppenkothen.

The tall, grim Heydrich and the small agile Canaris promised each other that they would be absolutely frank in future on all matters.

"But Heydrich said that if he made agreements with Canaris now he was doing so solely because of the war situation. After the war he must claim the whole work now being done by the military intelligence as the proper domain of the Gestapo," wrote Huppenkothen in his memorandum.

Canaris was silent. It was deep winter. The German armies lay frozen in front of Moscow. When the war was over . . .

Heydrich insisted that the Security Police must work in future in France and Belgium. Canaris declared that he would be prepared to put a large part of his Military Police there under the Security Police. He yielded to every demand of Heydrich. But when Huppenkothen received back his draft of the agreement from Bentivegni a few weeks later he was indignant to find that it was precisely the opposite of what had been said. Canaris explained that there was much hesitation, through no fault of his, in transferring the Field Security Police.

Heydrich wrote in anger to Canaris that he could see no sense in talks that seemed to be fully agreed, if it was necessary to have a shorthand writer present to prevent arguments afterwards.

"He could not negotiate with Canaris any longer and he had proposed to the Reichsfuehrer that they should take up contact with Keitel."

Canaris hastened round to Heydrich's office with Bentivegni. Heydrich sent out the adjutant to tell him that he was not there. Canaris waited several hours in the anteroom, then he departed, leaving Bentivegni with orders not to come away until he had seen Heydrich. Out came S.S. Mueller and prevailed upon Bentivegni to go away too. Canaris went to Keitel. Keitel rang up Heydrich, and Reinhard at length agreed to take up negotiations again. He even suggested a luncheon at Horcher's. In that suave atmosphere they formulated the new terms of reference and signed them afterwards. The Gestapo could take over in France. They would take charge of Odette and Captain Peter Churchill two years later, they would hunt the R.A.F. escape organisations, and break the British "circuits", they would round up the canisters of arms that the British dropped. They would liquidate the Maquis with terrible brutalities. Was success reflected in the surface of Heydrich's life mask? He had reason to be exultant; but it would be a year before the agreement was worked out in detail.

Meanwhile Huppenkothen saw something more of Canaris. The S.S. had made some play in conversation with the story of his Greek antecedents. Oh vanity of boasting illustrious ancestry! He may have claimed relationship with the Greek naval hero of 1820, Admiral Konstantin Kanaris; but the Greeks were now enemies, whereas the Italians, his real forebears, were allies. This confusion may have been faintly embarrassing. One day he handed Huppenkothen a copy of his family tree that showed that the Canaris family originally came from Italy.

"This will complete your dossier," he whispered.

Heydrich ranged through occupied Europe under his new title of Commissar General for the Security of Occupied Countries. Shoot them: senior officers, professors, communists, Jews and Maquis alike! The rule of General von Falkenhausen in Belgium was altogether too mild for him. He wanted the blood to flow. His master was after more blood, too. General Giraud had escaped early in 1942 from Konigstein fortress in Saxony and somehow contrived to find his way to unoccupied France. The Abwehr had been ordered to liquidate General Weygand in North Africa in 1940 after Hitler had written to Mussolini: "I am not satisfied with the choice of General Weygand to restore order in North Africa." He feared that Weygand would go over to the Allies. And now, Giraud. Then it was that Piekenbrock made his drastic remark that "Keitel must eventually be told quite clearly to report to his Herr Hitler that we of the military Abwehr are not an organisation of murderers like the S.S. and S.D.". The Admiral whispered something conciliatory to Keitel, and the Field-Marshal, who didn't like the idea of murdering generals anyway, agreed that the Abwehr should hand over the job to the S.D. Canaris said nothing further to anyone about it.

Heydrich had meanwhile added to his titles that of Protector of Bohemia and Moravia. Stagnation of the war in Russia made Czechoslovakia a future danger. Baron von Neurath was too mild a ruler. Heydrich, who succeeded him,

proclaimed a "state of civil emergency in September 1941"
and passed decree laws making the death penalty applicable to
minor offences of disaffection. Within two months some 1,100
prominent Czechs had been executed. He continued to inspect
the Security Police in other occupied countries and shifted
S.S. General Oberg from Poland to France on May 7th, 1942,
to cope with the swelling resistance. Then he went to The Hague
to supervise mass shootings, and in the third week of May was
back in Prague, where he told nominal leaders of the Czech
people that their young men would have to be conscripted for
military service.

The heavy boots of the senior officers of the Secret State
Police, the Criminal Police, the S.D., and the Abwehr echoed
in the stone halls of the Hradschin palace of Prague. Himmler
and Heydrich called a congress to announce the new order of
intelligence duties, with the S.D. taking charge of counter-
espionage and Abwehr III assuming a subordinate rule. By
now Heydrich's time was nearly run.

An R.A.F. bomber flew over Bohemia one night, possibly
while the Hradschin conference was being held. It dropped
three Czech parachutists of the Czechoslovak Brigade armed
with Sten guns and grenades. A reception group hid them and
showed them a sharp bend on a road near Leiben where
Heydrich's car frequently passed. It would be obliged to slow
down to take the corner.

Two bicycles were propped up near the corner, two men
loitered on the verge. As Heydrich's car slowed down, one man
hurled a grenade. The other opened up with his Sten gun. The
driver and the S.S. orderly were killed instantly, the officer with
the silver death's-head on his field-grey cap sank back mortally
wounded. The two Czechs fled for refuge to a little church in
Lidice.

Canaris met Huppenkothen at the funeral of Heydrich. The
intense blue eyes overbrimmed with tears, heavy tears rolled
down his cheeks.

"He offered us the condolences of his service and himself,"
recollected Huppenkothen. "He assured me that he had lost
a great man and a true friend in Reinhard Heydrich."

Himmler spoke the oration of "this man of purest character" and pinned a medal on Heydrich's breast. The S.S.
killed some one hundred and fifty hostages and proclaimed

that any men of military age found without identity cards would be summarily shot. A Czech wavered and Lidice was betrayed to them as the village that harboured the assassins. They surrounded the church, the parachutists died fighting. The Gestapo extinguished all human life in Lidice before razing every stone and planting grass over the foundations and the roads to conceal the very place where it had stood.

Some say that Canaris lost in Heydrich a man whose measure he had taken and could curb because he held documents proving his Jewish parentage. Others, that he lost an intimate colleague. If we believe Huppenkothen, we must doubt both suggestions.

Soon the whim seized Hitler again that he must have Giraud's blood. It was long overdue. The Abwehr must report exactly what steps had been taken or what had been arranged with the S.D.

"What about Operation Gustav?" Keitel, using the code name for the murder plan, fired this question at Lahousen, as departmental chief, when the Admiral was in France. Lahousen hurried anxiously to Paris and met his chief in the Hotel Lutetia. He related what Keitel had asked him. Canaris said nothing for a while, but over a glass of wine:

"Lofty, tell me the date that Giraud fled," muttered Canaris, "and the date that I was ordered to murder him, and the date that Heydrich was killed. Don't you see? We can say that we handed over that whole business in Prague—to Heydrich personally."

CHAPTER XVIII

THE PLASTIC BOMB

"WE PASSED ALL that on to Heydrich"—so spring and summer 1942 went and General Giraud was still alive. The battles in the western desert swayed to and fro and Rommel, still looking eastwards from El Alamein and counting up the opponents whom he had dealt with, Wavell, O'Connor, Cunningham, Ritchie, Auchinleck, found himself pitted against two more, Alexander and Montgomery. The German summer offensive in Russia that had been held up at Stalingrad developed into the death throes of the German Sixth Army. Hitler fingered the plan of Operation Attila, but he dared not move either to invade the rest of France or force his way into Spain. The battle of El Alamein broke upon Rommel on October 23rd; by November 5th the British had pushed him a hundred miles westwards and he was still going. Russian counter-attacks at Stalingrad increased.

It was reported that the British were collecting a great convoy at Gibraltar to relieve Malta. The shipping lay thick at anchor. Canaris had an Abwehr branch in the mainland at Algeciras and a senior officer in charge, whose duty it was to keep a constant check on the movements of Allied and neutral shipping. During these first days of November there was something brewing, and without any doubt Canaris, if anyone, would be able to find out what it was. He had his friends in the Spanish armada, his Abwehr men at Algeciras and in Tangier and Ceuta. He had himself stood many times on the Spanish coast and looked across at the Rock and the Royal Navy in the days when he and General von Richtofen were reporting to Hitler on the strength of Gibraltar. He had the Mediterranean situation in his blood. Now was the testing time for the chief of Intelligence.

Yet although the officers of the Spanish armada spoke emphatically of an impending invasion of Algeria and Morocco,

General Heusinger, the German Chief of Operations in the Army High Command, in early November gave this official view of the Mediterranean situation: "We are convinced that it is an attempt by the Allies to relieve the island of Malta which is being heavily bombarded. No landing in North Africa is to be apprehended; the British and Americans lack the forces and the experience for such an enterprise." In fact the Abwehr reports pointed to Malta as the destination of the huge Allied convoys in the Mediterranean and Atlantic approaches to Gibraltar. The British and U.S. forces were carried in no fewer than five hundred ships with three hundred and fifty naval escort vessels—it is hard to imagine that Malta alone could have been their destination.[1] On November 7th the German Ambassador, von Stohrer, and his naval attaché were at dinner with officers of the Spanish armada, who insisted that the convoys would land on the North African coast in the rear of Rommel. Stohrer hesitated for some hours before reporting to his government, and then he added his own views that these ships were destined for Malta or Alexandria. Before the telegram had been deciphered in Berlin, the landing of Lieutenent-General Eisenhower's Allied forces in Morocco and Algeria had begun. General Giraud arrived in Algeria on November 9th to assume leadership of the French in North Africa—it has always amazed me that a senior French general with one arm could have escaped from Saxony and made his way undiscovered across Germany into France. A British submarine had taken him on the first part of his journey from the Vichy state—safe from Hitler's Operation Gustav.

It is amazing, too, that Canaris came unscathed out of the German inquest on Operation Torch, because this was his peninsula and the sea was his element. Yet he had failed to guess or failed to report what the Spanish armada knew about the Allied convoys. I asked a senior British naval officer, well acquainted with Spain, Captain J. Hillgarth, what he knew of the Canaris reports from the peninsula.

"I don't think they ever did us any particular harm," was his reply. My friend, H. C. O'Neill (Strategicus), remembers seeing some of the Canaris reports after Wavell's victories over Graziani in the desert. "He vastly overrated Wavell's forces,"

[1] "I reported to Berlin from Hamburg about October 26th," writes Commander Wichman, "that the biggest convoy ever assembled was about to land Allied forces on the North Coast of Africa."

Strategicus told me. "Canaris must have known exactly how
many—or how few—divisions we really had in the Middle
East at that time to send elsewhere. Now that you mention
to me that Canaris was working against Hitler, I can see a
possible explanation for much that has long puzzled me."

Edward Crankshaw, an authority on Russia, who also
studied the secret reports of the Admiral in wartime, found
himself puzzled in exactly the same way. "There's something
wrong with this," was his reaction to some of them. Was
British deception so good, or were German agents so bad?
Lahousen offers a possible explanation: "Even if the Chief
doubted the reliability of an agent's report, he will have passed
it on if it agreed with his own line—that of impressing Hitler
and the party with the real strength of the Allies whom they were
continually underrating." It is, however, a wide step from that
to submitting misleading reports about impending operations.

Algeciras was one of his strongest points and yet it failed
him. "He was always going down there," remarked one of the
British officers whom I questioned. I remembered the picture
given by Abshagen of Canaris in Algeciras on the last night of
1942, dressed in a chef's cap and white apron and cooking
the New Year's dinner for the Abwehr officers at Algeciras.

"He was a first-class cook," a senior British intelligence
officer remarked to me in the course of conversation.

Some of the German officers went on from the dinner to the
Hotel Reina Maria Christina, where there was a New Year's
Ball, and danced there on the same floor as the British officers
from Gibraltar.

"Did you know that there was a British plot to kidnap
Canaris while he was staying in Algeciras?" This startling
question was put to me by a fellow journalist.

"It was in the time that General Mason-Macfarlane was
Governor of Gibraltar. The whole operation was prepared."

"What happened . . . ?"

"Gibraltar received a message from London cancelling the
operation."

"Did it say—leave our man alone?"

"No, it did not say quite that: it said that he was far more
valuable where he was."

The Axis forces in North Africa were taken unaware by
"Torch", and though German airborne troops were quickly

landed in Tunisia and Hitler pressed the button for Operation Attila and marched down the Rhone Valley, the Afrika Korps was lost; Italy quaked for fear or hope of liberation, and France under the Vichy police and the S.D. began to stir perilously. The German military governor had clashes of authority with the S.S. in their territory, as the dreaded "Night and Fog decree" took effect and men and woman were spirited away without trace beyond the reach of their kin.

Secret Operations Branch in London increased its weapons deliveries to the patriots in France. Canisters were dropped by parachute far and wide over France. Colonel Relling, Chief of Abwehr III, working from the Hotel Lutetia in Paris, reported in March that he had initiated Operation Grand Duke—the smashing of the French Resistance groups and the capture of their British confederates. One of his principal agents was that Hugo Bleicher, Serjeant-Major of Abwehr III, risen from the Field Police, who arrested Odette and Captain Peter Churchill in St. Torioz and so broke up an active British intelligence and sabotage circuit in France. Bleicher had phenomenal success in Operation Grand Duke, due to his gift for assuming the role of the sympathetic and enlightened German who wants to make common cause with the Allies against Hitler. So he won to his side the more gullible of the French patriots who fell into his hands, and, thinking Captain Churchill to be a relative of the British Prime Minister, he tempted him with curious offers that sounded like the mission of Rudolf Hess.

Bleicher in his heyday had broken in enough Frenchmen to form a team who went round among the Resistance sharing the task of collecting British arms canisters by night and stowing away tell-tale parachutes. He used to keep a tally of the secret weapons dumps of the Resistance and regularly arranged for them to be raided after some incident which might seem to have betrayed them, such as the arrest of one of the dump watchmen.

French traitors working for him told new British agents on arrival in Paris that their identity papers would be quickly supplied by a den of forgers. He cites one case in which the British agent in charge of a group, "Elie", and his secretary, "Denise", handed over a set of photographs of British agents for use in false identity cards, and adds that the papers were in fact made out for them in the Abwehr Office III in the Hotel

Lutetia. The photographs were copied for Gestapo and Abwehr files. Reports on the localities where these agents were active, and samples of the weapons and explosives dropped, were sent to Berlin.

The Abwehr showed an almost morbid interest in the new British plastic explosives and the silent acid capsule time fuses. The putty-like substance could be wound round a telegraph pole, pushed against a door lock, nudged under a rail or squeezed into a ship's cable. The acid capsule reacted on a wire. The time element depended on the thickness of the wire retaining the striker pin. Canaris received reports of German tests carried out with these materials by Abwehr II, the Sabotage Branch.

As winter deepened, the German Sixth Army disintegrated at Stalingrad, frozen, famished, out of fuel, cut off and attacked without respite by the Russian armies. Thousands of corpses strewed an area as big as East Anglia. The siege of Leningrad was raised on January 18th. Anybody not infected by war hysteria could see plainly that Germany was losing the war. Like a knell from Casablanca came the words of President Roosevelt: "Unconditional surrender." A month later Canaris's personal staff received a message from General von Tresckow of the Central Army Group in Smolensk that it was "high time to act". The Admiral set out for Smolensk in the second half of February, accompanied by many officers of his entourage. The occasion was a conference of army intelligence officers. A member of his staff carried a small package of the plastic charges and a set of time fuses. Hans von Dohnanyi of his personal office went into conference at Smolensk with General von Tresckow and Lieutenant von Schlabrendorff, his adjutant. They agreed that an attempt should be made on the life of Hitler when he visited the Army Group. They would engineer an explosion in the Fuehrer's aircraft so that his death might appear an accident. The Admiral knew what was afoot, but he left the detail to others.

That evening there was a party in headquarters mess, at which Canaris mentioned that he was flying to Berchtesgaden to see Himmler next day. He smiled at the chaff of the younger officers who asked him how he could possibly shake hands with such people. He had in mind to ask Himmler for the release of several Jews whom he would smuggle abroad after a pretence of training them as Abwehr officers. Hitler had exclaimed to Canaris in a frantic temper after nine young Nazi sabotage agents had been captured in America: "You should use criminals or Jews instead." "I have express orders from the Fuehrer to employ Jews for this work," was the argument that Canaris used with some success to Heydrich and Himmler.

A month later, on March 13th, 1943, the explosive charge was placed in the aircraft of Adolf Hitler, as he left Smolensk after a visit of inspection to Central Army Group. Lieutenant von Schlabrendorff had disguised the bomb as a package of brandy bottles which he entrusted to Colonel Brandt of the entourage as a "gift" to an officer at Supreme Headquarters. Hitler flew from Smolensk to Rastenburg in East Prussia with the package in his plane and the acid fuse ate its way through the retaining wire. When the wire parted, the intense cold had rendered the detonator unserviceable and the bomb failed to explode. The intrepid von Schlabrendorff flew to Rastenburg and retrieved the parcel before it had been opened. In this manner the explosives which the British dropped into Europe for the purpose of destroying German war potential found their way very close to the supreme target, via the man whose organisation was fighting the British Secret Service all over Europe. Dr. Abshagen says that Canaris "was more than half aware but did not want to be too much in the picture" when this attempt on Hitler was planned and that "Canaris knew that Abwehr Branch II was working on the fuses" and that "in fact he himself took fuses of this type in his aircraft when he flew to Smolensk". Some of the drawing-room opposition to Hitler was wont to chafe in inactivity and complain that "Canaris never did much". For my part, if I were told that he had a hand in the escape of General Giraud, I would not be a bit surprised. The truth is that he had a talent for doing an immense amount through other people so that detection was difficult.

"I have just had a message from Admiral Canaris."
Far away from the snows of Smolensk there was another nervous tremor. George Earle had descended from the rank of American Minister in Sofia to that of American naval attaché in Istanbul, since America and Bulgaria were now in the war on opposite sides. Cedric Salter, whom I have asked to search

F

his memory in this matter, recalls these facts from the days when he was correspondent of the *Daily Express* in Istanbul:

"It was early in 1943. George Earle was staying in the Parc Hotel in which I was also staying. He had been instructed to remain in Istanbul as a channel of communication between King Boris of Bulgaria and President Roosevelt to whom he reported direct and not through the State Department. Earle was approached by many German intelligence men, some wanting to plant false information, others convinced of Germany's impending defeat and wanting to lay evidence that they were anti-Nazi. Early in 1943, Earle told me that he had had a message from Admiral Canaris. Meetings took place, of which he did not tell me the details, but which included a vague exploration by Canaris of the sort of terms of peace that America would be prepared to consider."

It would be interesting to know the exact date of these communications from Canaris. It appears from the context in which Salter writes that the approaches were made to Earle about the time of the Casablanca Conference. Evidently Roosevelt had something very much in mind when he proclaimed Allied war aims to be "unconditional surrender". This formula is recorded in the Joint Chiefs of Staff minutes of January 7th, 1943, and will therefore have been discussed as a serious policy in Washington before Roosevelt left for Casablanca. There is no clue to any message received from Canaris in the Hopkins Papers. We have elsewhere the testimony of Allen Dulles that Canaris's man in Bern, Gisevius, had been trying hard to find out what Allied peace terms would be.

Did a revolt against Hitler no longer suit the Allies' grand strategy? Canaris, who knew of all the soundings and the hollow echoes that reached him from Berne, from Ankara and from Lisbon, had reasons to be pessimistic. His bomb did not explode, his overtures met with silence, and then the summons for "unconditional surrender".

Mr. Churchill has given in the fourth volume of his war memoirs his considered views on the meaning and effect of the "unconditional surrender" declaration on the history of the war. He tells us that the proposed peace terms, once set out in draft, looked far more severe than mere "unconditional surrender" did. Stalin about this time devised a more subtle declaration of his war aims when he said in a speech that he believed "that Germany cannot be destroyed, but that Hitlerism can and must be destroyed".

General Eisenhower has revealed in *Crusade in Europe* that the "unconditional surrender" formula was mentioned in the Joint Chiefs of Staff minutes of January 7th, 1943, and therefore must have been discussed as a serious policy before the President left for Casablanca. It seemed to those who studied the secret policy of nations that this meant that the war would be fought to the end, that no arrangement would be sought with the Nazis or with any other group opposed to Hitler, that the military power of Germany would be abolished and the consequent dominating position of Russia in Europe accepted as a basis for peace. A debate in the House of Lords in March 1943 shows what divergent views were held on this mighty problem at the time.

"Canaris reckoned with the 'unconditional surrender' policy and was not surprised when it was announced," Lahousen told me. "His mystic and pessimistic mind foresaw the end of Germany far off and he regarded it as the deserved punishment of destiny for the barbarities of the National-Socialist system. Canaris was at bottom a fatalist.

"'We will all have to pay for this, for we have all become responsible for it!' was one of his oft-repeated remarks.

"Nevertheless he thought that the Casablanca declaration was a calamitous mistake at the time, that could only prolong the war. For as long as there was no complete defeat, even the military leaders who were at heart opposed to Hitler could not be expected to accept such terms that were incompatible with their conception of honour. Canaris said to me after the Casablanca Conference:

"You know, my dear Lahousen, the students of history will not need to trouble their heads after this war, as they did after the last, to determine who was guilty of starting it. The case is, however, different when we consider guilt for prolonging the war. I believe that the other side have now disarmed us of the last weapon with which we could have ended it. 'Unconditional surrender', no, our generals will not swallow that. Now I cannot see any solution."

CHAPTER XIX

ASSASSINATE CHURCHILL!

ASSASSINATE CHURCHILL! THERE is no doubt from what senior German intelligence officers have revealed to me that orders to assassinate Churchill were given by Hitler about the time of the Casablanca Conference. Whether it was his reply to the declaration of "Unconditional surrender" is difficult to determine, as the war diary of Abwehr II, the Intelligence Section that dealt in sabotage and acts of violence, has been confiscated by the Allies and will probably not be available to historians.

It seems that there were two orders, one to assassinate him while abroad, the other to shoot down his aircraft. Of the Luftwaffe plans there is still something to be learned from Lisbon.

Lisbon lay athwart the Allies' lines of communication; from Portugal the passage of aircraft, ships and passengers could be observed by the Germans. It was plain from the first days of the war that here lay great possibilities, and so Admiral Canaris had first to test the ground with the German Ambassador, Baron Oswald von Hoiningen-Huene, who was well aware that he was in a country which, although neutral, was the oldest ally of Britain. It was a severely Christian state with a bias against both National Socialism and liberal democracy. Dr. Salazar, the Premier, was determined that it should not be drawn into the calamitous struggle between Germany and the Allies.

The Baron held a secret conference with Canaris in Lisbon at the beginning of the war. "We reached an agreement that no diversionary or sabotage actions would be undertaken by the German military personnel in Portugal," Baron Hoiningen-Huene told me. "Although certain German quarters envisaged several actions with time bombs to sabotage Allied ships anchored in Portuguese ports, Admiral Canaris and his representatives knew how to stop these attempts to my full satisfaction.

"Canaris was a man of integrity and good will. I saw very little of him when he was in Portugal. He usually came accompanied by one of his senior officers and conversed mainly with his own subordinates, the attachés, Colonel von Cremer-Auerode who also worked under the name of von Karsthof, and his deputy, Captain Fritz Cramer. I was also told nothing of his own activities while in Portugal, but he seemed to be seeking for links and contacts with the enemy in greatest secrecy and in contravention of the policy of Hitler."

Plainly this inactivity in such a promising area could not be allowed to last! Nor did it. The lull in Portugal seems to have got on the nerves of Hitler. Keitel at a conference at the beginning of 1942 abruptly ordered Canaris to get results on the Air Staff plan to sabotage the New York–Lisbon Atlantic Clipper airlines. General Lahousen was present. The Admiral nervously turned to him and passed the command straight on. They were apparently so disconcerted that the results were soon forthcoming. A time bomb was placed in the American Clipper flying boat shortly afterwards as she lay in the Tagus estuary. "There was a complete ban on all such acts of terrorism laid down by the Admiral and written on page 256 of my Departmental War Diary," General Lahousen told me. "M.I.5 has photo-copies of it. The original is in Washington."

But what use was a secret directive against murder and assassination if peremptory orders come from above? Canaris happened to be soon in Portugal and was told, to his consternation, by his officers that the bomb was already in the Clipper. He ordered it to be removed, and as the Clipper was delayed by rough weather this could be successfully done. "Trevor Roper is right when he asserts that Canaris was not always able to prevent acts of terrorism," concluded Lahousen. "Sometimes it was technically impossible. Sometimes it was a question of personality. That he was always opposed to it is without question."

It appears that the Germans knew of an impending meeting between Mr. Churchill and President Roosevelt in January 1943. Commander Wichmann in his Hamburg office learned about a week beforehand that a meeting was to take place. There was some rumour of it in Spain, too, where an indignant business man turned up after being ejected in advance from his room in one of the Casablanca hotels. The opinion in Berlin was, however, that the meeting was to take place at the White House and that the word "Casablanca", which had leaked out to them, was merely a code name for the "White House", the Washington residence of the American President. But the Luftwaffe was alerted, and Colonel W. Jenke[1] tells me that a special reconnaissance aircraft used by Department I of the German Intelligence (probably in Section I.L. (Luft)) and maintained at an airport on the peninsula for high level photography, was ordered out to reconnoitre and spotted from a great height a British bomber flying southwards with fighter escort, which turned around in the vicinity of Lisbon so that the bomber flew on alone. Was this the furnished hulk in which Mr. Churchill describes his uncomfortable journey with Lord Portal and others to the Casablanca Conference? Jenke believes that it was, and that the British bomber also sighted this German aircraft which belonged to the Rowehl reconnaissance squadron. Canaris had not organised the second stage of this operation, he said, which would have been fighter pursuit also from the peninsula.

"I know nothing of the air reconnaissance activities against Churchill," said Lahousen. "As to my own department, I do remember that after Mr. Churchill had arrived in Casablanca Keitel passed to me the request, probably from the Fuehrer, to have Churchill assassinated by nationalist Arabs. Hitler was probably thinking of some of our Spanish Moroccan agents. Quite apart from the technical impossibility of pulling an operation like that out of a hat, there was the Admiral's own ban on such activities. All attempts on Churchill, as far as I know, were ordered *after* his arrival in Casablanca."

I have received confirmation from Colonel of the Luftwaffe Theo Rowehl, commander of an air intelligence squadron, that Canaris mentioned to him in utmost secrecy the assassination order.

Of course the Luftwaffe was on its mettle when the Casablanca Conference had ended. The Biscay squadrons ranged far and wide. Otto John, a Lufthausa official, remembers how one of the Lufthausa air liners was suddenly ordered about this time to cancel its Lisbon–Madrid flight "owing to engine trouble" and make a "test flight" instead in a wide sweep out to sea; what the pilot was to watch for, John could not say.

[1] Adjutant to Canaris.

Mr. Churchill set out from England a second time five months later—this time really to the White House and returned via Algiers after the second Washington Conference, meeting Mr. Eden in North Africa on May 30th, 1943. There naturally his presence was reported to Berlin by German agents and the Luftwaffe alerted a second time to intercept his aircraft. It is probably to these circumstances that we owed the loss, so he believes, of the British Overseas Airways liner that was shot down on June 1st, 1943, out at sea by the Luftwaffe on its return flight to London. The thirteen passengers and the crew all lost their lives and the Wehrmacht communiqué of the day claimed it as a "transport aircraft". Leslie Howard and Mr. Alfred Chenfalls, a financial expert who bore a certain resemblance to Mr. Churchill and smoked cigars, were on board this aircraft and lost their lives with the rest, men, women and children. Mr. Churchill believes that Chenfalls, crossing over to the airfield to the B.O.A.C. plane, may have been mistaken for himself and so provided a motive for this singular crime— for the B.O.A.C. air liner carrying freight and some diplomatic correspondence to and fro had been allowed to run unmolested by the Luftwaffe all these years.

Soon after that Lisbon became the scene of a strange encounter, in which Canaris himself may have met an Allied officer.

Portugal had never accepted a Soviet ambassador or even a Soviet consul on her soil. Salazar and his people in their deep-rooted religious convictions saw atheistic states as their declared enemies. Her treaty with Russia had not made Germany any more popular in Lisbon. It followed that the Poles, because they were attacked by two powers that had forsaken Christianity, were treated with consideration by the Portuguese and allowed to maintain their Legation at Lisbon as well as certain intelligence agents.

Colonel Jan Kowalewski was an officer of the Polish General Staff with the deep-rooted mistrust of his nation for the Germans. During the years when he was studying as a young officer he had to travel to the military academies of Belgium and France and crossed Germany many times. "But I never spent a night in Germany," he told me. "Instinctively I passed through as quickly as I could." He served his country as military attaché in Moscow, escaped from the defeat of the Polish armies and was sent by General Sikorski to Lisbon to work as representative of the Free Poles. He kept his distance from the Polish Legation. It was one of his tasks to get in touch with the Polish communities of Europe, labourers in the Todt organisation, miners in France and Germany, and beyond, the people of enslaved Poland itself. He must be wary of his movements, even in Lisbon; for although British influence was strong, there were many nationalities in Portugal—Germans, Italians, Bulgarians, Rumanians, Hungarians, Spaniards and many more besides. Colonel Kowalewski was a man of simple habits, stocky and solid in appearance. With his broad face and blunt features, he could easily pass for a peasant or a labourer rather than a highly trained staff officer. He settled down unobtrusively in a small furnished apartment in Lisbon, took stock of his surroundings, informed himself as to who there might be in the diplomatic and consular services, friends, neutrals and enemies, and took up some of the threads that ran out of Lisbon into occupied Europe.

Colonel Kowalewski soon learned of the state of mind of the German ambassador, and perceived that fate had struck a bad blow at the Baron Hoiningen-Huene. Under Hitler's treaty of friendship with Russia all German minorities were withdrawn from East Poland and the Baltic states which Russia had occupied. The ambassador thus lost his ancestral home. His old mother was obliged to remove westwards, where a castle was found for her in the enslaved provinces of Poland. The castle in Lithuania was immense; an equally large castle in Poland was chosen, where the old lady was set down with her belongings. She did not move about much in her new domain to begin with, for, being over seventy, she had to overcome the fatigues of the journey, the strangeness of her new surroundings, the wrench of departure. After a time she set out to explore one story after another of the castle in Poland and in the course of her wanderings she suddenly encountered two ladies like herself walking about the place. She asked them who they were and whether she might do anything for them.

"This was our home," they answered. "The civil governor has given us permission to stay on in two rooms until we can find somewhere to go."

The Baroness Hoiningen-Huene realised to her amazement that a family of the Polish nobility were being turned out of their own castle to make room for her. This was a great shock to an old lady who still lived by the standards of the nineteenth century. She decided to go to Berlin and find out if people in the government really knew what was going on. At first the officials to whom she spoke in the Wilhelmstrasse showed some embarrassment, then she met other officials who showed no concern at all. This was merely part of the pattern of eliminating the Polish intelligentsia. That prompted her to go about saying many hard things to people in official positions, until she was told that she had better stop agitating about the Poles or she would be in trouble. The old lady died soon afterwards, early in 1940. The Ambassador went to Berlin for the funeral and returned embittered to his post at Lisbon hardly a trustworthy servant for the Fuehrer.

It was after the German war with Russia had started that Colonel Kowalewski, who had by then found stealthy contact with some of the small allies of Germany, in Lisbon, received a message from a Rumanian diplomat whom he could trust. It told him that the German ambassador had a confidential agent whom he wished to meet Colonel Kowalewski.

The Colonel took every precaution before the meeting. He rode out to the rendezvous with his Rumanian friend; a group of Poles followed him in a second car. As they reached it he caught sight of a smart Buick which he instantly recognised as the same luxuriously fitted model that was kept in a garage near his own apartment. The man who got out of the Buick was introduced to him. It was Captain Fritz Cramer, the Canaris attaché and military security officer of the German Embassy.

So began a series of secret meetings that were usually held at night in Kowalewski's rooms.

"You are Peter in Lisbon," asked Cramer.

"Yes, that is so!"

"We have arrested your man in Paris. He gave us your name. If you are anxious to save his life, perhaps we can do something about it."

Kowalewski was anxious to help the man in Paris and said so. Some days elapsed and Cramer came to the nightly meeting, bringing with him a bundle of papers. It was, he said, the reports of the man in Paris which he could see no harm in handing over. Kowalewski learned more of the state of mind of Baron von Hoiningen-Huene. Sometimes there was a little intelligence business to do, but he noticed that Cramer always tended to want to discuss the general situation, the future, the issue of the war, the frame of mind of the Allies. Kowalewski told him with great plainness what in his view had been the capital mistakes of the Germans. So began his secret contacts with the men of Canaris in Portugal.

One day, in the summer of 1943, one of the Canaris officers came to the appointment in a state of suppressed excitement. He spoke of strange new weapons that Germany was busy perfecting—rockets and bombs that were being mass-produced and could be fired at England in endless streams from bases in France. Aircraft could not intercept them; they could be launched night and day from bombproof concrete bases. When they were released they would fall in hundreds and London would be devastated. This was a full year before Hitler gave the order for the V-weapons to be used and the first buzz-bombs droned over Britain, though it seems that aerial reconnaissance had already revealed to the British what was going on in Peenemünde.

It was Cramer another evening who mentioned his "chief", who might visit Portugal and would like to meet Colonel Kowalewski. He would come at the time arranged for the Canaris men's talks. "That will be Canaris," the Polish diplomats in Lisbon told him beneath their breath. Kowalewski, who had never heard of this man, waited at his apartment at the time of the usual German visits. His visitor that evening was an older man, whose hair he remembers was nearly white, his skin sallow, who spoke rapidly and seemed to be in a high state of nervous tension. He did not introduce himself, moved about the room as he spoke and seemed to be a person of high authority.

"He wanted me to repeat to him what I had previously said to Cramer about the mistakes of Germany," Kowalewski told me. "I explained to him that the capital mistake in strategy was in allowing Russia in 1939 to advance westwards as far as the Carpathians. While Russian troops sat on the Carpathians, so close to Vienna and the Danube valley, the whole of Central Europe was permanently unsafe. Germany could neither move sufficient troops against England nor against Africa. Her main forces were tied to the eastern frontier.

"He cast questions at me, brusquely, with traces of the impatient authority that becomes a habit in some high officers, and had a rapid grasp for my answers. He asked me why it was not possible for Germans to get the co-operation of the countries that they occupied. I gave him a very simple answer to that. As long as Germany did not change her methods that was not possible."

"Why do you think that he should go to see you?"

"To exchange ideas on these strategic matters and Germany's mistakes."

Was this stranger Canaris? I recalled the Canaris conversations in Hitler's train at Ilnau in Silesia in September 1939, what the British intelligence officers had told me of his reports on the Moscow front and the Caucasus offensive. He did not need to travel to Lisbon at a certain risk to himself to recite the mistakes of Hitler in retrospect. Yet if it was not him it was certainly his technique. He was acutely reasoning the chances of finding allies among the Free Poles for a new course in German policy. They had the most formidable underground organisation of all. It would soon be playing havoc with the German communications. At this time, September 1943, the Russians were beginning to approach the frontiers of Poland. The dismayed Polish government in London saw their ravaged country about to become a battlefield for the second time. The Polish Resistance movement would present Canaris soon with a huge problem that the S.S. would try vainly to solve with more bloodshed. The Czechs were willing to welcome the Russians in their territory. The Poles were appalled at the thought. President Beneš in London and Washington was at this time the advocate of war to the end and he solemnly pledged himself to the American and British war leaders that Stalin desired an understanding with the West.

"During my work in Lisbon with these men of the German opposition, I could sense the malevolence of the Czechs," said Kowalewski. "I have no love for the Germans, but I could have made policy with them."

Nine months later he was in London reporting to the Polish Government in exile. On the night of June 13th–14th, he looked out of his hotel window and saw the widespread glow of fires from the first flying bombs which the Canaris men had foretold;

but the Allies had made good use of the interval to pin-point the V-bomb bases.

"I was forever making contacts with people in Lisbon searching for peace," Kowalewski told me. "There was a Bulgarian who was so nervous of the city itself that he would only meet me in quarries outside. There were many such people. I passed them on to the British Intelligence Service and then heard no more about them. They would transfer the talks to another capital for security reasons—say Istanbul—and I knew nothing further. It was disappointing. It made you feel that opportunities were not being exploited."

"Do you think that it was Canaris with whom you spoke?"

"Perhaps you could show me a photograph of him," suggested Kowalewski.

I produced two or three taken of the Admiral about that time in plain clothes.

"Yes, that may have been him," said Kowalewski as he stared at the pictures. "Perhaps his hair was not quite so white as it appears here; it is possible that this was the same man."

Fritz Cramer, whom I traced from Lisbon to Hamburg early in 1951, told Leverkuehn that it was not Canaris, and he should know. But he did not say who his "chief" was on this occasion.

Three or four visits by Canaris to Portugal during the war years were noticed by the Allies. His arrival caused less apprehension than it did in Madrid where the silent warfare of Abwehr and the Secret Service was more intense.

Whenever Canaris did visit Portugal he saw Cramer and spoke something of what was in his mind. He enjoined him earnestly against acts of sabotage, and he never mentioned the order of Hitler to assassinate Churchill, though he yarned a bit to him about the British war leader.

"I used to have some contact with Churchill before the war," he said vaguely. "The most important statesman of our times—after Stalin."

The star of Canaris was waning in the peninsula. The British Secret Service at lower grades was pressing the Abwehr hard in Spain; his own position at home was threatened. A new emissary appeared, a young official of the German Lufthausa civil air lines, Otto John, who found his way to British officials in Lisbon in the summer of 1944 and told them that a revolt against Hitler was imminent. Within a year of the meeting between the stranger and Kowalewski, destiny was to set its heel on both the secret movements that they represented. The Polish patriots rose in Warsaw and fought their terrible battle with the S.S., while the mistrustful Russians let the blood of these heroic men run unsuccoured. These fighting Poles were not the men that Stalin wanted to emerge in command. The German revolt in Berlin about the same time was forlorn and unspectacular by comparison and the S.S. mastered it with one hand.

CHAPTER XX

THE RAT RUN

"SAVE US FROM the security sense of our ambassadors!" said the security officer.

I asked him whether ambassadors were any more fallible than ordinary people.

"It is not that they are worse than anyone else," he answered, "but the result of their rashness can be so much worse."

"Are you thinking of the case of Cicero?" I asked.

"No, not at the moment. I was thinking of the Ambassador's pearl necklace. Cicero was by no means the first valet or butler to spy on a British ambassador. I cannot imagine why we don't make English butlers obligatory in the diplomatic service. They are the finest in the world."

"But the Ambassador's pearls?"

"Oh, yes—there is one thing that makes the security of an ambassador a difficult matter. By the time he has reached that height he has a fair claim to know about the world and its pitfalls; but if he has lived for so long in diplomatic society without noticing a missing key or a document out of place he may think that his security is in order or that if somebody else warns him that person is being an alarmist. He may regard a warning as a reflection on his character. That is what happened in this case—it was before the war."

"Then somebody warned the Ambassador——"

"Oh yes, but he was fairly haughty about it. No matter what arguments were used, he would not get rid of the man. There was no proof against the valet. It was very worrying. He refused to part with him."

"Suppose the Permanent Under-Secretary——"

"Yes, but it's ticklish going over a man's head in his own service. Something else happened."

By now I had forgotten Ankara in the story of the Ambassador's pearls.

"Some people say the British Intelligence Service is very stupid. Others say it is good. I wouldn't know. I don't suppose they would either. I wonder if anyone does. But the Ambassador's daughter was going to be married and the family pearls were brought out from England. The Ambassador kept them in his bedroom against the day when he would bestow them on his daughter. Do you know, they vanished out of his bedroom——? Who could it have been? Of course, suspicion fell upon the butler. There was not a bit of proof in the matter, either; but this time the Ambassador was quite firm—and the butler went. There was no other servant who could be suspected in the same degree. Oddly enough the pearls were recovered soon afterwards—in time for the wedding."

"Sounds very odd," I ventured.

"Odd is the word—but the main thing is that the butler went. . . . Yes, that was long before the days of Cicero."

"I am interested in the activities of the German espionage in Turkey," I said. "Can you suggest why, for instance, Admiral Canaris should have employed deaf mutes, particularly in Ankara?"

"Did he, eh? Poor old Knatchbull! First of all Cicero, and then be followed around by deaf mutes. Sounds eerie, doesn't it?"

"Not followed around, watched in restaurants. Reading his lips—a German Abwehr officer told me about it."

"Ah, yes." The security man nodded slowly. "I see some sense in that. In Ankara there's only about three restaurants he could go to. Not like Madrid or Istanbul!" Here he pulled out a scrap of paper and began to trace out a sketch map of Ataturk's capital.

When Kemal Ataturk moved his capital from Istanbul into Asia Minor, he dragged the diplomatic corps after him up the three-thousand-foot plateau on which stood Ankara, hot and dry in the summer and severely cold in winter. It was a new city, though the ruins of the citadel were pre-Hittite, and its whole life went up and down the three-mile length of acacia avenue that was called the Boulevard Ataturk. In the older and grander embassies and legations of Istanbul, the Consuls-General and their staffs and the naval attachés spread themselves after the Chanceries had moved to Ankara and enjoyed the cosmopolitan life of the Porte. The Ambassadors came down to Istanbul in the summer months; although it was just as hot as Ankara, there were sea breezes.

The new embassies and legations in Ankara were all grouped round the Boulevard Ataturk. The British Embassy, then consisting of a residence and a chancery in a sort of compound of several acres, stood on a hill at the eastern end not far from the President's palace. The Swiss and Czechoslovak are nearby, the French and American Embassies set a little back from the boulevard across the way from the Poles, the Persians, the Chinese, the Iraquis and the Brazilians. The Italian and German compounds lie on the south side of the boulevard adjacent to the Soviet Embassy. Further west, on the north side of the boulevard, the Greeks, Dutch and Belgians, and then the only restaurants of Ankara, Soruia, or Serge's, open in winter only, Papa Karpics, and, near the Palace Hotel, Phaia and the Station Restaurant. Now no British ambassador could ever dine at a place called the Station Restaurant however good the food, so that the choice was narrowed down to three. Papa Karpics was a favourite resort; the German diplomats and the British both frequented it. Herr von Papen and Sir Hugh Knatchbull-Huguessen sometimes found themselves dining there on the same night. That is how Ankara lived, all in one place or the other. If you stood at a window and looked out at the Boulevard Ataturk, you would see in one day all the diplomats and officials who mattered in Turkey passing up and down. So one of the diplomats christened it "The Rat Run".

Turkey lay athwart the path of Germany to the oil wells of the Middle East and the delta. This friend and later ally of Britain, staunch, discreet and immensely valuable even in neutrality, was perhaps the greatest acquisition to the British side between the two wars when we gave up the friendship of Japan to reassure America and lost our influence in Italy. The firm neutral attitude of Turkey deflected Hitler from the road to Baghdad and the Persian Gulf and was a powerful factor in bringing about the clash between Germany and Russia. Yet Turkey watched this gigantic struggle disconsolately, because, whichever side won, she would suffer for it. The security of Turkey was best guaranteed if Germany and Russia were of fairly equal strength. Such was the view that a senior British officer in Turkey wishes to report home, and when His Excellency disagreed with him, he remarked: "The only reason for

not sending home this telegram is that the argument is obvious."
Turkey feared the defeat of either side and was almost tempted
to enter the war against Germany in order to save the Balkans
from Russian domination.

Mr. Churchill and President Inonu met secretly in Adana in
January 1943 and discussed the security of Turkey and how
she might be defensively equipped from the arsenals of the
Middle East. General Sir Alan Brooke, Chief of the Imperial
General Staff, and Sir Alexander Cadogan were present. The
year 1943 rolled by and Allied victories mounted. Mussolini
resigned in July and was arrested; Italy surrendered in September. President Roosevelt, Mr. Churchill and General
Chiang Kai-Shek met in Cairo on November 22nd to agree
upon future operations against Japan. The meeting with
Stalin at Teheran took place a week later. Stalin was angry and
impatient that there should be no second front yet, and he
definitely did not want such a front to start in the Balkans.
He was emphatic that there must be a direct assault in
Western Europe, and President Roosevelt was inclined to see his
arguments. To pacify him, Mr. Churchill gave a rough outline
of Operation Overlord, the invasion plan for Western Europe.
According to the Royal Institute of International Affairs'
Chronology of the War, "the approximate date of invasion of
Western Europe was decided" at Teheran.

Then the scene shifted to Cairo again, where President
Roosevelt, Mr. Churchill and President Inonu met, with
Harry Hopkins, Mr. Eden, the Turkish Foreign Minister, M.
Menemenjoglu and Sir Hugh Knatchbull-Huguessen present.
Mr. Churchill discussed with the Turkish President the pos-
sibility of secretly placing 7,500 British service personnel at
Turkish airfields as a preliminary to Turkey entering the war.
It is disturbing to think that the minutes of some of these
meetings and the outline of Operation Overlord should have
fallen almost at once into the hands of the Germans. "The
results of the Teheran Conference were soon known to Hitler,
but he failed to draw the proper conclusions," writes General
Hans Speidel, Rommel's last Chief of Staff.[1] How did it happen?

An Albanian valet, named Diello, in the service of Sir Hugh
Knatchbull-Huguessen made himself known mysteriously to
the German Security Service agent in Ankara, L. C. Moyzisch.

[1] *Invasion 1944.*

Herr von Papen thought of the code name of Cicero for him and his services were accepted. Cicero kept the Germans supplied with films of documents that he had extracted by night from the Ambassador's dispatch box and photographed. From October 1943 until April 1944 Cicero brought Moyzisch rolls of film for which he was paid £20,000 and £15,000 a time, mostly in counterfeit sterling banknotes. So the Foreign Office most secret dispatches were betrayed one after another to the Germans as fast as the cipher signals went out from London. Moyzisch reported home to Berlin in person during November 1943, so interested were the big men of the Third Reich in the Cicero papers. He found Ribbentrop coldly sceptical and unwilling to believe the contents of telegrams that outlined the immense Anglo-American war effort and their concerted strategy, in which his own doom was written. Among them lay the outline of Operation Overlord mentioned by its code name—the invasion of Normandy. Ernst Kaltenbrunner, a big scarred fellow with an evil temper, the successor to Heydrich as Chief of the Security Service, wanted to know all he could about this Albanian and what his motives were. He was powerful enough to take over "Cicero" from Ribbentrop as a "Security Service matter". Moyzisch noticed his violent dislike for Ribbentrop, his temper; he, too, noticed his huge hands. The fat, sallow Albanian, who nursed a grudge against the British because an Englishman had accidentally killed his father during a shooting party, continued to slip away from the British compound in the evening and carry his rolls of film down to agreed meeting places, where Moyzisch waited for him with rolls of bank and counterfeit notes. The Cicero documents continued to flow in until the Turks became suspicious that Herr von Papen knew an amazing amount about their secret understandings with the British. Then another rat ran, in the other direction—Moyzisch's own secretary, Elizabeth Kapp, opening a diplomatic bag for him, came upon a letter from Berlin in which Cicero was mentioned. She was spying on Moyzisch for the British, so it seems, and perhaps for the Americans also. The secret of Cicero became suddenly in danger of discovery. The plump Albanian fled from Ankara with his German forged banknotes, leaving the British Embassy in no doubt any longer how it was that Herr von Papen had known of the plans to infiltrate British flying personnel into Turkey, and adding up, with consternation, the state secrets that must have been lost this way. A new security officer was attached to the British Embassy in Ankara. All sorts of precautions were taken now that the rat had run.

"Ambassadors can be careless," it was Paul Leverkuehn, the principal German intelligence officer in Turkey, telling his side of the story, as we sat in a Greek restaurant in London. Nearby there hung a portrait of the old Greek hero, Admiral Konstantin Kanaris. The waiter brought us a carafe of Spartan wine.

"I mean von Papen this time." Leverkuehn, former German assistant military attaché in Istanbul, returned to his respectable peacetime profession of the law, thought back to the days when Herr von Papen gave away to the Turkish Foreign Minister how much he had learned about the Turkish military agreements with the Allies.

"Hitler placed von Papen in Ankara so that he might sound the Allies on a peace solution," Leverkuehn concluded.

"But he never trusted Papen and never let the entire Papen family out of Germany at any one time," said Thomas Marffy, one of the Hungarian diplomats in Ankara. "As for Cicero, I believe he was really a Turkish agent making a little on the side."

CHAPTER XXI

CONSTANTINOPLE

THE CHIEF GERMAN intelligence officer in Turkey, Dr. Paul Leverkuehn, was a tall, studious, soft-spoken lawyer with the polish of a German who has lived several years in America. He was a student of Moslem countries and had spent part of the First World War in northern Persia. General Warlimont of the High Command picked him out in the winter of 1939 for a special mission to Persia. Warlimont feared that General Weygand with the French army in Syria would strike through Asia Minor at the Russian oilfields of Baku and destroy one of the main German sources of oil— the oil with which Stalin was buying off Hitler. Leverkuehn travelled through Russia by rail to reach Persia, where he remained in a consular post until German consuls were banished from that vital transit land for lease-lend goods. He reported to Warlimont early in 1940 that there was a real threat to Baku—the British were studying naval and air attack, the French a land march on Baku from Syria. Soon, by the irony of war, the Germans would be plotting to destroy Baku, and the Canaris agent who protected the Ploesti wells from the British, Herr Kuechler, would be ordered to plan operations against the Russian wells.

Captain Leverkuehn was reporting one day in 1942 to a military conference in Sofia, when he noticed that Admiral Canaris was looking at him very intently. His report had been uncomfortably frank and had implied criticisms of German direction of the war. That summer Leverkuehn was in Berlin and was ordered to report to the Chief of Intelligence.

"Very bright, animated and talkative, like a little old lady! He had an extraordinary disregard for military conventions," so Leverkuehn described him. He noticed a characteristic of the family. Canaris had thin blood and was always shivering even in the heat of the Berlin summer of 1942. He wore a naval great-coat as they drove together through Berlin. The wide-brimmed

Panama hat that Leverkuehn was wearing pleased the Admiral so much that he seized it and put it on in place of his uniform cap. So they rode on together, the Admiral quietly enjoying the novelty of his headgear.

"Then he asked me whom I would recommend for this or that intelligence post—quite regardless of the fact that I was a mere captain and these were the posts of colonels and generals. That was entirely unheard of in the German forces."

They drove to the villa in Schlachtensee for lunch, where Leverkuehn saw a modest good taste in his style of living. He remembered a coloured print on the office wall of Konstantin Kanaris in flowing dress with a scimitar in his hand. In the villa a parrot stood and chattered on a perch; on a music stand lay a flute. Canaris talked at length to his dachshunds, a maddening habit sometimes, said Leverkuehn, if you had a whole range of subjects to discuss with him.

Canaris asked Leverkuehn to go to Istanbul and organise his intelligence service for Turkey. To those who imagine the Abwehr as a thorough and efficient organisation, it will be of interest that Leverkuehn set up his service in an empty room of the big German Embassy building in Istanbul, without a secretary, without register or indexes, and without a typewriter. He did not attempt to create a system of German-born agents, but used the material that lay to hand, émigré Austrians, Turkish political leaders, small Moslem sects who served him with the zeal of hatred because the British were using Levantines and Armenians for preference. Finally he came into collaboration with the Turkish Intelligence Service and interrogated some of their Russian security suspects. What did the Turks get out of it? They listened and noted from the sort of questions he asked what it was that the Germans sought to know about Russia.

"Canaris had never spoken a word to me about peace negotiations," said Leverkuehn, "but I have no doubt now that he posted me to Istanbul to take up whatever threads might be put in my hand. He knew that one of my American friends of pre-war days was General William Donovan who became Chief of U.S. Strategic Services."

As Leverkuehn's work grew more exacting, he asked for an assistant and was sent the son of an old friend and business associate of Hamburg, young Erich Vermehren, son of Dr.

Kurt Vermehren. Erich came to Istanbul with his wife, née Countess Plettenberg, a woman of redoubtable intelligence and energy with emphatic religious views. The Abwehr thought that she would work with the Christian minorities in Turkey, just as Leverkuehn had worked with the Moslems. This pale, rather stolid young man with an obstinate chin and a singular, sceptical mind had been proposed before the war for a Rhodes scholarship and turned down on the grounds of his negative attitude to National Socialism.

Leverkuehn does not know of any peace approaches in Ankara or Istanbul earlier than 1943. Canaris went to Turkey twice during the war, and Helmuth von Moltke, one of his assistants, also visited Turkey twice early in the war.

"Then you passed no message from Canaris to George Earle?"

"No."

"Perhaps Moltke did."

"It was about the time of the Stalingrad disaster that the first peace feelers reached me from the Americans," said Leverkuehn. "An intermediary came to me——"

"From George Earle?" I asked.

"Yes, that is it. They complained that it was so hard to find common ground with Germany. The Germans had no good word to say for any living American. Could we not at least say a friendly word about a dead man. I told the Ambassador about this approach and Herr von Papen composed a little speech for our war memorial ceremony in February.

"We have always had great esteem," said Papen, "for the men who made history across the ocean, and created the land of unlimited opportunity through their initiative and dynamism. We bow to Washington, Abraham Lincoln, Monroe and many others. But we would not find it unfitting if the Monroe doctrine were extended to Europe."

The last remarks were meant to mollify Ribbentrop, but he was angry and mistrustful. The Kremlin listened. It was deeply suspicious that Papen aimed at a separate peace with the West. An attempt had already been made on the life of Papen in Ankara on February 24th, 1942, by an obscure agent whose defective bomb blew himself up instead. The Turkish police discovered indication in his mangled remains that he was a Russian, and his two Russian accomplices, Pavlov and Komilaff, were sentenced to imprisonment.

"The next contact came from the Turkish Foreign Minister, Numan Menemenjoglu," related Leverkuehn. "He told Papen in March 1943 that Cardinal Spellman would visit American churches in the Middle East as Roman Catholic primate of America and would like to speak with Papen or a man who possessed his confidence. Herr Moyzisch, the security officer at the Embassy, got to hear of this offer, so Papen was obliged to report it to Ribbentrop and suggested that I should take up this invitation. There was a sour negative reply from Ribbentrop that 'it was no use discussing peace' and a violent reaction from Papen who cabled that he saw no sense in that case in maintaining missions abroad.

"There was another message from George Earle in April 1944, that was transmitted to me in Germany. He let me know that Allied preparations to invade Europe were technically so complete that the invasion must succeed, but victory in the West must also mean victory in the East and the end of European civilisation. Was there then no possibility for another talk about a solution? I reported this to Colonel Hansen, the new chief of Military Intelligence, but I was not allowed to return to Turkey. The talks were conducted with Herr von Lersner who was living in Istanbul as President of the German Orient Society, and I believe that Herr von Papen had talks with Americans also."

In the meanwhile an awkward mishap had overtaken the German Intelligence Service in Istanbul.

It was the business of the German Abwehr office in Istanbul to pass out genuine and spurious information to the British, to serve certain purposes and perhaps gain some goodwill. But in this dangerous contact with the enemy inward loyalty meant everything. Every man in the German consulate and attaché group in Istanbul watched his neighbour. Was X really spying on the British, or was he working with them? Vermehren was already known to the Gestapo for his negative attitude to National Socialism, and when it become a question of his returning to Germany fear for his wife and himself seized him and he took up contact with the British with the idea of finding refuge with the Allies.

The British Secret Service decided to spirit the Vermehrens away, giving the affair a mysterious aspect so that the Germans could hardly guess whether this was a "Night and Fog" action or a simple desertion, but news of the scandal leaked out to the Allied press and tactics had to be changed. *The Times* reported Vermehren's defection and subsequently published extracts of a statement by him under the sarcastic heading "A German and his Conscience".

Vermehren had high ideas of putting his knowledge at the service of a propaganda campaign against Hitler. "You will not find the same understanding in London," the British officials warned him, "as you have found out here. You may be disappointed." He wanted to go, nevertheless.

This was a scandal that shook Germany, not so much because there were not other traitors stirring. The Ernst Kaltenbrunner Security Service could afford to lose Moyzisch's secretary, Nelly Kapp, "Elizabeth" to the Allies, without being weakened but Canaris and the Abwehr were in a precarious position. We shall see how this incident of Vermehren was used by Hitler for his own designs.

The Germans related among themselves that Vermehren had run with the code books of the Abwehr.

"Did you take the code books with you?" I asked him years afterwards when we met at a London dinner party.

"No, I did not take the code books," he said emphatically, and I naturally accept his word in this matter.

His wife, the Countess Elizabeth, upright, incisive, dressed in stiff gold brocade, led the conversation.

"Ah, Canaris," she said, smiling, "him and his dogs!"

German society in Berlin talked for days of nothing else than the defection of the Vermehrens. In gossip they ascribed it to the religious antipathy of the Countess Vermehren towards the Third Reich. The story circulated that the Vermehrens had been approached by a distinguished member of the Trinity and warned to flee from the damned state of Germany, "but," said the Voice as they were about to leave, "do not forget to take the code books with you."

So these two fled from Asia Minor from the city of light opera in the intelligence war, where British and German intelligence agents met by moonlight or lamplight and tried to guess who was fooling whom; and Greeks, Albanians, Levantines, Turks, Austrians, Bulgarians, Italians came and went across the Bosphorus. The Vermehrens hoped that they would be able to achieve some understanding and enlighten some of their own people from an independent position outside Germany, but, like many human purposes that run counter to destiny, the effect of their striving was the opposite to what was intended. The force within Germany that was secretly working for peace was shaken.

"Vermehren tells me he did not take any code books," I said to Leverkuehn when he had finished his narrative.

"Yes," replied Leverkuehn, "I have met Vermehren and had it out with him. He had every right to save himself. They were really in danger from the Gestapo."

"What did the Countess mean about the dogs?"

"Ah, that will be the dachshunds. You see, when he travelled, Canaris often used to book a double room and the dogs slept on the other bed."

"That's not at all the German way with dogs."

"He could be quite infuriating the way he talked about them——"

"And the stories of high treason?"

"The Admiral and I became good friends, but he never even spoke of secret peace talks to me. He may have informed neutrals and through them the Allies of some facts that he wanted them to know for reasons of high policy."

"The truth, in fact!"

"Oh yes, when some salutary counter-action could be hoped for—he wouldn't just give away military information like a common spy."

"He didn't get much credit for his intentions—from either side."

"Perhaps not, but if you write about him, try to make this clear. He saw quite clearly what he was doing and why he was doing it. Maybe the British expected more action of him; but violence was not in his nature. I hope you will make a true portrait of him, because we loved him although he was the most difficult chief in the world. He had that greatness of mind that we cannot find today to start up a new intelligence service."

CHAPTER XXII

A UNIFIED SECRET SERVICE

THE IRRITATING RAIDS of the Mosquitoes on Berlin gave way on the night of August 23rd–24th, 1943, to a large bomber raid, in which 1,700 tons were dropped on the capital. Hitler walked up and down the corridors of the shelter under the Reich Chancellery and spoke his thoughts to Martin Bormann. Perhaps this first big raid on Berlin brought something home to him.

"I wonder how that little outfit of Admiral Canaris is doing," he mused. "I don't seem to have heard anything from him for a long time."

Martin Bormann conveyed these words to the Intelligence Service, and Colonel Jenke, the adjutant, remembers how the Admiral exclaimed:

"You see, he wants something from me." When he had thought again he remarked: "But what use is it really?"

The entourage had driven Canaris away, said Jenke, because they disliked his reports. Perhaps Hitler disliked them, too, and Canaris knew that the entourage was really the pack of yes-men that Hitler wanted. Hitler could not reproach him for inadequate results. The Fuehrer made a remark in his Reichstag speech on December 11th, 1941, that if he had not known beforehand exactly how strong the Russian Army was on his Eastern front, since the campaign he had seen from their offensive dispositions how justified his action was; but when Canaris called on him with his back reports to expostulate that he had given the exact order of battle in advance as far back as the Urals, Hitler smiled. He said that he knew and appreciated the Admiral's intelligence, but that he had to make that statement for political reasons. "No nation went to war with such complete information about the enemy as we have had about Russia," Canaris told his own staff. Hitler dismissed his Commander-in-Chief of the Army when he failed to reach Moscow in the first year and did not replace von Brauchitsch. In the following year Canaris was as gloomy about the Caucasus offensive as he had been about the attempt to reach Moscow. He relinquished the duty of making the situation reports on the Eastern Front to his deputy, the Chief of the Foreign Intelligence branch (Amt Ausland Abwehr), Vice-Admiral Bürckner, who unfortunately conformed to Fuehrer Headquarters standards. Jenke remembers him fussing round the intelligence map as it was being prepared for the Fuehrer with blue flags for the German units and red flags for the Russian saying:

"Ach, don't put so much red on the map!"

Did Hitler sense that the greater betrayal came from creatures of his own liking? "What is that little outfit of Admiral Canaris up to—I haven't heard from him for a long time?"

The Intelligence Headquarters moved south of Berlin to Zossen, where lay Army High Command Headquarters. There were two huge concrete citadels separated from each other by a cordon—they were known as Maibach I and Maibach II. The General Staff occupied Maibach I and the Intelligence Service was put in Maibach II. Even intelligence officers could not pass the barrier into Maibach I without a special pass. Each citadel had three storeys above ground and three below, and every room had its replica below ground with a branch telephone plug, so that when an air-raid alert sounded the staff could remove its telephones, descend three storeys and begin work again without interruption. A small cottage stood in the grounds of Maibach I, the residence of the Chief of German General Staff, Colonel-General Franz Halder. It was known as Halder's cottage. Halder lent it to Canaris and he lived there snugly and safely, for the S.S. was not allowed into the Maibach complex. His adjutant noticed how Canaris disliked leaving Halder's cottage and venturing to Berlin or East Prussia. He felt himself perpetually watched outside the citadel. He was afraid for his life. He forsook his abstemious habits and his one glass of red wine and began to drink rather more than his nervous system would stand.

The commotion about Erich Vermehren and his wife would not by itself have upset the precarious footing of the German Intelligence Service. A whole series of misfortunes and curious incidents occurred throughout 1942 and 1943. The Vermehren affair was only the culminating blow at the authority of Canaris.

The adroit Josef Mueller came and went between Munich and Rome without hindrance from September 1939 up to December 1942. Colonel Helferrich, the intelligence liaison officer in Rome who suspected his motives, had been moved at the orders of Canaris. Otto John, an authority on the German Abwehr, tells me that a cautious question from a cleric in the entourage of the Pope about the standing of Mueller in Germany filtered through to the Gestapo and put them on their guard again. In December 1942 Customs officials in Prague detained an Abwehr agent named Schmidt-huber on suspicion that he was involved in currency offences. Schmidthuber confessed to carrying money on behalf of the Abwehr and explained that there was a group of generals who were sounding the Allies through the Vatican as to peace terms. He mentioned the names of Oster and von Dohnanyi of Canaris's own office as being concerned in this affair. He was himself attached to the Munich office of the Abwehr. Mueller of the Gestapo was at once acquainted with the case. He sent a criminal inspector to work with a Colonel Roder of the Judge Advocate General's department. They started slowly, and it was April 1943 before they first visited Canaris and obtained his permission to search the office of Dohnanyi. There they discovered a file lying about in which a Pastor Dietrich Bonhoeffer, known to the Gestapo as an opponent of National Socialism, was recommended for exemption from military service because of his valuable foreign contacts. (Bonhoeffer had secretly met the Bishop of Chichester in Stockholm and informed him in some detail of an impending plot against the life of Hitler, but there was no inkling of this in the file.) Dohnanyi and Pastor Bonhoeffer were arrested, General Oster was removed from his appointment, and then Josef Mueller was put under military arrest.

"I appeared before court-martial," he told me, "on charges of treasonable activities and undermining the war effort. My line of defence was that I had taken part in talks about peace, which as an intelligence officer I was qualified to do, but that I had not undertaken any negotiations. Now there was no documentary evidence whatsoever in Gestapo hands to show that there had been negotiations with the Allies. The draft proposals that I had brought from Rome lay safely in the steel chest of Colonel Schrader, a trusted friend of Admiral Canaris, in Army Command Headquarters.

"I said to the court, conducting my own defence, either I was absolutely innocent or entirely guilty and that I demanded acquittal or the death penalty. The court acquitted me, but I was kept in military arrest because the Gestapo would otherwise have taken me into custody for special interrogation."

Canaris had his first official conference with Ernst Kaltenbrunner in Munich in February 1943, when these investigations were still not completed. It so happened that two students, one a girl, had just been hanged at Munich University for making propaganda against the regime out of the Stalingrad disaster. The Admiral found Kaltenbrunner wary and critical. Though less cunning than his predecessor, Heydrich, he was a grim and uncouth opponent. Canaris sized up the broad shoulders, massive head and thin violent eyes and was consternated by the size of his hand; "real murderer's paws," he described them to one of his officers afterwards. Kaltenbrunner criticised one of Canaris's men, the Chief Intelligence Officer of Vienna, Count Marogna-Redwitz. He asserted that the count was in close touch with the Conservative opposition in Hungary and was on friendly terms with suspect members of the Hungarian Intelligence Service marked for their pro-British attitude.

Kaltenbrunner was in fact implying that a senior member of the German Intelligence Service was in touch with such persons as were most likely to be themselves in touch with the British.

His officers noticed that Canaris reacted instantly, speaking in the rapid, persuasive manner that he showed when excited. There were, he argued, the very best reasons for watching Hungarians of all parties. The duties of an intelligence officer demanded that he should have some knowledge of the activities of all groups. It seemed as if Kaltenbrunner was partly reassured.

"The Hungarian Intelligence Service never lost touch with the British throughout the war," a senior Hungarian diplomat told me when I mentioned this incident. "It is easy to understand the menace that Kaltenbrunner's criticisms embodied. Hungary kept such good contact with the British that we

signed articles of surrender on board Sir Hugh Knatchbull-
Huguessen's yacht off Istanbul in October 1943—eighteen
months before surrender was actually possible."

Ulein-Revicky, Hungarian minister in Stockholm, who
maintained contact with the British during the latter years of
the war, has added a detail to my picture of Hungary. "The
General Staff was pro-German," he told me, "the Ministry
of the Interior was pro-British. The friends of Canaris were in
the latter Ministry."

The contacts with the Vatican had been scented, the activities
with the Hungarians noticed, his Protestant emissary to
Stockholm had been arrested. His man in Istanbul, Dr. Paul
Leverkuehn, was in constant danger of being accused of
indiscretion or treason. Canaris must have had nerves of quite
unusual resilience to pursue his course against Hitler.

"Oh yes, Admiral Canaris warned Switzerland again in
October 1942." August Lindt, the press attaché of the Swiss
Legation in London told me. When Ribbentrop was at length
convinced that the Allies would soon be thrusting at the "soft
underbelly of the Axis," the position of neutral Switzerland
attracted his blundering attention. He sent a questionnaire to
the German Minister in Berne instructing him to report what
reserves of food and raw materials Switzerland possessed. No
doubt Ribbentrop thought of another bloodless occupation
for which the Allies could be blamed. A little advantage would
be gained by possessing this linking territory between the
Italian front and Germany. The German Minister in Berne,
Dr. Köcher, emphasised the hardy and soldierly character of
the Swiss people and the strength of their national redoubt in
the mountains. There was contact thereupon with Canaris's
men in Berne, and the Councillor, Dr. Theo Kordt, informed
the Intelligence Chief what was afoot. Thereupon Canaris
sent a warning to the Swiss Government. The danger may not
have been imminent. He wanted to omit nothing that would
help to shorten the war.

We have already seen that the Allies achieved surprise in
their North African landings. They achieved surprise on the
Anzio beachheads in January 1944.

"Canaris was a bad intelligence officer," said General
Westphal, one of Rommel's Staff officers, when asked for his
opinion about the Admiral. "I recollect that just before the

Anzio landings I asked him where the British battleships were.

"'We are looking after them—don't you worry,' answered the Admiral, but he gave no positive answer on their whereabouts.

"When they appeared in support of the Anzio landings immediately afterwards, we knew where the British battleships were. That's why I say he was a bad intelligence officer."

Doubtless the Admiral was genuinely unaware that Anzio was impending. I find it hard to believe the same of North Africa. Herbert Wichmann from Hamburg, perhaps in the face of conflicting reports, gave him the correct destination of the "Torch" convoys. Maybe Canaris had an idea, too, but simply let the General Staff and the High Command draw their own conclusions. It is positive that he knew of the impending defection of Italy and made a point of reporting to the S.D. in the opposite sense. It is impossible to say whether he knew of Count Grandi's visit to Portugal to treat with the Allies; but he was on the most friendly terms with his Italian colleague, the Chief of Servizio Informazione Militare, General Cesare Amé. It appears that Canaris was acting like a man who is trying to demolish a condemned building by dismantling the roof first and then the topmost stones, Bulgaria, Italy, Hungary, so that the final collapse would be less disastrous, whereas others were intent on keeping every stone together so that when the foundations went the collapse would be all the more disastrous.

Mussolini resigned and was arrested on July 25th after a vote of censure by the Fascist Grand Council. It was then a delicate matter for Hitler whether to believe the professions of King Victor Emanuel and Marshal Badoglio. He could ill afford to disarm his Italian ally while Italy was still fighting the Allies; but he brooded over plans to kidnap the King of Italy and the Pope and to free Mussolini. Skorzeny was able to carry out the last of these plans for him. Canaris, when he heard that such plans were in the mind of his Fuehrer, decided that he himself could very well make a personal journey to Italy on the pretext of assessing the will of Italy to resist, but General Lahousen tells me that his purpose was to warn the Italians of the Fuehrer's intentions.

So he arrived at Venice in August 1943 and stayed at the Danieli, the same hotel where he had met and persuaded the Rumanians in 1940 to let him infiltrate Germans into Ploesti as a guard for the oil wells. The scene had changed mightily in those three years.

Amé, a tall blond Tyrolean type, slow of speech and more German in appearance than Italian, brought a number of his officers to Venice. Canaris was accompanied by Lahousen, who was about to leave him and go to field duties, and Colonel von Freytag-Loringhaven, who would take over from Lahousen Department II of the Intelligence.

Lahousen relates that there was a large and formal breakfast at the Hotel Danieli. Canaris and Amé went alone to the Lido that afternoon and spent an hour and a half together. It was during this time at the Lido that Canaris warned his friend of the kidnapping plans. He indicated to Lahousen on his return that the warning had been given and that Amé for his part had been equally frank with him. Capitulation was in the air. Italy was about to change sides. Amé and Canaris met next day for a formal leave-taking in the presence of their assembled staffs. The Italian loudly and clearly assured the Germans that the brotherhood in arms was sacred and inviolable and that Italy was determined to resist to the utmost by the side of Germany the onslaught of the Anglo-American powers. Canaris heard him out with wonderful seriousness in the presence of them all.

Back at Zossen Canaris sat at dinner table and regaled Ernst Kaltenbrunner and Walther Huppenkothen with his memories of Italy. Huppenkothen remembered and noted in his report how Canaris emphasised that General Amé had assured him personally that he considered it out of the question that Italy should take independent steps to end the war. Huppenkothen noted also that after the surrender of Italy on September 8th, 1943, Canaris told a slightly different story to Schellenberg, the S.S. deputy intelligence chief. He passed Schellenberg a thick bundle of all the reports he had ever made to Keitel on the unreliability of Italy as an ally and the intrigues of the Italian General Staff for a separate peace. Amé? Well yes, he had since learned that Amé had been sent to command a division immediately after the Venice meeting. Badoglio had returned him to field duties, but he, Canaris, had been told that Amé disappeared on his way to his new appointment and assumed that he had been murdered by the anti-German party.

In what silence or with what disbelieving stares Schellenberg heard this story, Huppenkothen does not say.

If the treachery of Italy did not come entirely as a surprise and the S.S. was able to round up and transport to Germany large numbers of Allied prisoners of war in Italian camps, it was due to other information than that which Canaris brought back from his personal visit to Italy. The Intelligence Division of the British Control Commission interrogated an Abwehr specialist officer in 1947 who had been at a Wehrmacht listening post in France on September 1943 picking up Allied signals. The Germans had managed to master the secret of the P.E. or scrambler telephone that blurs all conversation to thwart "tapping" and only restores it to articulate sounds through a special attachment at the receiving end. This is secure enough if the line used is a telephone cable, to which it would be unlikely that a spy could attach the bulky unscrambling apparatus. But if the telephone conversation is beamed by wireless, a variable "unscrambling" instrument in enemy territory could be fairly quickly attuned to the same frequency as the two other P.E. sets.

Thus it was that the German Abwehr in the Pas de Calais picked up a scrambler telephone conversation between President Roosevelt and Mr. Churchill that had been passed over the transatlantic wireless link instead of the cable unknown to the two war leaders. There was a guarded reference in their conversation to "arming our prisoners".

"This made it plain to me," the Abwehr officer told the Intelligence Division of the British Control Commission, "that the defection of Italy was at hand; there was an S.D. man beside me reading every word I wrote down."

As Russia advanced in the East and Kesselring fell back out of Italy, the drawing-room Fronde in Berlin grew more vocal and in January 1944 the Gestapo pounced on a group of disaffected Germans. A Gestapo agent informed against Frau Solf, widow of the former German Ambassador to Japan, after being at a tea party in her home. There had been present among other disaffected persons a retired diplomat, Otto Kiep, who was at the time one of Canaris's subordinates, attached for war duties.

G

Count Helmut von Moltke and his friends were arrested as a consequence of this. General Oster had been finally relieved of all intelligence work and retired in December 1943. Then Kiep was arrested. After that the Vermehrens and then two other agents fled from Istanbul to Cairo. Yet the final rupture between Hitler and Canaris did not simply arise out of a desertion or unorthodox peace talks. He had been careful to pass on to the High Command or to Ribbentrop reports on any new peace soundings from unknown quarters—lest by failing to do so he should fall into a trap set for him by Kaltenbrunner. Thus in 1943, when Madame Kollontai, the Soviet Ambassador in Stockholm, started talks with the Abwehr in the hope of discovering a military group that would make peace with Russia, Canaris passed on his man's report to the angry and suspicious Ribbentrop, who nevertheless took some further bearings on this peace offer.

The fact that a Jew was the intermediary between Madame Kollontai and Wagner, the German intelligence officer in Stockholm, did not deter Ribbentrop.

Richard Protze was told by Canaris himself of the last big storm that rose over his reports on Russia. Hitler, perhaps primed on his defeatist views, ordered him to report on the situation on the Russian front. Canaris arrived with a bundle of intelligence reports and began to describe the military situation. Hitler watched him as he spoke for some time, Himmler stood by. Suddenly Hitler sprang forward, overturning the table and seized the Admiral by the lapel.

"Are you trying to tell me that I am going to lose this war?" he yelled.

"Mein Fuehrer, I have said nothing about losing the war. I have tried to explain the military situation on the Russian front."

This may have been the same occasion as Canaris was overwhelmed with abuse about the desertion of Vermehren and the peace talks of Leverkuehn. At any rate he was dismissed the presence and told to leave his intelligence behind.

Hitler's patience was exhausted. He spoke savagely of "typical Canaris men" in foreign posts. Kaltenbrunner and Schellenberg closed in on the Abwehr. After conferences with Himmler, Keitel and Jodl, the text of a Fuehrer decree was submitted to Hitler and signed by him. Huppenkothen quotes it as follows:

(1) I order the establishment of a unified German secret intelligence service.

(2) I appoint the Reichsfuehrer S.S. to command the secret
service. He will agree with the Chief of High Command on
what conditions the military intelligence service is to be
incorporated in the secret service.

"Is there anything else you require?" asked Hitler when
Kaltenbrunner showed him the scheme for the new unified
intelligence organisation, and Kaltenbrunner promptly laid
claim to the intelligence service of the Foreign Ministry. But
that would have gone against Hitler's own policy of "divide and
rule".

Canaris ceased to be Chief of Military Intelligence in
February 1944, a little more than nine years after taking up the
appointment, but to cover the real causes for his dismissal an
economic job was found for him in the Wehrmacht. Kaltenbrunner took over in such haste that Canaris had no time to
make the turnover of duties required by the customs of the
service. The faithful Jenke flitted round the secretaries to
ascertain that no portions of the Admiral's diary were left
behind. The S.D. were now in the Maibach citadel, next to the
General Staff. They ordered Canaris to leave the Halder cottage
and not return to it.

He sat alone in his Schlachtensee villa, and the military
intelligence service that he had held together disintegrated
rapidly.

"When the Admiral was no longer there," said Richard
Protze sadly, "I no longer forwarded everything to Berlin from
my intelligence office in Holland. We had no confidence in the
service without him."

"Canaris was unprotected," said Willy Jenke. "He was afraid
for his life, and yet he would not budge. We urged him to flee
to Spain with his wife and family. General Franco would have
seen to his safety. The Military Intelligence could have put an
aircraft at his disposal; but he would not go."

Jenke shook his head as he recalled his vain arguments with
the Admiral, who was facing up to calamity, and prepared
to atone for the crimes of his countrymen.

CHAPTER XXIII

OPERATION VALKYRIE

THE GERMAN FRONT in Normandy was strained to breaking point in the middle of July 1944 and the Russian armies were lapping through Rumania and Poland towards the Reich. At last the younger men of the German Army took action into their own hands. Colonel von Stauffenberg, who had gone home from the war in Africa after losing an arm, an eye and two fingers from his remaining hand, was not the ideal man to manage an attempt to blow up Hitler, but the Fuehrer had withdrawn so much upon himself in the "Wolf's Lair", the name for his East Prussian headquarters at Rastenburg, or in his Berchtesgaden enclave, that it was very difficult for anyone to approach him. His own entourage had been carefully chosen by the Personnel Office of the Army and most of them fell under his strong hypnotic influence. The conspirators whom the course of war had sometimes brought together and sometimes scattered again had managed to draw up an operational plan for seizing power in Germany which they sent out in sealed envelopes to be opened only on receipt of the code word "Valkyrie". It went to the Headquarters of Military Districts from the Headquarters of Home Forces which was commanded by General Fromm. His Chief of Staff was this same Colonel Klaus Schenck von Stauffenberg.[1] The conspirators had at times been very few; but now that the situation was boiling up it became alarming to them how many adherents came in. Everybody wanted to bring his friend and actually quarrelled over the ministerial posts before the coup was even ready. The conspirators tried to widen their circle to include representatives of labour, but the Nazis had their own spies well distributed among the workers. Julius Leber, one of the most prominent of the Social Democratic adherents, was arrested on July 5th, and by July

---

[1] Not to be confused with Franz von Stauffenberg, alias Uncle Franz, who ran the German military intelligence in Switzerland.

16th the Gestapo had learned enough to issue a warrant for the arrest of Karl Goerdeler, the political leader of the whole conspiracy. No wonder that Stauffenberg and his friends hastened their plan of action. It was very nearly foiled altogether.

Canaris sat in his house in Schlachtensee and waited pessimistically on events. Although no more than fifty-seven, intensive and nervous concentration over the past nine years had worn him physically.

Working in the heights of intelligence, though his brain was as keen as ever, his powers of action had receded; moreover, the soundings that he had taken with the Allies in past years seemed to offer nothing positive to the insurgents to build upon. He had sent his wife and two daughters to Bavaria, where they were safe from the mass air raids, and in July he was living alone in Berlin with his Polish cook and Mohammed, his Algerian servant—his distractions the parrot, the rough-haired dachshunds, occasional visits from neighbours and the work in his new economic study group in Eiche.

Stauffenberg carried a bomb constructed of the same materials as Canaris's staff had taken to Smolensk in 1943—British plastic charges and detonators with acid-tube time fuses. This was concealed in the brief-case which he intended to leave in a conference room with Hitler, Himmler and as many other Nazi leaders present as could be found together. It was not easy to concoct a service pretext for reporting to the Fuehrer, still less easy to find Hitler and Himmler in one room. Once Stauffenberg was ready to make the attempt, but the Fuehrer did not appear. On July 15th he managed to be present at a conference in Berchtesgaden where Hitler and Himmler were both in the room, but just when he was about to press the acid capsule Hitler walked out and did not return. Twice he reported failure and the reports ran to the British Intelligence Service in Lisbon that there had been a postponement. Finally Stauffenberg was given the task of reporting to Hitler on July 20th at Rastenburg on the subject of replacements out of Home Forces for casualties on the Russian front. He flew from Berlin to Rastenburg with his adjutant, Lieutenant Werner von Haeften, passed through the three security cordons and reached the citadel, where he reported to Marshal Keitel a few minutes before the twelve-thirty conference, clutching the brief-case in his three sound fingers. As they walked together to the conference,

Stauffenberg noticed that it was to take place in a wooden hut with its windows wide open. If it had not been such a hot day they would have met in the concrete citadel. Hitler appeared not to recognise Stauffenberg, so Keitel presented him. The conference assembled, with the adjutants General Schmundt and Colonel Brandt, the secretaries and the reporting officers. Stauffenberg leaned his brief-case on his knee, squeezed the acid capsule of the ten-minute fuse and then stood up the brief-case against the table within a few feet of Hitler. Colonel Brandt found that the brief-case cramped his feet and moved it slightly away. General Fellgiebel, the liaison officer of the conspiracy at Supreme Headquarters, called Stauffenberg out on the pretext of answering a telephone call. Keitel looked up and noticed that Stauffenberg left the room. It was then a few minutes after twelve-forty. Stauffenberg went through the security check point to the M.T. Park and waited there. A flash, a deafening roar, and a cloud of smoke over the shattered hut as the debris flew in every direction. They watched men running to and fro and stretcher-bearers hurrying up to take away the bodies. He had no doubt that the bomb had done its work, so he argued his way with some force past the security officer who had arrived at the outer barrier with orders to let no one in or out, drove to the airport and flew back to Berlin.

The conspirators in Berlin sat waiting for the first news. An officer brought a report to Headquarters of Home Forces at the old Defence Ministry in the Bendlerstrasse at 3.30 p.m. that there had been an explosion at Fuehrer Headquarters and several officers had been seriously injured. General Beck, who had resigned from the post of Chief of German General Staff in 1938, had taken charge at the Bendlerstrasse with those generals who were prepared to risk everything in a revolt. He had all the network of East–West army teleprinters under his control there. General Fromm, Commander of Home Forces, did not know what was afoot for at least an hour after that. Beck tried to contact the Army Group Commanders in the East and the West personally and ordered a large withdrawal of the exposed left flank of the German armies on the Baltic coast. Rommel, one of his main hopes in the West, had been severely injured by an R.A.F. fighter attack on his car three days previously. Marshal von Kluge, Commander-in-Chief West, could perhaps have asked Eisenhower for an immediate parley; but he was uncertain of himself and, after telephone conversations with Beck, Fromm, Hoeppner and others in Berlin, he decided to do nothing. Meanwhile the plotters sent out the code word "Valkyrie" to Home Forces, the garrison of Berlin was ordered out to protect the Bendlerstrasse from the S.S., the nearest troops outside Berlin were ordered to march into the capital—and Fromm was told about 4 p.m. by General Olbricht that Hitler was dead.

"Who has told you that?" asked General Fromm cautiously.

"The information comes from General Fellgiebel."

The wary Fromm took the precaution of demanding to speak to Fuehrer Headquarters and immediately was connected to Marshal Keitel.

"What is happening at headquarters? There are the wildest rumours here in Berlin," asked Fromm.

"What do they say? Everything is in order here," parried Keitel.

"I have just had it reported that the Fuehrer has been assassinated."

"That is nonsense. An attempt has been made, but it failed. By the way, where is your Chief of Staff, Stauffenberg?"

"Stauffenberg has not yet arrived here."

Unaware that the orders had been unsealed all over Germany and troops set on the move, Fromm decided to take no further action. At 4.30 p.m. Stauffenberg arrived in Berlin and reported to the Bendlerstrasse to tell Fromm that he had seen Hitler carried dead out of the wreckage. Fromm confronted him with the words of Keitel. Stauffenberg retorted:

"Keitel is lying as usual," but he knew that Keitel had been in the hut and that he at any rate had survived. The revolt must go ahead cost what it might! The plotters had to overpower the reluctant Fromm and put him and other staff officers under arrest.

Stauffenberg had telephoned to Canaris, probably from Staaken Airport, Berlin, as soon as he arrived to say that Hitler was dead after a bomb attempt on his life.

"Great heavens, dead?" replied the Admiral. "Who did it? The Russians?" He was well aware that even telephone calls to his home were noted and recorded. Within an hour of this call, soon after 4.30 p.m., there was a second telephone call from another of the conspirators to say that the attempt had been made, but that it had failed and the Fuehrer was still alive. Thereupon Canaris drove to his office at Eiche and arrived just in time to approve a staff telegram of congratulations to the Fuehrer on his lucky escape.

Meanwhile the generals in the Bendlerstrasse had ordered the watch regiment to seize Berlin radio hoping to prevent the news from spreading; but Major Remer, commander of the regiment, became suspicious of his instructions. One of his officers suggested that they should ask Dr. Goebbels for confirmation of the reports that Hitler was dead. Goebbels acted quickly, connected Remer with Hitler himself, and the Fuehrer in that unmistakable vibrant voice gave Remer full powers to suppress the revolt. Two officers in the plot, arriving at the office to arrest Goebbels, found themselves arrested in turn. It was obvious to the plotters by 6 p.m. that Hitler was still alive. They saw copies of signals from Fuehrer Headquarters going out direct to commands countermanding the "Valkyrie" orders and their own communiqué. Remer turned his cordon round on the Bendlerstrasse and would let nobody out. They were trapped. Fromm broke out of his mild state of arrest about 10 p.m., turned the tables on the plotters and ordered the summary execution of Stauffenberg, Olbricht, Colonel Merz von Quirnheim and Lieutenant Werner von Haeften. They were shot in the glare of motor transport headlights in the courtyard before Himmler could intervene to forbid any more executions and demand that all suspects should be turned over to the Gestapo. Beck attempted to take his own life, wounded himself, and was given the coup de grâce as he lay dying. Hitler broadcast to the nation at midnight. He said that "a miserable clique of military traitors had attempted to annihilate him and with him the High Command". That day he appointed one of his most trusted generals, Guderian, to the post of Chief of General Staff. This was the same Guderian who had so much bother over Sosnowski's thefts from I.N.6 at the beginning of our story.

What had happened meanwhile at Rastenburg? Hitler had been leaning on the map table when the bomb exploded. The force of the plastic charge was so instantaneous that it blew the flimsy walls of the hut apart and spent its fierceness in the open. Had the conference taken place in the concrete citadel from which the explosive force could not have escaped, the history of the world would perhaps have taken another course. A cone of immunity remained in the centre of the hut and in it stood Adolf Hitler leaning on the table which collapsed under him. They were all blown flat, the Fuehrer's trousers were scorched off, his hair singed, his shoulder badly bruised—and that was all his superficial injury. The first voice heard in the wreckage was that of Keitel: "Where is the Fuehrer?"

Colonel Brandt was dead, one stenographer and a secretary. Others were more or less seriously injured; but Hitler had his wounds dressed and was quickly on the move again, wildly exhilarated as he glided round the casualty ward beds with the film unit behind him, touching the bandaged forms that lay like large white mummies and squirmed despite their cerements at his approach. He joked about having had a short haircut, and when somebody sniggered at his painful attempt to give the Nazi salute, Hitler did not turn on him, but merely remarked that he could not raise his arm properly and must be content with the bourgeois greeting. That afternoon he hurried to the railway station to receive Mussolini and Marshal Graziani, who had arrived from Italy to seek aid and counsel. There was a tea-party at Rastenburg with Goering and Ribbentrop. This was the famous occasion when Goering threatened the Foreign Minister with his baton, and the inevitable reaction to the shock of the explosion came in a violent brainstorm with the Fuehrer raving before the appalled Italians that the German people were unworthy of him and that he would wreak terrible vengeance on his enemies. Then he lapsed into moody silence.

The revolt lasted altogether no more than eleven hours. Those connected with it, if not already shot or arrested, committed suicide, disappeared into hiding, or just went about their daily work as if they were in no way implicated. Guderian and Keitel promptly turned over all military suspects to the Gestapo.

Canaris made no attempt to escape. Apart from a chance remark to an old friend—"Of course you can't do things *that* way. Ring me up in a few days' time"—he went about his work in the economic staff, as if he had never plotted against Hitler.

General von Tresckow, one of the chief architects of the plan to seize power in Germany, chose the other course. He walked out into the no-man's-land of the Central Army Group towards the Russians, said farewell to his A.D.C. and then drew the pin out of a hand grenade which he held against his neck so that it blew his head off his shoulders.

Himmler was not in Berlin when the insurrection started but he arrived in the afternoon of July 20th and ordered that his own counter-operation should begin at dawn next day. He had plans laid to arrest all enemies of the regime, no matter how highly placed, no matter how renowned were their names in Germany. This operation started at dawn on July 21st and lasted for several days during which time hundreds of eminent men were rounded up. Ewald von Kleist-Schmenzin was among the first to be taken. The S.S. had found his name listed as future Political Officer for Pomerania in an administrative annexe to Operation "Valkyrie". The Gestapo went through his writing desk at dawn and seized a letter with a foreign address on it. They were astonished to find that it bore the signature of Winston Churchill. It was the warning missive written at the request of Lord Halifax in August 1938 to strengthen the movement for peace among the generals.

Two more days passed. Then an S.S. car drove up to the villa of Canaris in Schlachtensee. Out got Schellenberg, Himmler's deputy, and a few minutes later Canaris walked out of the house in the Dianastrasse and was driven away in the car with the man who had become his successor.

CHAPTER XXIV

THE LAST THROW

THE CELLS OF the Reich Security Office were full of the most prominent men in Germany that winter: generals, officers, diplomats, politicians, landowners, lawyers and clergymen sat in the small cells—men like Goerdeler, Halder, Hassell, Oster, Schulenberg, Fromm, Popitz, and among them Schacht trying to look, as he did later at Nuremberg, as if he did not know his companions. Josef Mueller was taken out of military detention and transferred to Gestapo keeping. Kaltenbrunner gave special orders for the security of Canaris. He was to be kept in a lighted cell with the door permanently open and permitted to speak to nobody. No prisoner was allowed to speak to another, but when the air-raids alerts sounded they had all to shuffle out to the shelters and that gave them a chance for whispered conversations. Their doors were left open for rounds and then they could whisper through the hinges to each other. It surprised his fellow prisoners and the Gestapo that Canaris still talked with an up-to-date knowledge of the war, although he was cut off from all outside contact. He was thereupon forbidden to ask his guards for the Wehrmacht communiqué of the day. Yet his grasp was still amazing, as if his mind still assimilated intelligence from the air when the threads were severed. Lieutenant von Schlabrendorff was in a nearby cell and recalls the vague and naïve questions with which Canaris tricked his guards into giving him situation reports.

"I suppose by now we are pushing the Russians back over the Vistula."

"Ach, what nonsense! They are approaching the Oder."

One day in midwinter a Gestapo detachment went to fetch von Schlabrendorff from his cell and take him to the Sachsenhausen Concentration Camp. They had suspicions that General von Tresckow had taken his own life, and so opened his grave. When they prised open the coffin and examined the corpse their suspicions deepened and they decided to cross-examine his former adjutant, Schlabrendorff, who had been arrested on supposition of treasonable activities. Thinking that his last day had come, he walked out of his cell.

"Put on your overcoat," shouted the guards.

"I have no overcoat," he answered.

"Then borrow one from the nearest prisoner."

The only cell door that stood open was that of Canaris, as it stood, day and night, with the lights on. He must have suffered much that winter from his thin blood in a cell sometimes unheated, but he flung his overcoat out of the cell into the gangway. Schlabrendorff picked it up gratefully and put it on, and when he had settled his hands in the pockets he found a scrap of paper there. He read it furtively in the black maria that drove him out to be confronted with the corpse of his general. The note read:

"Your case comes up on the 23rd."

Kaltenbrunner with his security branch man, S.S. General Mueller, and the painstaking Huppenkothen began their search for evidence against Canaris. They sent an agent to Switzerland to spy on the Allied military attachés. It was hard to find anything that implicated Canaris directly. His case baffled them. A man who had been in such a high position, a friend of General Franco from whom they hoped perhaps still for mediation and peace terms with the West, could hardly be hanged on a meat hook just like those other blundering staff officers. But Huppenkothen noticed that Colonel Schrader, an intimate friend of Canaris, had committed suicide immediately after the insurrection of July 20th had failed. He interrogated his driver; the man could not think of any reason why his master should have been implicated—he lived a quiet life and did not see many people—but the driver did remember certain files entrusted to him, for which Colonel Schrader had enjoined him to particular care. Where were they? The S.D. searched his home, the War Ministry offices in the Bendlerstrasse, and then the Army H.Q. citadel at Zossen. There, after some weeks, they discovered Colonel Schrader's steel box and broke it open.

The box contained a miscellany of papers. There were the medical history sheets of Corporal Adolf Hitler containing the observations of the Commandant of the military hospital at

Pasewalk in Pomerania, where Hitler had lain gassed after the First World War. The remarks referred to his symptoms of hysterical blindness and suggested a psychiatrist's report on his sanity. There were copies of certain service reports of Admiral Canaris, some latter pages of his diary, a series of intelligence papers on National-Socialist atrocities and the correspondence on the Vatican negotiations with the proposed peace conditions drafted by the Pope's secretary going between Sir D'Arcy Osborne and Josef Mueller, with the visiting card of Laiber still attached. The Germans had not been so careful to destroy these drafts as their adversary had been.

"I had to accept this post (the Reich Security Office) at a time when suspicion fell on Admiral Canaris of having collaborated with the enemy for years," stated Ernst Kaltenbrunner in his final plea at Nuremberg. "In a short time I ascertained the treason of Canaris to a most frightful extent." When he said this he was probably thinking of Colonel Schrader's safe.

"Yet for months Canaris baffled them with one ruse after another," related Schlabrendorff. "His skill in acting a part, his cunning, his imagination, the ease with which he affected naïve stupidity and then emerged into the most subtle reasoning disarmed the security agents who interrogated him."

"It was not so much lying," said Lahousen with a chuckle, "as the artistic distortion of the truth."

Kleist was interrogated about the letter from Winston Churchill that had been found in his desk. "That was simply the result of an official mission to find out whether the British would make war on us over the Czechoslovak issue," explained Kleist to S.S. Mueller. No doubt Canaris gave the same answer.

I have tried from the shreds of evidence on his behaviour to work out what his replies would have been if, for instance, the Gestapo had discovered his "Viking" line to Switzerland and the warning of an impending threat he gave to the Swiss in 1943. To the accusation of treason in giving the Swiss a hint to mobilise it would have been possible for him to reply in this manner:

"The case is entirely different. We did not warn the Swiss of a real danger that they would be invaded. The Abwehr had information on Allied pressure on the Swiss to cut all rail communications between Germany and Italy, slow it down, and allow Allied agents to blow up the St. Gothard tunnel.

Our intention with the warning was in fact to convey a threat and so keep our rail communications open, which in fact we did. Nobody in their senses wanted to invade Switzerland."

I emphasise that the above is an exercise of the imagination and that Canaris may never have been asked that question or have given that answer. It serves solely to show what fine constructions can be put on any one of his actions and gives an idea of the time and study that would be needed to disprove such an explanation.

The peace negotiations with the Allies could also be explained as attempts to size up their determination, their unity, their war aims, their trust or mistrust of Russia and generally soften their purpose by suggesting that Germany was not going to prosecute war to the full. Unless Kaltenbrunner really knew what Canaris's agents had told the Allies, he could not say for certain that such activities were treason—and there must have been always at the back of his mind the subconscious hope that Canaris had in fact found what they must all eventually seek—acceptable terms.

So the months went by until, on February 3rd, 1945, the Reich Security Office received a direct bomb hit and Himmler decided that the prisoners must be removed to concentration camps. He dispatched Josef Mueller on February 7th to Buchenwald and Canaris was sent further south, to Flossenbürg, in the "redoubt". Since the discovery of Colonel Schrader's safe, he had been kept in irons day and night.

Kaltenbrunner and Schellenberg, the Security Chief and the Intelligence Chief of the new unified Secret Service, were appalled by the odour of treason that they had found in the papers of Admiral Canaris, but they were more than appalled. The possibilities of survival for themselves and their whole order peeped out of the new evidence. The foreign contacts that Canaris had taken up in a treasonable sense, as they suspected, might have to be taken up by themselves perhaps as a legitimate task. But this process of thought was not without some pangs of the Nazi conscience. When Count Folk Bernadotte of Wiborg, of the Swedish Red Cross, appeared in Berlin on February 16th, Kaltenbrunner regarded the visit as a suspicious omen. His obsession with the treason of Canaris had bitten deep into his mind. Schellenberg says that Kaltenbrunner suddenly turned on him and threatened to produce proof that he, Schellenberg, was an agent of the British Secret Service. Kaltenbrunner had by now got the eerie feeling that there were secret service agents everywhere—he suspected that Canaris was a British agent and extended his suspicions to the Intelligence Chief.

But Schellenberg, half in the cloudland of the Third Reich, was a sworn Nazi himself and had a practical and crafty side to his character. Had he not invented the Venloo trap? He suggested that he, Kaltenbrunner, might well succeed Ribbentrop as Foreign Minister if Schellenberg could patch up peace terms with the Western Allies through this Count Bernadotte. It had been Kaltenbrunner's hope that he would succeed Ribbentrop, so he acquiesced in the secret meetings and was later even party to Bernadotte meeting Himmler. All this seemed to give him a hold over the biggest pieces on the chessboard, while Martin Bormann, Hitler's palace chamberlain, kept in touch with Kaltenbrunner and was ready at a propitious moment to whisper "treachery" to his master. Bernadotte told in *Fall of the Curtain* how he had seen General Eisenhower in the autumn of 1944, but gives no hint of any mission entrusted to him other than his own purpose of serving the welfare of some Swedish women married to Germans, whom he hoped to repatriate to Sweden. I suspect that the Allies hoped he would disrupt the Nazi leaders. To ingratiate himself with Himmler he bought him a gift of a book on Nordic runes, which Himmler received with tears in his eyes. Then began the struggle of Schellenberg to break the loyalty of Himmler to his leader and induce him secretly to negotiate a surrender.

"You may think it sentimental, even absurd," Himmler confided in Bernadotte when they first met, "but I have sworn an oath of loyalty to Adolf Hitler, and as a soldier and a German I cannot go back on my oath."

So he and Kaltenbrunner havered through March and April, looking East and West at their torn and shrinking fronts and watching the glowering Hitler in his Chancellery, intervening to no purpose in the battle and yelling his imprecations upon his hypnotised staff. By the early days of April the Russians were in the outskirts of Vienna, the Ruhr was encircled, the British passed through Minden, the Americans crossed the Weser at Hamelin. The Germans strained to hold the Oder front. Hitler alternated between insane and terrible paroxysms of rage and strange periods of calm, when he would walk out and engage sentries in philosophical talk interspersed with mystic and childish remembrances of his youth, his father Alois, his home life and early career, wandering thence into abstract speculations on the world and eternity. Sometimes between his rages and his calms he must have instructed Kaltenbrunner to deal with the prisoners in Flossenbürg, and Kaltenbrunner sent Huppenkothen off to Bavaria with instructions for a summary court.

"These men must be snuffed out, without much ceremony," raved Hitler after the terse pages of the Canaris diary and Oster's literary curios had been laid before him.

Flossenbürg, set among woodland in a forbidden zone of Franconia, contained "the prominent men", destined either to be hostages or to await death. They did not know which. When Canaris arrived there after leaving Berlin on February 7th, he remained two months in a separate block, in which the brains of the German Intelligence Service were kept apart from the rest. General Oster was there, Josef Mueller was brought in from Buchenwald in April with Captain Gehre, Roland Strünck, Dietrich Bonhoeffer, Schlabrendorff and other associates. Canaris was put in a cell next to that of Colonel Lunding, Director of the Danish Military Intelligence Service, arrested under suspicion of working against Germany during the occupation of his country. Destiny had brought other victims strangely together in this extermination camp—Lieutenant-Colonel Jack Churchill, Captain Peter Churchill thought to be a valuable hostage because the S.D. believed Odette's story that he was related to Winston Churchill. There was Giles Romilly, a nephew of the Prime Minister, captured as a War Correspondent in Narvik. "One British agent whose real name we never knew," Josef Mueller told me, "had been captured after an attempt to blow up the Iron Gates and block the Danube shipping. He could not even write home lest his name should be revealed."

Men of all European nationalities now sat in the same grim confinement with the chief whose organisation had hunted them—all victims together of Himmler's unified secret service.

The interrogations of Canaris continued in Flossenbürg; the Gestapo, bringing down fresh evidence extracted from prisoners under torture, questioned him again and again. He still eluded them. Lunding and he recognised each other in the corridors and started a tapping code between their cells at night-time while the guards were out of earshot. They used the prisoners' system of dividing the alphabet into five groups and tapping out the group first and then one tap for each letter in the group. So these two chiefs of the Intelligence Service kept in touch through the cell wall.

Colonel Lunding noticed that the Admiral still wore civilian clothes, whereas others wore convicts' uniform. He was treated as if his guilt had not been positively established. One day Gestapo Commissioner Starvitzski came down to confront Canaris with some fresh revelations and Lunding could watch through a chink in the door how they walked up and down together, while Starvitzski spoke in loud and angry tones and Canaris remonstrated and gesticulated. At the time Lunding mistook this big Gestapo man for Kaltenbrunner.

This was the second week in April. Huppenkothen arrived and ordered that a summary court should deal immediately with the chiefs of the German Intelligence. Huppenkothen admitted at his own trial six years later that a summary court was held on April 8th with S.S. Judge Thorbeck presiding, which found Canaris guilty of high treason, and that he then returned to Berlin. Others assert that he waited to see that the sentences had been executed before leaving. Josef Mueller was sitting fettered in his cell on April 8th, when the door was flung open and an S.S. man shouted to him to get ready to leave. Mueller tidied his cell. He was taken out still in fetters and led away towards the gallows yard.

"Now the play is ending," shouted one of his guards. "This is the last act. But you will be hanged a head lower than your chief Canaris."

As he stood at the gates of the execution yard, Stavitzki shouted to him:

"Happy journey, gallows bird."

After standing half an hour motionless, Mueller was led away to his cell. He had not been there long before he was led out a second time.

A second time he stood at the threshold of the gallows, as if some authority were awaited for his execution. Then the S.S. came to lead him away again, shouting:

"You've been forgotten for today."

Did the distant rumination of Himmler save him, or the remonstrances of Mueller himself, who knew all the laws of the Third Reich, and protested that he must have a proper trial. Late on that same day Canaris was brought back to his cell from what was named a summary trial, but could have been no more than an interrogation with torture. Colonel Lunding in the next cell could hear him moving and then the last slow tappings began.

"That . . . will . . . have . . . been . . . the last . . . I think. . . . Badly mishandled. . . . Nose broken. . . ."

Then as far as Lunding remembers he tapped out the words that his gaolers had been trying to extract from him for months. The Danish Chief of Intelligence subsequently repeated this important message when giving evidence in court in the Huppenkothen trial.

"I die for my Fatherland. I have a clean conscience. I only did my duty to my country when I tried to oppose the criminal folly of Hitler leading Germany to destruction."

He tapped out a last message to his wife, with whom he had never shared the secrets of his most dangerous actions, then living destitute somewhere in Bavaria with her two daughters.

By first light on April 9th the S.S. were round the cells of the Intelligence Service again.

"Out, out," they shouted. Lunding could hear the shackles fall from Canaris's hands and feet, and heard the command: "Clothes off." Through the chink in his door he saw the prisoners led naked away.

Dr. Abshagen concludes that the prisoners, Admiral Canaris, General Oster, Dr. Strunck, Judge-Advocate-General Sack and Captain Gehre were killed quickly in short succession.[1] I have discussed with him particularly his deductions, which are based on the rapidity of the summons: "The next," which showed that one was already hanged. "They met a speedy end," he writes. This is unconvincing in face of the persisting rumours that Admiral Canaris was hanged twice. The S.S. had no time indeed for the finesses of a long drop—they must die in their own time. All the evidence shows that although he

---

[1] The S.S. executioners giving evidence at the trial of Huppenkothen in February 1951 admitted that there was room for at least six on the gallows and that they did not wait for one to die before hanging up the next.

was treated without brutality until the last few days, the amazed hatred of the S.S. pursued Canaris as their greatest victim.

"On the 10th of April a drunken S.S. guard told me that the day before they had again been hanging some men of the Intelligence Service," related Schlabrendorff in his book, *Revolt Against Hitler*. "Those guards who had taken part in the execution had received extra rations of spirit and sausage. The victims had not been executed in accordance with a court sentence; Himmler had ordered their liquidation by hanging on his own responsibility. When I asked for their names, the guard gave me those of Admiral Canaris, General Oster and Bonhoeffer."

"My cell was not far away," Schlabrendorff added when I questioned him on this point. "The guards told me that same day that Canaris was hanged twice."

"To give you a foretaste of death"—is one version of what the S.S. said when they revived him. Did they want to extract a last confession before they hanged him up again or merely prolong their revenge on the man whose organisation had, so they suspected, lost them the war. I have asked a high officer of the British Intelligence Service for his opinion—and the British accept the version that was related by his guards on that same morning as they returned to their breakfast.

The stoic Ewald von Kleist who had plotted with Canaris before the war was hanged in Berlin on April 16th.

Five years afterwards I met Dr. Josef Mueller in Munich. He was preparing the trial of Huppenkothen.

"One of the S.S. prisoners waiting to give evidence," said Mueller, "alleges that Canaris was hanged in an iron collar and took half an hour to die."

So his supreme intelligence was quelled, and the intense blue eyes that so many witnesses remembered. To keep the act secret, a wooden pyre was lit under the bodies not far from the cells. Josef Mueller shuffled to and fro in his cell to keep his feet warm while he waited his turn for execution. Then there was some knocking on the door of his cell and a voice said:

"Do you speak English?"

"Yes."

"Are you one of those high officers who were meant to be hanged?"

"I believe so."

"That does not seem to be so. They are being burned at this moment."

Mueller, on the verge of hallucinations, believes that it was Captain Peter Churchill who whispered this to him.

"No, I could not have done," Peter Churchill told me. "I did not know about the executions. I only whispered to him something like—keep cheerful, the Allies are not far away."

Mueller sat and waited for the summons to death that had passed him by, either because he was still a counter in Himmler's game or because an order had gone astray. The wooden pyre outside burned badly. Corpses are not consumed easily in the open. The ashes of the dead floated in through the bars of his cell and settled down all round him—"and that was the worst of all".

What had happened in the S.S. summary Court? Did Canaris confess? For a time Huppenkothen walked about Munich after the war as if he had nothing on his conscience, still wearing his uniform leather coat but with the badges removed. After Josef Mueller had returned from a rest cure, which he had certainly earned, Huppenkothen was apprehended and treated to the reverse of summary justice. It was five years before the case against him was complete.

Then S.S. Judge Thorbeck popped up from his post-war legal practice in Nuremberg to give evidence.

"Why did you not come forward before?" asked the amazed Judge Ackermann.

"I was never questioned about this case," replied Thorbeck. "I found no space provided for such matters in the Allied questionnaire."

When confronted with Thorbeck, Huppenkothen became less assured in his demeanour. He admitted that he had been mistaken as to the date of the trial and that defence counsel had been denied to the prisoners. But he said that he knew nothing of overheated cells, of arc lamps and other instruments of confession.

It had been his object as prosecutor to establish that Canaris had been connected with the revolt against Hitler. His scope did not extend to contacts with the Allies.

All the intelligence officers tried that day with Canaris admitted their guilt, he said. The Admiral did not. The S.S. agreed that Canaris defended himself with remarkable skill.

In that nightmare twilight of the Third Reich, words and imposture were his last weapons. At length Judge Thorbeck, well briefed by Huppenkothen, confronted him with his former Chief of Staff, General Oster. By then Oster was no longer of this world. I can imagine him standing there nonchalant and dreamy with no denials to make. Perhaps he had been drugged.

Thorbeck exhorted Canaris to confess his complicity. Oster would say that he knew of the plots.

"Of course I had to know about such things," parried Canaris. "After all, I was the Chief of Intelligence. I had to be ready to prevent it at the critical moment."

Oster demurred, according to the S.S.

"Oster," cried the Admiral, advancing a step towards the man whom he had so often protected, "allow me to say that I only pretended complicity."

"I cannot say anything more than I know," was the answer ascribed to Oster. There were times when he had kept secrets better.

Upon that the S.S. Court passed its sentences as Hitler had instructed it, and snuffed out the Chief of Intelligence.

CHAPTER XXV

THE POST-MORTEM

SOMETHING OF THE pathos of his death affected those deeply who had been once his rivals, the Chiefs of the Allied Secret Services. Although in itself an insignificant event in the catastrophic war still raging in the world, I examined such accounts as exist with the same sense of tragedy as I felt when reading of the murder of Admiral Coligny in the religious wars of France. The man himself is old and past the age of impetuous quarrelling, but the cause he represents must be annihilated if the tyrant is to have peace, even for a short while. At first nobody in the Western zones of Germany came forward to testify that he saw the body of Admiral Canaris, and there was some doubt about the exact manner and time of his death until February 1951. Lunding saw him go naked to the place of execution; but Josef Mueller described to me how he himself was twice led to the gallows on the previous day and taken away again "as a valuable hostage". Was the Admiral less valuable? His guilt may have been greater, but it was less evident than that of Mueller. So legends flourish.

I heard one myself in December 1950 when a tall old man, spare and handsome, with light-grey hair, was shown into my study. Willy Jenke, the adjutant of Canaris, had come up from Hanover to clear up some points of detail. I asked him what he knew of the circumstances of the death of Admiral Canaris and he held out a typewritten letter to me. "One of my friends of the Abwehr," he said, "has just written to me with a new account of the matter. He has spoken with Toeppen, the chief accountant of the Abwehr, who declares that Canaris was seen in Berlin about April 20th under close escort and adds that he was subsequently told that the Admiral had been shot and buried in a bomb crater on April 23rd at a time when Hitler was ordering some of the last executions."

It seemed possible that Canaris stood under the gallows like Mueller and saw his companions hanged, perhaps was even given his own "foretaste of death", and then driven to Berlin as a last hostage. Maybe even the story of his first hanging and revival could be reconciled with this strange version. But none of the many witnesses whom Trevor Roper has interrogated mentioned Admiral Canaris in their account of the last days in Berlin. It is, incidentally, worthy of note that Trevor Roper, who as a British intelligence officer might have perceived the real game of Canaris during the war, vouchsafed him in *The Last Days of Hitler* no more than a few disparaging remarks as an inefficient intriguer, but has since revised these opinions in his favour.

The survivors of Flossenbürg were driven off to Dachau, as the Americans advanced, and then taken still further south, until the disintegrating morale of their guards and the fortuitous arrival of German Army units saved their lives.

"We were to have been liquidated," Captain Peter Churchill told me, "by order of Hitler himself from the bunker. But the S.S. officer in charge of us saw that things had gone so far by then that he would do better to stay his hand."

Trevor Roper describes the afflicted and shaking Hitler shouting for hostages to be shot after one of his transcendent brainstorms. American forces freed Dachau Concentration Camp on April 24th and pushed on southwards. Goering had telegrammed to Hitler from the Bavarian "redoubt" on the previous day and offered to try and make peace. On April 28th the Allies revealed that Himmler had been discussing peace terms with Bernadotte, but that they were unacceptable. The tyrants were falling apart. Mussolini was captured and shot on April 28th. Hitler married Eva Braun in the Chancellery bunker on the morrow. She took poison. He shot himself on April 30th. His guards made a pyre for them in the Chancellery grounds and burned his body and that of Eva Braun after soaking them in petrol. So whatever the truth is about the death of Admiral Canaris, the tyrant whom he had secretly thwarted whenever he could for seven years outlived him by twenty days at the most. I daresay that Canaris often wondered which of them would go first.

That was the end of Kieker, "the old man" to his staff, "father of the unfortunate", as difficult a subject for a biography as can be imagined, secretive, mistrustful, of high intelligence and humane principles, yet different by a shade in his appearance and mentality to everybody who knew him. Loquacious in an appointment that seemed to demand silence, eccentric where a steady man would have seemed more suitable, indiscreet and yet calculating. "I tell them what they want to hear and what can be repeated."

"Was he a British agent?" The grey, worn face of Jenke reflected no astonishment as I put that direct question. "That is a figure of speech. A British victory might have served his purpose, but he hoped that the last catastrophe to Germany could be averted."

"Why did the British not use Canaris better if they knew about him?" I asked a senior British intelligence officer. His answer was exactly what I had always suspected:

"We would have liked to do so, but the Foreign Office was against it. They were afraid of offending Russia. That was not our view, but the Foreign Office view prevailed."

I remembered the answer that I had been given myself in the Foreign Office in 1943.

"We want no problems in Europe after this war." In other words, if the German General Staff was destroyed there would be peace. I do not think that after January 1943 the nature and aims of Canaris and his friends were properly understood by the British and American cabinets; probably they were not fully represented to them in intelligence reports.

The inmates of Flossenbürg sat together in Capri for a while, recuperating from their ordeal. In the first days of liberation they lived together, as Europeans should, in the comradeship that comes from common suffering and fortitude. Then General Eisenhower's "no fraternisation" order reached even their remote abode and they were separated and dispersed with dignity and regret.

Josef Mueller returned to his native Bavaria, where he became one of the leaders of the Christian-Socialists and Minister of Justice. The experiment of democracy was painstakingly begun and the Allied decrees and ordinances began to rebuild what was left of Germany and put it up in a new shape. The Nuremberg tribunal dealt with the big survivors and suddenly Erwin Lahousen appeared before it, discovered in a prisoner-of-war camp, to accuse the defendants of criminal inhumanity in the name of his dead chief, Admiral Canaris. Ribbentrop, Jodl and Kaltenbrunner, sitting in the dock, stirred uneasily.

They were haunted by the thought of the German Intelligence Service, "that he had served the enemy for years" as Jodl put it in his last plea, while Kaltenbrunner said in his that he "had ascertained the treason of Canaris to a terrible degree". The angry and defeated militarists, such men as Guderian and Remer, talked in scandalised tones of the grand treason of Canaris, while his widow and her children and the widows of his friends sat on the verge of starvation in a liberated land. "You must know something about Admiral Canaris," the junior American intelligence officers, who apparently knew little themselves, said to his nephew Joachim Canaris, and they interned him for a year as a good measure. What use was it to try and explain his uncle's "European ideas"?

The Russians arrested the secretary of Canaris, Fräulein Schwarte, and plied her with questions about the missing diary.

A British member of Parliament tried in vain to obtain a small pension for Erika Canaris from the Bavarian Government. She was deprived of all means of subsistence by Allied regulations that both "froze" the bank accounts of General Staff Officers and their dependants and stopped their pensions. American troops were billeted in the Bavarian home of the Canaris family and plundered it thoroughly.

One day in 1948 two Spanish diplomats arrived in Munich and arranged in utmost secrecy for Frau Canaris to go to Switzerland. On arrival there she was invited by General Franco to proceed to Spain as a guest of the state, where she was given a home in Barcelona. The Caudillo was remembering a promise and paying a debt of gratitude.

Another old friend, Fabian von Schlabrendorff, went to the remote house on the Luneburger Heide where Frau Schrader had been entrusted with the only complete diary of Admiral Canaris, in which he had secretly noted his acts and missions during these terrible years. Frau Schrader declared that under the strain of the events after July 20th, 1944, fearing that the Gestapo investigations would lead to its discovery, she had removed the diary from its hiding place and burned it.

"I do not believe it is destroyed," Willy Jenke told me as we talked over the closing scenes of the tragedy; but he could not produce any argument to bear out his assertion. The S.S. at the trial of Huppenkothen admitted to having made microfilms of such parts of the diary as they had seized in Zossen.

I remembered hearing a naval intelligence officer say that the Foreign Office had possession of some diary and wondered whether it still survived in the material about Admiral Canaris to which I had been refused access, but he was probably referring to the departmental diary of Abwehr II that was taken to Washington.

"Did Canaris ever meet the British himself?" I asked Jenke. "He seemed to be always expecting them to throw him a lifeline."

"Not that I know of," replied Jenke. "I can't vouch for his activities abroad; but I do remember making arrangements in 1943 for an English visitor who was to have come out to Germany——"

"What, to Germany in wartime?"

"So it seems, but nothing came of it. They dropped the idea on the other side."

He nodded vaguely across the Elbe over Hamburg and the North Sea.

"So his liking for the British was instinctive and perhaps part of his fixation against Hitler?"

"I never heard him tell of any English friends," said Jenke.

We agreed that the head of a secret service has to be careful whom his meets.

Finally I came to examine with some of his officers what influence Canaris may have had on the course of the war. One reproach that has been held against him is that he did not make enough use of his position to work for what he sincerely believed to be the right course. His men sat round the table with me and we surveyed his work. I discussed this subject with General Lahousen, Josef Mueller, Willy Jenke, Dr. Leverkuehn, Kumerow (Piekenbrock's principal staff officer), Wichmann, the specialist on Britain, and Richard Protze.

Their pictures of him all varied slightly, but all agreed that he was a man who detested violence, disliked war and was reluctant to act himself. It would remain an unsolved question whether if Britain had given him a firm lead he would have taken action against Hitler. His policy of condoning contact with the enemy supplied the Allies with intelligence of inestimable value. His moderation and humanity prevented the war from taking yet more violent forms than it did.

"There is no doubt we could have killed Winston Churchill," said Jenke, "if the Admiral had carried out his orders. Mr. Churchill gave us plenty of opportunities, being as active as he was in the war. We could also have murdered other war leaders, Giraud and Weygand among them."

Canaris did not manage to deter Hitler from his fatal course, and he encouraged revolutionary movements rather than led them. His omissions in the intelligence field helped the Allies to achieve surprise and brought their certain victory mercifully closer.

He warned Great Britain of the impending mobilisation against Czechoslovakia in 1938 and advised strong action which might have prevented war altogether. He helped to prevent the war from spreading to Spain and Portugal and kept silent at the crucial moment when Italy was changing sides. His service warned Great Britain of the V-weapons and so gave us opportunity to reduce their destructive effect. If he did not in the course of his secret talks with Hitler pull out a pistol and shoot the man, it was simply because that did not lie in his nature—and a man is only capable of acting within his own capacity. But the historians who want the flesh and blood and the spirit of this era and are not content with the massive bones of the document centres will see his elusive anxious figure hovering behind the brutal tragedians and spoiling their destiny. Could any man in like position have achieved more than that without being detected?

The German Intelligence Service was scattered by the dissolution of the armed forces. Piekenbrock, for a long time Chief of Department I, was captured in the field by the Russians; Bamler, the Spanish specialist and then Chief of III, deserted to them from his own command; his successor, General von Bentivegni, shot himself after the failure of the July revolt. Lahousen spent some uncomfortable weeks in Nienburg internment camp before he was discovered and taken out to give evidence in Nuremberg. Then he retired to the Tirol to live out his days in quiet. Leverkuehn found a powerful friend again when General "Bill" Donovan of the office of Strategic Services arrived in Germany. Leverkuehn made a name for himself in the defence of Marshal von Manstein. Willy Jenke withdrew to life in the country near Hanover. Richard Protze sat down in the old inn on the Baltic coast of

Holstein and brooded on days past. Everywhere they had to
contend with Allied lawgiving which forbade their employment
in positions of responsibility. The Western Allies, though they
had found the German military intelligence a negligible force
in its later years and in some respects an ally, nevertheless
mistrusted the organisation as such. The politicians of Western
Germany found it convenient not to employ these men. Old
Admiral Patzig, with whom our story began, put up hope-
fully as a candidate for the post of Security Chief created
in 1950 in the West German Republic, but he was passed
over.

Whatever signs of friendliness the British Intelligence
Service might privily show them, it could not in the nature
of the settlement with Russia and France bestow any recogni-
tion, let alone accept any commitments. The incomparable
Russian section of the Abwehr which Canaris had built up was
unbuilt by the Soviet security police in part and what was
left either fell apart or was clumsily drawn into surviving
services.

Not long after the Treaty of Potsdam was signed, the British
and American Intelligence Services found themselves involved
in a struggle if anything more grim and pitiless than the last.
It lay in the nature of things that there would be no peace
between the secret services of the East and West, whatever
the open professions of friendship might be. The Western
Intelligence Services did stage a round-up of National
Socialists at large just before the 1947 Moscow Conference of
Foreign Ministers, known as Operation Selection-Board; but
it roused no enthusiasm in the Kremlin and resulted in no
trials. What mattered most to the Soviet Government was to
exert its influence on the future of Western Germany and to
obtain from the Western Allies those thousands of Russians of
all ranks who had deserted to Europe during and after the war.

So the struggle went on, but instead of opponents with some
common philosophy, and some division in their own ranks,
the Western Allies found themselves dealing with the secretive
and fanatical trainees of world revolution. Beria had long been
the chief of a unified intelligence service. Hitler had made the
mistake of dividing to rule. Stalin unified first.

The German intelligence men sat by as spectators in the
front row; for the new dispute was mainly about their own

country, which remained the key to the world situation, for all the attempts to neutralise it. But there was no chance now of finding an opponent who would suppress the worst orders or warn small victims of impending aggression.

Whereas the Nazi ideology had found few adherents in the democracies, there was a nameless fascination in the Communist system for many in Western Europe. The opportunities for the Soviet Intelligence Service are greater than those of Nazi Germany, and in this modern world of interlocking minds it is easy to imagine that Comrade Beria is well served. Conversely, the work of the Allies beyond the Iron Curtain is hampered by the destructive mentality of the enemy and his disregard for the rules on which the intelligence game operated hitherto. Well might they look back to the comparatively civilised duelling with Admiral Canaris.

"As Colonel Nicolai says in his book on the German Secret Service in the First World War, it is important that the head of an organisation wielding such power should be a gentleman. What a tragedy the death of Canaris was!"

I have saved to the end this oblique tribute to Canaris from his chief opponent in Britain—a tribute to a man who often thought too rapidly for his opponents, even when he helped them, who opened his mind to them to an extraordinary degree and was not fully understood until it was too late. The understanding which he sought in Europe against one tyranny may be achieved against another.

.   .   .   .   .

The inquest was over.

We have seen little of the Canaris family in these years. They did not go out in the gaudy society of the Third Reich, not to Goering's hunting parties or Goebbels' island festivals. They knew little about the work that was done by the Chief of Intelligence, except that he was up early and home late and often vanished to the office on Sundays. The Abwehr was to Frau Erika Canaris a book with seven seals.

Their reticence and my desire to write an independent study of the man were two reasons why we did not meet at the outset of this book. His widow had first to run the gauntlet of the war correspondents eager for the story of the master spy and enquiring after the diary. What could she tell them?

—about as much as the scientist's wife might have gathered at table about atomic fission. After seeing the whitewash brush applied so liberally to much less worthy memories, it was refreshing to encounter this dignified silence.

She recoiled every time she heard of new publications about her husband, knowing how terribly hard to define he was, even for those who knew him. She had no family papers on his work—nothing except her personal memories of him and his personal letters. They had both been very cautious and there was nothing in them about intelligence matters or politics.

The Abwehr had remained to her a book with seven seals, perhaps instinctively because she knew that it was very dangerous territory. Occasionally she picked up a thread at table from the conversation of guests, and discussed with him alone some imminent topic. But time and the tragedy itself weakens memory, and she could hardly summon up any recollections on Service matters.

She was not anxious for her husband to be discussed in books, even if it was a question of vindicating his memory.

Yet it seems as if the truth is emerging slowly everywhere. Our times and our generation are not capable of grasping the situation in which they stood, and the ethical motives of those men. Perhaps later when these things can be treated with less prejudice, the historian will discard the sneers of their contemporaries and see them as they were.

Canaris rendered account to no earthly tribunal for his deeds and omissions and cared little for the approval or censure of men. He followed what Goethe has called 'the independent conscience'. To those who knew him well, the verdict in the Munich trial of Huppenkothen[1] was a matter of no significance. A man like Huppenkothen had his role appointed for him by the inexorable laws of the Greek tragedy.

I met Brigitte Canaris, daughter of the Chief of Intelligence, in Munich before the Huppenkothen trial and we walked together for some time in the park of Nymphenburg castle. A quiet, melancholy girl who had, I noticed, a hereditary characteristic of her father in that she shivered a little even in bright sunlit weather. The G.I.s strolled in the sun, the gardeners trundled by, the newsvendors offered the latest from Korea. The world looked anxiously into the future. It had

[1] Three years' imprisonment.

seen dimly the tragedy of the past, and was already beginning to forget it. What would these strollers ever know of the deeper story? What did she know? What question was there still to ask? Wilhelm Canaris had done his duty according to his own lights.

BIBLIOGRAPHY

Records of the Proceedings of the International Military Tribunal at Nuremberg.

Canaris, by Karl Heinz Abshagen, Union Verlag, Stuttgart.

Offiziere gegen Hitler, by Fabian von Schlabrendorff.

The German Secret Service, by Colonel Nicolai. Harrap.

Odette, by Jerrard Tickell. Chapman & Hall.

The Last Days of Hitler, by Trevor Roper.

Operation "Cicero", by L. C. Moyzisch. Wingate Press.

Germany's Underground, by Allen Dulles. Macmillan.

The Russo-German Alliance, by A. Rossi. Chapman & Hall.

The Venlo Incident, by Captain S. Payne Best. Hutchinson.

The Second World War, by Winston S. Churchill. Cassell.

Vom Anderen Deutschland, by Ulrich von Hassell. Atlantic Press.

Selected official German documents relating to the Spanish Civil War, published by the U.S. State Department.

A General Against War, by Albert Forster.

The Huppenkothen Statement (unpublished), by Walther Huppenkothen.

Entre les Pyrenees et Gibraltar, by R. Serrano Suner. Les Editions du Cheval Aile.

Defeat in the West, by Milton Shulman.

Hitler and his Admirals, by Anthony Martiensen. Secker & Warburg.

Birth of the Third Reich, by Konrad Heiden. Europa Verlag, Zurich.

The Polish White Book on Polish–German Relations 1933–39. Hutchinson.

Outbreak of Hostilities Between Great Britain and Germany. British Blue Book, H.M. Stationery Office.

Documents on German Foreign Policy, Series D, Vol. III. *Germany and the Spanish War.*

British Naval History of the First World War.

Chronology of the Second World War, published by the Royal Institute of Foreign Affairs.

The Private Papers of Ewald von Kleist.

Correspondence with members of the German Intelligence Service.

Lightning Source UK Ltd.
Milton Keynes UK
UKOW04f1024151213

223027UK00001B/105/A